TRADITIONS AND TRANSFORMATIONS

Traditions and Transformations

The Rise of German Constitutionalism

MICHAELA HAILBRONNER
Humboldt Research Fellow at the Institute for International and Comparative Law at the University of Pretoria, South Africa

OXFORD
UNIVERSITY PRESS

OXFORD
UNIVERSITY PRESS

Great Clarendon Street, Oxford, OX2 6DP,
United Kingdom

Oxford University Press is a department of the University of Oxford.
It furthers the University's objective of excellence in research, scholarship,
and education by publishing worldwide. Oxford is a registered trade mark of
Oxford University Press in the UK and in certain other countries

First Edition published in 2015

Published in the United States of America by Oxford University Press
198 Madison Avenue, New York, NY 10016, United States of America

British Library Cataloguing in Publication Data
Data available

Library of Congress Control Number: 2015945235

ISBN 978–0–19–873542–7

This book is dedicated to
Martin Drath

Martin Drath (1902–76) was a Justice at the early German Constitutional Court and a constitutional scholar, who is today largely forgotten by German lawyers and legal academics (although there has been some recent rediscovery of his work by political scientists). A convinced Social Democrat and critic of National-Socialism, Drath was dismissed from his position as a law lecturer in 1933. After becoming a full professor after the war, Drath soon left East Germany for the West when political pressure on him started to mount. Appointed to the Constitutional Court, he was later to be one of the few Justices whose tenure would not be renewed as a result of exaggerated criticism for his role in the creation of the Eastern German administrative justice system (Manfred Baldus, 'Wer war und wofür steht Martin Drath?', *Recht und Politik*, 43 (2007), 86). He remains to date one of the few legal realists Germany has produced and is, if only for this reason, worth remembering.

Hier liegt die entscheidende Schwierigkeit: Es wird die legitimierende Kraft, die die sonstige Gerichtsbarkeit in unseren Verhältnissen erworben hat, benutzt für eine Institution und ein Verfahren, für die und in denen die Voraussetzungen dafür zwangsläufig fehlen. Es wird im Sinn der Gewaltenteilung als Funktion der **richterlichen** Gewalt gekennzeichnet, was tatsächlich im größten Umfange einer **anderen** Gewalt angehört.

(This is the decisive difficulty: The legitimacy the ordinary judiciary has gained in our time is used to shore up an institution and a procedure that themselves lack the conditions essential to this legitimacy. One describes as a matter of separation of powers something as a judicial function, which in fact belongs mostly to another branch.)

(Martin Drath, 'Die Grenzen der Verfassungsgerichtsbarkeit',
Vereinigung der deutschen Staatsrechtslehrer Heft, 9 (1950), 17, 96)

Acknowledgements

This book was written from a particular background, that of a young German lawyer who sees herself—after six years of rather rigid German legal training—suddenly confronted with the chaos and freedom of the common law and a US law school. After two German law exams, however, Yale's legal education appeared less like a bramble bush than a tropical rainforest full of exciting new species, and I ended up staying much longer than I had intended, altogether nearly four years.

Perhaps the first and certainly the most important person who helped me to rediscover the joys of thinking about law has been Bruce Ackerman. He not only displayed an infectious enthusiasm in the classroom which revived my interest in law, but has also accompanied my academic journey first as a faculty adviser and later as a doctoral supervisor in the most honest and generous way any student could wish for. Without his advice and support, I would first have embarked on the wrong project and then done the right one badly. Unsurprisingly, therefore, this book owes much to his criticisms and comments. I have also learned a lot from Robert Post and James Whitman, whose incisive comments were extremely valuable and have prompted a number of significant revisions of the original JSD thesis in the current book. I owe to Alec Stone-Sweet my first encounters not only with comparative law, but also with a more realist political science perspective than I had previously encountered or held. Maria Dino, the heart and soul of the graduate programmes at Yale, deserves mention too for her unfailing support and patience in replying to dozens of emails, most of them, of course, entirely unnecessary. On the German side, I am particularly indebted to Christoph Möllers at Humboldt University, initially my doctoral supervisor until it became clear that a cooperation between Yale and Humboldt would not be possible. He and his work provided important inspirations and also helped convince the German Studienstiftung that this was a project worth funding. Without their monthly stipends over two and a half years I could not have written a doctorate in essentially two countries. This, too, was very important to me—in particular, in grappling with my mother's justified objection that she did not raise her daughter to run away so far. Yet, it turns out I have my father's temperament and this, too, shows in the book. Finally, there is James Fowkes, whose contribution is immense and mostly intangible; countless discussions over dinner, late-night drinks, and his repeated patient review of the following chapters have significantly shaped my ideas in this book.

Small parts of this book have been previously published. Some pages, mostly in the Introduction and Chapter 1, have appeared in a separate paper that addresses the role of National-Socialism for the Court's authority in greater detail than I do here and otherwise provides an introduction to the themes discussed in this book ('Rethinking the Rise of the German Constitutional Court: From Anti-Nazism to Value Formalism', *International Journal of Constitutional Law*, 12(3) (2014)) and I have previously published the descriptive part of my analysis of the German Bundestag protocols in Chapter 6 in German ('Zu viel Vertrauen, zu wenig Kritik? Das Bundesverfassungsgericht im parlamentarischen Diskurs', in *Festschrift für Kay Hailbronner zum 70. Geburtstag*, ed. Georg Jochum, Wolfgang Fritzemeyer, and Marcel Kau (Heidelberg: C. F. Müller, 2013), 713–24). From a somewhat different angle than here, I also discuss the concept of interpretive communities mentioned in Chapter 6 in more detail in another German paper ('We the Experts. Die geschlossene Gesellschaft der Verfassungsinterpreten', *DER STAAT*, 53 (2014), 425).

Contents

Introduction

> One reason why the law of the constitution is imperfectly understood is, that we too rarely put it side by side with the constitutional provisions of other countries. Here, as elsewhere, comparison is essential to recognition. (Dicey, 1885)[1]

In 2011 the German Federal Constitutional Court celebrated its sixtieth anniversary. All agreed that the Court had significantly contributed to the building and shaping of post-war Germany. Chancellor Angela Merkel called it the 'reliable spine'[2] of the new German democracy and the prominent German newspaper *Frankfurter Allgemeine* declared: 'Without the controllers from Karlsruhe, the Federal Republic would not have taken this path of success.'[3] This praise represented more than mere birthday ovations—it reflected what has come to define the contemporary consensus about the German Constitutional Court as a protagonist in the success story of post-war Germany. Today, the Basic Law and many of the Court's jurisprudential innovations have become export models around the world.

Only rarely, however, do we ask how German constitutionalism and the Court came to succeed. In retrospect, it often seems as if the way things turned out was obvious, natural, and could not have been any other way. For official purposes, the story we tell is one of the abuse of power and its taming by law. In Chancellor Merkel's words, 'it was the contempt of law which preceded the unspeakable horrors of the National Socialist tyranny.

[1] Albert Venn Dicey, *Lectures Introductory to the Study of the Law of the Constitution* (London: Macmillan, 1885), Lecture VI: The Rule of Law: Its Applications, p. 218.

[2] Angela Merkel, speech at the occasion of the Federal Constitutional Court's sixtieth birthday, 28 September 2011, reprinted in Stichworte zur Sicherheitspolitik, Nr. 9/10, September/October 2011, pp. 93 et seq., <http://www.bundesregierung.de/Content/DE/PeriodischerBericht/StichworteSicherheitspolitik/2011/2011-11-28-sipo-september-oktober-2011.pdf?__blob=publicationFile>.

[3] Reinhard Müller, '60 Jahre Bundesverfassungsgericht—Verfassungstreue', *Frankfurter Allgemeine*, 28 September 2011, <http://www.faz.net/aktuell/politik/60-jahre-bundesverfassungsgericht-verfassungstreue-11372361.html>.

Therefore, those who created our constitution drew two central lessons from history: Law before power and effective control of power by law'.[4]

Foreign observers, too, tend to understand German constitutionalism as a story about the victory of the rule of law. They view the German Court's extensive authority as an inevitable reaction to the catastrophic violation of human rights by the Nazi regime, which came to power with the consent of the German people. And undoubtedly, German history under the Third Reich and National-Socialism played an important role in the considerations of the men and women who drafted the Basic Law (*Grundgesetz*). The decision to place a bill of rights at the beginning of this constitution that affirmed in its first article the inviolability of human dignity reflected the desire for a new beginning. It marked a break not only with Nazi ideology, but also with what many thought of as its precursor, the German tradition of putting the state first, a strand of thought most famously theorized by the philosopher Hegel.[5]

And yet, none of this quite entailed the idea of a constitutional court that would enjoy the authority of the current Constitutional Court, as we will come to see. The main reasons for this are three. First, the assumption that Nazi history warranted a strong court in order to control the parliament cannot be upheld. Not only did the judiciary massively take part in the administration of Nazi horrors, whereas parliament was already disempowered in 1933, but this was also well recognized in the post-war years where lawyers and judges in particular were among the most mistrusted professions.[6] Second, the framers paid little attention to the new Constitutional Court or indeed to rights review, the basis for the broad expansion of the Court's powers until today.[7] This should not surprise us. No model for a court with

[4] Merkel, speech.

[5] Georg W. F. Hegel, 'Dritter Abschnitt: Der Staat', in *Grundlinien der Philosophie des Rechts*, ed. Georg Lasson (Leipzig: F. Meiner, 1911); Dietmar von der Pfordten, 'Zum Begriff des Staates bei Kant und Hegel', in *Internationales Jahrbuch des Deutschen Idealismus: Der Begriff des Staates*, ed. Karl Ameriks and Jürgen Stolzenberg (Berlin: Walter de Gruyter, 2004); for what has remained of this intellectual tradition of the state in German constitutional law see Christoph Möllers, *Staat als Argument*, 2nd edn (Tübingen: Mohr Siebeck, 2011).

[6] See e.g. Martin Hirsch, Diemut Majer, and Jürgen Meinck (eds), *Recht, Verwaltung und Justiz im Nationalsozialismus* (Baden-Baden: Nomos, 1997), pp. 390 et seq., 488 et seq.; even after the war, 80–90 per cent of all county judges had previously been members of the Nazi party, see Michael Stolleis, *The Law Under the Swastika: Studies on Legal History in Nazi Germany*, trans. Thomas Dunlap (Chicago: University of Chicago Press, 1998), p. 176.

[7] See Chapter 1; generally on the framers' lack of interest in the new Court: Heinz Laufer, *Verfassungsgerichtsbarkeit und politischer Prozess: Studien zum Bundesverfassungsgericht der Bundesrepublik Deutschland* (Tübingen: Mohr Siebeck, 1968), pp. 52 et seq.

a strong rights jurisprudence existed in the 1940s: the 'rights revolution' in countries such as the United States would only really develop in the 1960s and 1970s.[8] To imagine that the German framers would have conceptualized a constitutional court with even roughly the authority and power of the current German Court hence misunderstands the spirit of the time. Third and most importantly, the Court only built up its strength slowly over the course of decades and many of its most expansive cases today simply do not fit with the anti-Nazi paradigm. If the Nazi thesis were right, it should have been a dominant idea the Court was called upon to follow right from the beginning and we would expect to see the Court being especially active in fields such as the protection of minority rights. This is, however, not the case. What role, then, does the legacy of 1933–45 play in explaining the rise of the Court? My answer is: a reasonably small role. The real influence of Germany's Nazi past is much more indirect and less important than the standard narrative suggests.

It is not surprising, therefore, that other scholars have emphasized the continuity in German constitutional thought rather than its break with the past. The German emphasis on rights, so some have suggested, stems from an entrenched nineteenth-century legal paradigm that understood constitutional law as a *limit* to rather than a *basis* for power, and therefore emphasized individual rights over questions of organizational constitutional law.[9] Although their account is less concerned with explaining the Court's authority than the dominance of rights review as a particular feature of German constitutionalism, these two things are connected. Individual complaints based on constitutional rights not only make for more than 95 per cent of the Court's docket,[10] but they are also at the core of the Court's public perception as a 'rights tribunal'. Rights doctrine and theory moreover dominate German constitutional theory to the neglect of organizational and institutional questions.[11] Nevertheless, I am not convinced that the emphasis on rights over organizational and institutional questions can really primarily be understood as a

[8] Compare e.g. Charles R. Epp, *The Rights Revolution: Lawyers, Activists, and Supreme Courts in Comparative Perspective* (Chicago: University of Chicago Press, 1998).

[9] See especially Christoph Möllers, 'Pouvoir Constituant—Constitution—Constitutionalisation', in *Principles of European Constitutional Law*, ed. Armin von Bogdandy and Jürgen Bast (Oxford/München: Hart Publishing/C. H. Beck, 2009), and Oliver Lepsius, 'Rezension von: Frieder Günther: Denken vom Staat her. Die bundesdeutsche Staatsrechtslehre zwischen Dezision und Integration 1949–1970', *Sehepunkte*, 4 (2004), <http://www.sehepunkte.de/2004/05/5714.html>.

[10] See official statistics for the years 1951–2014, <http://www.bundesverfassungsgericht.de/DE/Verfahren/Jahresstatistiken/2014/gb2014/A-I-4.html>.

[11] Möllers, 'Pouvoir Constituant—Constitution—Constitutionalisation', pp. 169–204, at p. 174. See also Lepsius, 'Rezension Günther'.

nineteenth-century heritage. Nor, as I will argue, is German constitutional law today best described first and foremost as a limit on state power. It is much more than that: it is a framework for governance meant to steer and guide state action as much as restrain it.

Still, it is not hard to see that any good explanation of contemporary German constitutionalism will involve elements of both change and continuity: Of course, changes happened, and some of them in response to National-Socialism. And of course, there is also continuity with deeper German legal traditions. However, precisely what kind of changes occurred remains contested and vague in our current understanding. What is perhaps most interesting about those accounts that emphasize continuity is that they approach German constitutionalism broadly from a comparative perspective. Its emphasis on rights over institutional and organizational law stems from a comparison with the more institutionally and politically aware constitutional jurisprudence and scholarship of the United States.

This book takes a similar starting point in comparative law. For when we ask how and why German constitutionalism and the Constitutional Court have succeeded, we often in fact ask a more specific question. This question is not how West Germany established for the first time stable political institutions, among them the Constitutional Court; instead, it is a narrower one. We want to know why the German Court *compared to other constitutional courts* has been doing so well and how we can understand its particular style of jurisprudence. Our methodological starting point is therefore difference-oriented.[12]

And differences abound—in particular, when we compare German constitutionalism to US constitutionalism, as we will throughout this book. US and German scholars speak in very different ways about their courts and constitutions, as do their courts. The US Supreme Court tends to focus more on institutional themes and, in particular, democracy, whereas the German Court typically concentrates on substantive rights questions. Germans have moreover preserved much greater trust in the rationality of law than Americans, and legal doctrine (*Dogmatik*) plays a much more important role in judicial decisions.[13] And perhaps most importantly, the German Constitutional Court's authority is well accepted both by legal academics

[12] Mitchell Lasser, *Judicial Deliberations. A Comparative Analysis of Judicial Transparency and Legitimacy* (Oxford: Oxford University Press, 2004), pp. 145–65.

[13] See e.g. Oliver Lepsius, 'Kritik der Dogmatik', in *Was weiß Dogmatik? Was leistet und wie steuert die Dogmatik des Öffentlichen Rechts?*, ed. Gregor Kirchhof, Stefan Magen, and Karsten Schneider (Tübingen: Mohr Siebeck), pp. 39–62; also Armin von Bogdandy, 'The Past and Promise of Doctrinal Constructivism: A Strategy for Responding to the Challenges Facing Constitutional Scholarship in Europe', *International Journal of Constitutional Law*, 7(3) (2009), 364.

and in the broader public when compared to the US 'obsession' with the counter-majoritarian dilemma.[14]

My interest in differences also explains why much of the more general political science literature does not answer the questions I am asking here. This book builds heavily on previous empirical and historical research on the Constitutional Court, much of which is owed to political scientists, but it ultimately seeks to address a different question. As I argue in more detail later, this question is not one that can reliably be answered by blow-by-blow accounts of individual decisions or with reference to the Court's high approval rates. If politicians and the public support the Court, this tells us nothing about the Court's comparative success and moreover begs the question why they support the Court. Here, suggestions quickly run dry.

Yet, starting with the differences comes with its own problems. For one thing, it is always hard to say if differences matter. Are there not more similarities between the German and other courts, and should we not perhaps focus on these? Or more precisely: Is the lack of a counter-majoritarian obsession in German discourse really relevant to what the German Court can do and does? After all, the US Supreme Court, too, enjoys a comparatively high level of public support and has not shied away from taking expansive decisions that shape political outcomes significantly. Is the German Constitutional Court, in other words, really more powerful compared to other courts?

If we look at the scholarly literature on this question, we quickly find ourselves confronted with a confusing array of widely differing descriptions and opinions of the Court's comparative power. Often, we will be told that the German Court is the 'most powerful' or one of the most powerful courts worldwide.[15] But taking a look at the more detailed studies on judicial self-restraint, we will be confronted with rather contrary descriptions, emphasizing the wide discretion left to the other branches by the Court and its overall modesty.[16] Digging deeper yet by looking at the doctrinal criticism of individual decisions, accusations of judicial expansionism surface again, and

[14] Barry Friedman, 'The Birth of an Academic Obsession: The History of the Counter-majoritarian Difficulty, Part Five', *Yale Law Journal*, 112 (2002), 153.

[15] See e.g. Christoph Grabenwarter, 'Verfassungsinterpretation, Verfassungswandel, Verfassungsfortbildung', in *Soziokultureller Wandel im Verfassungsstaat: Phänomene politischer Transformation. Festschrift für Wolfgang Mantl zum 65.Geburtstag*, ed. Hedwig Kopetz, Josef Marco, and Klaus Poier (Wien: Böhlau, 2004), p. 61; Douglas P. Kommers and Russell Miller, *The Constitutional Jurisprudence of the Federal Republic of Germany*, 3rd edn (Durham: Duke University Press, 2012), p. xii; Georg Vanberg, *The Politics of Constitutional Review in Germany* (Cambridge: Cambridge University Press, 2005), p. 17.

[16] Compare Christian Rau, *Selbst entwickelte Grenzen in der Rechtsprechung des United States Supreme Court und des Bundesverfassungsgerichts* (Berlin: Duncker & Humblot, 1996), pp. 240 et seq.

scholars often charge the Court with assuming the function of lawmaker and thus overstepping its competences. The resulting confusion is rooted in a number of methodological problems with which such inquiries are often fraught: To assess if a judgment is deferential or restrained, we need a perspective from which to make this judgment, a baseline against which we can measure what the Court does. Many legal scholars stipulate what the right decision in a given case would have been and then criticize the Court if it deviates from this position. Of course, by doing so, they merely substitute their own opinion for the Court's and thus hardly provide us with an objective standard. Another, more modest approach is to take the Court's word for what it is doing. Again, however, this is a doubtful enterprise: The Court is not actually exercising restraint every time it claims to do so. Nor can we avoid problems by turning to a statistical analysis of cases. Sure, the German Court's general record of invalidations is, at approximately 10 per cent per year, comparatively high, even though less than half of all norms challenged are actually invalidated.[17] Yet, here, too, methodological questions loom large: How do we compare this with a court that functions as a general appeals court and, more importantly, how can we account for the political setting, the parties, and the facts of the case at hand, all of which are relevant for determining whether or not a decision is expansive?

The challenge is therefore to move beyond this kind of analysis. Whether there are more differences or similarities is ultimately not a question we can usefully answer. And rather than seeking to measure different degrees of judicial deference or expansionism, we need to get a better understanding of German constitutionalism and the Court's authority. Only then will we be able to answer the question if the differences we observe are merely superficial, or do indeed matter and for what. In terms of comparative methodology, we might say that we need to integrate functionalist with expressivist considerations that take the broader legal and political culture into account.[18] This book hence understands itself, at least in parts, as a project of 'constitutional ethnography', to borrow Kim Scheppele's term, rather than in terms of classical functionalist analysis.[19]

As a result, our inquiry must be both wide-ranging and deep. How citizens view the state and law influences the role of courts in a society: Do they think that all government is inherently oppressive and law should therefore limit state power as much as possible? Or do they conceive of the state as a

[17] Sascha Kneip, 'Rolle und Einfluss des Bundesverfassungsgerichts in international vergleichender Perspektive', *Zeitschrift für Politik* (2013), 72 and 81 et seq.

[18] Marc Tushnet, 'The Possibilities of Comparative Law', *Yale Law Journal*, 108, 1225.

[19] Kim L. Scheppele, 'Constitutional Ethnography: An Introduction', *Law and Society Review*, 38(3) (2004), 389.

beneficial force and of law as its primary tool? Nor can we confine ourselves to looking at constitutional courts merely as strategic actors seeking to carve out a maximum of power for themselves, because this isolates them from the legal traditions and the larger cultural context in which they are operating. Justices at constitutional courts are first and foremost individuals who have been educated in, work in, and are socialized into a legal system for decades before their appointment to the Court. Unsurprisingly, these lawyers will be influenced by their specific legal culture, and by the more general attitudes towards legitimate authority in their society.

Once we take such a broader cultural and comparative approach, we begin to see not only the differences, but also the similarities—sometimes where we would not have suspected them. With societies as far away and different as South Africa or India, for example, Germans share the idea that the state has to play a central role in shaping society. Like them, Germans understand law as the key instrument to bring about a better and more just society. Looking at things from a different angle, we see another group of family resemblances with many of Germany's European neighbours, but also countries as far east as Japan. Like Germany, these societies organize the exercise of state authority hierarchically, entrusting highly specialized administrative tasks to professionals who will usually be career bureaucrats. In such systems, law is treated as a science and the exercise of legal tasks requires long and intensive periods of study and training. As a result, the division between law and other disciplines is a key tenet of the professional self-understanding of lawyers.

As we look back and forth between the German Court and other constitutional courts around the world, we also start to better understand the relationship between change and continuity. German similarities with South Africa's transformative constitutionalism show that the changes we see in German post-war jurisprudence are not confined to a more robust attempt to realize individual rights as limits on government. Rather, they indicate a shift to a different paradigm of constitutional law, where law becomes a driver for state action as much as a restraint on it. And we also realize that the many differing descriptions of German constitutional law are not accidental. For the German Court turns out, after all, to be all of these things: pragmatic, open to policy arguments, but also formalist, dry, and technical at the same time. But this wealth of seemingly contradictory adjectives now no longer marks our surrender before the complexities of the real world. Instead, it holds the promise of its success. For it is the successful reconciliation of these somewhat contradictory elements that gives German constitutional jurisprudence its particular style, a style I call 'Value Formalism' and will be discussing in detail later.

The book begins by setting out its analytical framework for understanding German constitutionalism from a broader comparative perspective. This framework builds on previous research by Mirjan Damaška and Bruce Ackerman, and it operates with two binary variables or ideal types. The first variable concerns our understanding of the kind of state the constitution envisages and the constitution's role in this state: Does it set up a traditional 'reactive' constitutional regime, concerned primarily with protecting individual liberty and making sure that no one institution holds too much power? Or is it 'activist' and transformative, setting out its own vision of a just society that requires active state engagement in order to realize this goal? As we will quickly recognize, the German Constitutional Court not only operates against the background of a tradition of activist statehood, but has also adopted a broadly transformative understanding of constitutional law: in German legal parlance the Basic Law constitutes an 'objective order of values' (*objektive Werteordnung*). Consequently, the constitution is thought to have a 'radiating effect' (*Ausstrahlungswirkung*) throughout the whole legal order, informing the application of legal rules in any field of law—the famous German *Drittwirkung*. Second, we need to understand how judicial authority is constructed: Is it exercised by a hierarchically ordered bureaucracy staffed with professional experts, or is it typically shared between different offices that derive their legitimacy from their connection with the public or the social elite? Even though the days of Weber are gone, the hierarchical paradigm of authority still retains considerable explanatory power in relation to German understandings of legal and constitutional legitimacy. This allowed the Constitutional Court to build up an exclusive authority, based centrally on its apolitical professionalism.

Equipped with these categories, I then move on to look more closely at the German case. As we will see in Chapter 2, the German Court's turn to an activist conception of constitutional law in the late 1950s constituted a break with the entrenched nineteenth-century understanding of rights as negative rights, protecting individual spheres of freedom against state intervention. With its conception of the Basic Law as an order of values, the Court created an ever-expanding field of constitutional law. But while the turn to a transformative vision of constitutional law in the 1950s provided the basis for the Court's later expansionism, we will see how the Court initially exercised its new powers only cautiously, because it was yet unclear how it would fit into the established legal culture and hierarchies.

The novelty of the legal questions arising under this activist paradigm was for a long time perceived as a threat to legal certainty and judicial consistency, as we will see in Chapter 3. Certainty and consistency are important ideas in any legal system, but even more so in one that relies on professional expertise as its main basis for authority. Nevertheless, activist law and hierarchical authority—while sometimes in tension—are not polar opposites and could eventually be reconciled. The story of this reconciliation is the story of the rise of the German Constitutional Court from 1951 until today. Over time, as the new institution assumed a distinct identity as a court, it could draw on the traditional resources of judicial legitimacy within the system and thus stabilize its own institutional authority.

In reconciling transformative constitutionalism with the traditional hierarchical approach to judicial authority, the German Constitutional Court and scholars created a particular style of constitutional jurisprudence, Value Formalism, which I and will explore in Chapter 4 in more detail. In spite of its success, Value Formalism comes with a number of shortcomings and problems that are frequently ignored in German scholarship. We will discuss one of these problems in more detail in Chapter 5. As I argue there, the hierarchical conception of judicial authority has undermined the Court's capacity to adequately reflect on its own role vis-à-vis the other branches in its jurisprudence. This heightens the risk of judicial expansionism, especially in those cases where strong political pressure is absent.

The hierarchical paradigm is not only key to understanding constitutional jurisprudence, but it also influences the way the public and German parliamentarians perceive the Court. A short study of parliamentary discourse about the Constitutional Court in Chapter 6 demonstrates that legislators, too, have come to accept and indeed appreciate the Court's authority in these terms. In light of these insights, we will have to clarify the nature of German constitutional patriotism as a 'Catholic' form of constitutional faith in contrast to the US 'Protestant' model.[20] The book closes with a short normative critique of the standard arguments in favour of German-style constitutionalism, but argues that the chances for a major change in the German model are slim.

Before we now dive into the deep waters of German constitutionalism, a final word of caution should be addressed to the reader: Though this book sets out a particular framework to understand German constitutionalism, it should not be read to present a causal explanation in the strict sense. To give such a causal account, my theory would have to take many more factors into account. Any story of how a particular court acquires its status and power is inevitably a complicated and multi-faceted thing. Instead, what this book offers is *one*, hopefully insightful way of understanding the German Court and the most important features of German jurisprudence from a broader

[20] Compare Sanford Levinson, *Constitutional Faith* (Princeton: Princeton University Press, 2011).

comparative perspective. Second, even though my frame of reference is comparative and historical insofar as I include two chapters of constitutional history and many references to the United States and South Africa (including some remarks on Japan and India), I offer neither a comprehensive account of German constitutional history nor indeed of these other countries' constitutional systems. Inevitably, my account of history and foreign legal systems will remain piecemeal here. My aims are more modest: I merely seek to get a better sense of what makes the German case distinctive by looking at other examples.

And distinctive it is with its particular synthesis of two so different paradigms of law and legal authority. Yet, it is this particular synthesis that plays an important role in explaining the global success and admiration for German constitutionalism: With its proto-transformative idea of constitutional law, German constitutionalism fits the spirit of our times better than the more traditional liberal US model of constitutionalism. At the same time, the German Court's commitment to a hierarchical culture of authority means that its jurisprudence is something richly and distinctively *legal*, even though it significantly shapes German politics. For constitutional drafters elsewhere who consider copying parts of the German Basic Law, this second dimension, German legal culture, is particularly important. For it is easy to transplant provisions and even adopt a transformative constitution, but one cannot manufacture a legal culture from scratch. This may not be a bad thing, of course; as we will see, the German model comes with its own faults and downsides, and as I argue in the Conclusion, there is much to be said for a more open and dialogical approach to judicial authority. However, whether we seek to borrow or reform, without an appreciation for this legal culture we cannot hope to grasp the distinctive recipe of the success of German constitutionalism.

1

Constitutional Paradigms and Judicial Authority

Law and courts are essential parts of human societies, both old and new. But not everywhere do they fulfil the same functions or fulfil them in the same way. In this chapter, I ask two questions: First, how do citizens understand the role of law and in particular of constitutional law? And second, why do they accept and follow judicial authority, including that of constitutional courts?

To address these questions, I use a set of binary variables, which build on the work of an earlier generation of scholars.[1] These variables represent Weberian ideal types that can help us to better understand the particular features of German constitutionalism, as compared especially with the United States. My first two variables are reactive and activist (constitutional) law: Reactive constitutions are oriented towards protecting individual liberty and limiting state power. They stand opposed to transformative or activist constitutions, which lay out a more comprehensive vision of justice that mandates state intervention in society in order to achieve change. Previous scholarship also distinguishes between two modes of legal authority: Authority can be constructed hierarchically, perceived as founded on professional expertise, or it can be coordinate, shared among many institutions and persons, and tied firmly to a socio-cultural basis of common sense.

These ideal types, of course, represent abstractions. Law is never only reactive or activist in real societies, and it may even serve different purposes altogether. The same is true for our ideas of authority. The reason I work with these ideal types is first and foremost because of their explanatory power for this particular project. Second, while life is varied, variety is not endless. The model of authority and law I adopt here builds on previous comparative studies, most notably Mirjan Damaška's important *The Faces of Justice*

[1] Bruce Ackerman, *Reconstructing American Law* (Cambridge: Harvard University Press, 1984); Mirjan Damaška, *The Faces of Justice and Authority: A Comparative Approach to the Legal Process* (New Haven: Yale University Press, 1986).

and Authority and Bruce Ackerman's *Reconstructing American Law*, but it also draws more broadly on the comparative studies of civil and common law systems[2] as well as the literature on transformative constitutionalism.[3] Finally, while my ideal types do not exist in their pure form in real societies, by drawing on them we can nevertheless identify the broad patterns, the platonic ideals that exercise a gravitational pull in the system for matters to fall along certain lines, and not along others. To illustrate them, I draw on examples from countries such as the United States, South Africa, and Japan.

A. Previous Literature

My theoretical framework builds on Mirjan Damaška's theory of comparative law (*The Faces of Justice and Authority*, 1986) and has been complemented by Bruce Ackerman's thoughts on the rise of activist law in the United States (*Reconstructing American Law*, 1984).

I am relying on these two authors most importantly because I have found them particularly useful in understanding German constitutionalism. Beyond that, however, Mirjan Damaška is one of the very few scholars in comparative law who offers a general comparative framework encompassing a wide range of legal systems. This framework builds and develops further not only the existing literature on the difference between civil- and common-law systems, but also Max Weber's groundbreaking work on legitimacy,[4] and hence unites two major strands of work in comparative law and comparative sociology. Damaška develops his analytical categories of hierarchical vs coordinate authority and activist vs reactive ideas of statehood as a way of

[2] See especially Wolfgang Fikentscher, *Methoden des Rechts in vergleichender Darstellung: Band 2: Anglo-amerikanischer Rechtskreis* (Tübingen: Mohr Siebeck, 1975) and Wolfgang Fikentscher, *Methoden des Rechts in vergleichender Darstellung: Band 3: Mitteleuropäischer Rechtskreis* (Tübingen: Mohr Siebeck, 1976), and of course the godfather of theories of legitimation Max Weber, *Grundriss Der Sozialökonomik. III. Abteilung: Wirtschaft und Gesellschaft* (Tübingen: Mohr, 1922).

[3] To name just a few of the works in the South African literature where the term 'transformative constitutionalism' has first been employed, see e.g. Karl Klare, 'Legal Culture and Transformative Constitutionalism', *South African Journal on Human Rights*, 14 (1998), 146; Pius Langa, 'Transformative Constitutionalism', *Stellenbosch Law Review*, 17 (2006), 351; Dikgang Moseneke 'Transformative Constitutionalism: Its Implications for the Law of Contract', *Stellenbosch Law Review*, 20 (2009), 3; Marius Pieterse, 'What Do We Mean When We Talk about Transformative Constitutionalism?', *South African Public Law*, 20 (2005), 155; Theunis Roux, 'Transformative Constitutionalism and the Best Interpretation of the South African Constitution: Distinction without a Difference?', *Stellenbosch Law Review*, 20 (2009), 258; Andre J. Van Der Walt, 'Transformative Constitutionalism and the Development of South African Property Law (Part 1)', *Tydskrif vir die Suid-Afrikaanse Reg*, 4 (2005), 655.

[4] Weber, *Wirtschaft und Gesellschaft*, chapter III.

understanding different approaches to the administration of justice and the roles of those involved in it. His main focus is on civil and criminal procedural law, but his models run much deeper and provide us with the analytical tools to understand the broader typologies of different legal cultures around the globe and they are therefore invaluable for the project pursued here. Bruce Ackerman's work, in turn, sharpens some of Damaška's categories from a US perspective and therefore complements my framework. Ackerman is primarily concerned with the changing role of the state in the United States since the New Deal and the consequences of this change for the US legal system. His goal is to provide a new legal language (constructive legal argument) that transcends Legal Realism in order to be able to better address the problems arising in the activist post-New Deal state. Yet, even though both Damaška and Ackerman make occasional suggestions about how their models may apply to constitutional law, neither is explicitly conceived as a model for constitutional jurisprudence.[5]

Damaška's concept of *authority* requires relatively little development and adaptation to make it a useful tool for constitutional analysis. My variable of *activism* as a concept of constitutional law is, however, somewhat further removed from Damaška's original concept and closer to, though not entirely identical with, Ackerman's understanding in *Reconstructing American Law*. If I have tried to go beyond his concept it is because the US case for activism is, compared to countries such as India or South Africa, not particularly well developed or strong. This is hardly surprising. When both Ackerman and Damaška were writing their books, they could not very well have taken account of these countries, since an explicit concept of what I call activist (or transformative) constitutionalism[6] was only just beginning to emerge. It made its perhaps purest appearance in the South African post-apartheid model of constitutionalism. Similarly, the Indian Supreme Court's post-emergency activism was neither yet firmly established nor thoroughly researched at that time. But while the Indian and South African examples inform my thinking here, I do not provide a full-blown inductive comparative study in this

[5] See, however, Damaška's later paper, 'Reflections on American Constitutionalism', *American Journal of Comparative Law*, Supp. 38 (1990), 421, which applies parts of his framework to US constitutional law. I have nevertheless found *The Faces of Justice and Authority* more useful for my enterprise.

[6] Please note that the term 'activist' is used here in a very *specific* sense that refers to Ackerman's and Damaška's work and as broadly equivalent to what has been termed 'transformative' in the South African context. It is thus distinct from the use of 'activist' as a description of a particularly expansionist or even aggressive style of jurisprudence or description of courts, as it is frequently used in the literature!

book that seeks to identify common features of transformative systems,[7] but instead proceed from a more abstract perspective.

Similarly, I have avoided in this chapter to speak in categories of common law vs continental law, even though my framework strongly builds on features that can be identified as classical attributes of common or civil law, respectively.[8] If I nevertheless take a different, more abstract analytical approach here, it is not because I am trying to obscure these roots. Rather, it is because both common- and civil-law jurisdictions have evolved significantly over the last centuries and much that we would identify as classical common-law features may have been long discarded in actually existing common- or civil-law systems. For example, many common-law countries are today rather activist states that are strongly involved in the welfare of their citizens. Moreover, differences between them can be considerable, as demonstrated, for example, in Atiyah and Summers' comparative research about form and substance in US and British law[9] or the different role of juries in these two countries.[10] Nevertheless, in the following chapters I sometimes refer to continental law when I take a more historical perspective.

B. Concepts of Law

Activist or transformative constitutional law is a relatively new thing in the history of constitutionalism. Activist constitutions seek to change and improve state and society. They are aspirational. In contrast, reactive constitutions attempt to protect society and individuals against state intervention. They are first and foremost concerned with safeguarding individual rights and preventing the state or any one institution from holding too much power. In other words: They want to keep government out, whereas activist

[7] But see for this Michaela Hailbronner, 'Not Only in the Global South: Transformative Constitutionalism in Comparison' (conference paper, Younger Comparativists Conference, Portland, USA, April 2014).

[8] Damaška, *The Faces of Justice and Authority*, p. 1. For a German–US comparison working with the common-law vs civil-law framework see Shu-Perng Hwang, *Verfassungsgerichtlicher Jurisdiktionsstaat? Eine rechtsvergleichende Analyse zur Kompetenzabgrenzung von Verfassungsgericht und Gesetzgeber in den USA und der Bundesrepublik Deutschland* (Berlin: Duncker & Humblot, 2005), pp. 104 et seq., pp. 149–50.

[9] Patrick S. Atiyah and Robert S. Summers, *Form and Substance in Anglo-American Law: A Comparative Study of Legal Reasoning, Legal Theory, and Legal Institutions* (Oxford: Clarendon Press, 1991).

[10] John H. Langbein, Renee L. Lerner, and Bruce P. Smith, *History of the Common Law: The Development of Anglo-American Legal Institutions* (New York: Aspen Publishers, 2009), chapters 8 and 11.

constitutions seek to bring government in and to make use of its powers for the greater good.

In the following pages, we will examine these two legal paradigms in more detail. If I spend more time on the concept of activist constitutionalism than reactive constitutionalism, there are two reasons for that: first, reactive constitutionalism is historically older and we are therefore more familiar with it; and second, activist constitutionalism is ultimately the more important concept for Germany and thus deserves more attention here.

Activist constitutionalism depends on three conditions: political, legal and cultural. First, we must have an activist state concerned with enhancing public welfare and constructing a just society, rather than merely with preserving peace and order by settling individual conflicts. Second, we must have a constitution and a court endowed with the power of constitutional review, which people can access. Finally, this constitution must be understood as the fundamental legal and ethical programme laying out the state's transformative vision. An activist constitution will therefore typically a) provide for the direct or at least indirect *application of constitutional rights to private conduct*, b) include *enforceable state duties*, and c) its interpretation will focus on *substance* over form and require considerable flexibility in order to provide for the best possible realization of constitutional values under changing circumstances. Before I turn to explaining these two different models of constitutionalism in more detail, however, we need to take a closer look at the ideas of law underlying these two concepts of constitutionalism which shape our understanding of what a constitution does and should do.

I. Reactive law

For a considerable time our understanding of law has been strongly reactive, its main function being to solve conflicts and protect individual liberty.[11] With the global trend towards constitutionalization and juridification, this understanding of law has become nearly universally accepted. What is contested today is therefore no longer whether constitutions should indeed protect individual rights and set limits on government, but rather *what other functions* they have and should have, in particular whether they should incorporate a thicker, aspirational idea of justice.

Reactive law appears in its purest form in *reactive states*. By reactive state I mean a minimalist state, in the sense of, for example, Robert Nozick's concept.[12] The reactive state confines itself mainly to securing peace and order,

[11] Compare Damaška, *The Faces of Justice and Authority*, pp. 73 et seq.

[12] Robert Nozick, *Anarchy, State and Utopia* (New York: Basic Books, 1974).

and intervenes only for that purpose—and if so, in minimal ways—in society.[13] But reactive law does not *depend* on the existence of a reactive state. In a weaker form, reactive law may also develop in states that are quite actively engaged in the welfare of their citizens. Such activist states then typically use other means than law and rights to engage in the task of social engineering, such as administrative decrees and hierarchical command and oversight. The emergence of a public–private divide historically enabled law to take on a reactive character even in activist states: Law here served to protect the boundaries of the private against the public realm, by safeguarding negative individual rights and solving conflicts between private parties while still leaving ample room for state intervention in the public domain. As we will see in the next chapter, the German nineteenth-century legal paradigm in many ways reflected just this kind of reactive attitude in the context of often rather activist states.

The characteristic *legal form* of reactive legal systems is the contract.[14] Because individuals are free in their private relationships with one another and at liberty to seek what is best for them, the state does not usually intervene in private interactions. Only when disputes arise is state intervention required. Even then, however, reactive law tends to leave as much as possible to the parties, letting them determine much of the content of subsequent legal proceedings. Substantive rules will be minimal and handled with flexibility where both parties consent.[15] If possible, the state confines itself to providing merely a procedural framework in which the parties can settle their disputes, without prescribing any idea of justice on its own. The classical common-law conception of 'natural justice' as a (procedural) right to a fair hearing[16]—as opposed to the thicker continental concept of natural law—illustrates this.

Reactive *constitutions* therefore primarily contain mechanisms to curb governmental powers by providing for individual rights and institutional checks and balances. They will not, in contrast, seek to steer positive state action. Positive rights allowing citizens to demand things from the state are anathema here. So is the direct application of fundamental rights in private conflicts, which is thought to interfere with individual freedom as expressed in the freedom of contract. How far reactive constitutions go in restricting state action will, of course, vary between states. The stronger the checks on concentrations of power and the more far reaching its individual rights, the more reactive a state is likely to be. More checks and veto gates are in reactive

[13] Damaška, *The Faces of Justice and Authority*, pp. 73–5.
[14] Ibid., pp. 75–6.
[15] Ibid., p. 76.
[16] Compare e.g. for details, Frederick F. Schauer, 'English Natural Justice and American Due Process: An Analytical Comparison', *William & Mary Law Review*, 18 (1976), 47.

legal systems generally considered better than less, since it is not the efficient administration of governmental tasks that counts but avoiding concentrations of power. The same rationale applies to individual rights: More is always better for individual freedom, which is the ultimate aim of reactive constitutionalism.

II. Activist law

Activist law in contrast is importantly a tool for social engineering and state-driven change.[17] It envisages an energetic state that has set itself the task of overcoming existing injustices and problems by regulation and management, and law here furnishes the state's main instrument in achieving its transformative agenda. An activist constitution hence lays out a vision of a just society and provides directions for realizing it. And because realizing a comprehensive vision of justice is a challenging task, activist constitutions will typically require the transformation of society and individual behaviour. There are hence no social or individual spheres that are considered private, sacrosanct, and above legal intervention. State planning and the administration of governmental programmes extend to potentially all areas of its citizens' lives.

Not *all* activist states, however, will cherish an activist idea of law. Some of them may use means other than law and legal regulation to realize the aim of social transformation and change. In such activist states (most notably many of the former Communist states) individual rights that exist merely for the individual's sake have no place.[18] Individual entitlements are at best part of certain state policies and schemes that seek to implement some overarching policy, but they do not confer independent rights. However, with the global human rights movement and the trend towards constitutionalization, this brand of activism has become more rare. More often than not, activist states today turn to law as their primary means of implementing state policy and lay down their constitutional vision in a document that is to be enforced by courts. After all, in democratic politics there is always a risk that legislators may favour short-term political gains over their long-term duty to realize constitutional values.[19] It is therefore important to establish checks that can

[17] Though my framework does not follow any particular conception of transformative constitutionalism, I have drawn on the South African literature on the subject, most notably Klare, 'Legal Culture and Transformative Constitutionalism', and Langa, 'Transformative Constitutionalism' (see also note 4 for further references).

[18] Damaška, *The Faces of Justice and Authority*, p. 83.

[19] There are also other potential reasons for activist states to convert to an activist model of law. Especially when the regime in power has changed and the old administrative branch appears as insufficiently reliable to implement the new political agenda, it may be costly and difficult to

bring legislators back on track to concentrate on their most important tasks when necessary.

To fulfil this function, courts need the power of *constitutional review*. They also need to have a sizeable *jurisdiction*. In activist regimes, state institutions will typically be able to raise constitutional issues with the court in order to ensure the efficient implementation of the grand plan and abstract review provides just for that possibility. However, allowing for abstract review may often not be sufficient because it depends on the willingness of political actors to appeal to the court. It is therefore important that individuals, too, can access the court—not so much in order to defend their individual liberties, but rather to act as agents of the public interest in realizing the constitutional agenda.

Finally, interpreting and enforcing an activist constitution is no easy task. Where reactive constitutions seek to delimit spaces of private freedom from state interference, transformative constitutions have a much broader understanding of justice at their core. From this more comprehensive aspirational character of the activist constitution some further characteristics follow.

1. Individual rights

Individual freedom may play an important role in transformative constitutional regimes, too, but it is likely to be understood in a different way than in reactive ones—as something that has to be actively pursued and that depends on the state providing certain material conditions for its enjoyment, such as housing or food.[20] Realizing individual freedom thus understood hence becomes a task that may well require heavy-handed government intervention. Rights in transformative constitutions will therefore typically not be absolute, but rather subject to the imperative of implementing the best policy: Substantive liberty for all citizens may often require infringements of classical (formal) liberal rights to be left alone. Governments will therefore have to intervene in spaces previously considered private and hence restrict the room of (negative) freedom from government intervention.

establish the necessary internal control mechanisms. In this situation, courts may appear more reliable to the new regime and more suitable to be charged with the task of transformation. If an activist state emerges out of a former reactive regime with a well-functioning judicial branch, it may be both cheaper and easier to use the existing judicial mechanisms rather than put new ones in place. Or states may want to express their allegiance to the emerging international trends towards legalization and judicialization, as in the case in post-apartheid South Africa, which wanted to express its conversion to the established international human rights paradigm.

[20] Ackerman, *Reconstructing American Law*, pp. 32 et seq.

a) Horizontal application

To transform society according to the constitutional mandate, it is first of all necessary not to confine constitutional rights to the relationship between citizens and the state. If society is to change, so must the relationships between private citizens. Because the constitution represents the fundamental ethical and legal matrix guiding the transformation, constitutional rights need to apply—directly or at least indirectly—between private persons as well as between individuals and the state.

b) Justiciable state duties

Second, a truly activist constitution will recognize the state's key role in realizing the constitutional vision of justice. Courts thus cooperate with the political branches to maximize good outputs. While this may involve taking a stance against government in some cases, it does not imply opposition to the government's activist role, but rather the opposite. Courts will consider above all if the government has lost track of the grand plan of society as it is laid out by the constitution and will attempt to improve governmental measures instead of limiting them. An activist constitution will therefore entail justiciable state duties.

2. *Focus on substance and flexibility*

Finally, constitutional interpretation and jurisprudence in activist systems tend to emphasize substance over procedure. This is because it matters little who carries out the relevant tasks as long as someone does and does it well. Procedure only matters insofar as it is necessary to ensure a good result, but it carries little value of its own. If procedural requirements get in the way of efficiency, they need to be handled flexibly.[21] However, when it comes to realizing the constitution's substantive precepts, flexibility is less valued and may indeed even be thought dangerous. There is little room for discretion on the part of individual state actors when it comes to results.[22] At the same time, the delegation of authority to specific institutions may be necessary to ensure efficient outcomes, as the implementation of complex policy agendas may require considerable expertise. But while delegation may provide the necessary knowledge and expertise to successfully engineer social change, it is also problematic: It risks that subordinate institutions may apply the law in an arbitrary and inconsistent way and thus endanger the realization of

[21] Compare the policy-implementing process in activist states, Damaška, *The Faces of Justice and Authority*, pp. 82 et seq. and pp. 150 et seq.

[22] Damaška, *The Faces of Justice and Authority*, pp. 82–3.

constitutional goals.[23] Finding the right balance between sufficient flexibility and rigidity is therefore one of the main legal challenges in the activist state.

III. Examples

1. Reactive constitutional regimes: the United States

Even though few contemporary states can still be characterized as reactive, reactive *law* is well and alive today. Reactive legal attitudes characterized most notably mainstream US eighteenth- and nineteenth-century political and legal philosophy, and its traces can still be identified in US political and legal culture today.

The Declaration of Independence proclaimed the sanctity of individual liberty as the aim and limitation of every government. Though providing for a stronger national government than the previous Articles of Confederation, the US Constitution nevertheless strongly reflected fears of government overreach and tyranny, as the Federalist Papers emphasized.[24] Insofar as the national government had been granted powers, many of these were moreover—at least in their Madisonian conception—understood as a counterweight to democratic excesses within the individual states.[25] Unsurprisingly then, the US Constitution equipped the national government only with a limited set of competences, making Congress the key institution. In contrast, it showed little concern for the establishment of a national administration. Though vesting the executive power in the President, it provided almost no explanation as to what exactly this meant.[26]

Once established, the national government under the administration of Hamilton took on considerable tasks, mainly in the fields of taxation, finance, banking, and military affairs. Nevertheless, national government remained comparatively limited until the New Deal. Moreover, even the early expansions of national power were severely contested at the time and partly reversed under the reign of later presidents such as Thomas Jefferson or Andrew Jackson, who cherished a thoroughly reactive idea of national government.[27] After the Civil War, opposition to what was polemically

[23] Ibid.

[24] Alexander Hamilton, James Madison, and John Jay, *The Federalist Papers*, ed. Isaac Kramnick (England: Penguin, 1987).

[25] Gordon S. Wood, *Empire of Liberty: A History of the Early Republic, 1789–1815* (Oxford: Oxford University Press, 2009), p. 33.

[26] Jerry L. Mashaw, *Creating the Administrative Constitution: The Lost One Hundred Years of American Administrative Law* (New Haven: Yale University Press, 2012), pp. 311–12.

[27] See e.g. Gordon S. Wood, *The Radicalism of the American Revolution* (New York: A. A. Knopf, 1991), p. 328.

understood as paternalism was strong and widespread. A general laissez-faire attitude dominated legal thought, emphasizing the freedom of contract as key to individual liberty.[28] Before his appointment to the Court, the later Chief Justice Fuller declared: 'Paternalism, with its constant intermeddling with individual freedom, has no place in a system which rests for its strength upon the self-reliant energies of the people.'[29] The Supreme Court's later (1905) Lochner decision famously exemplified this reactive spirit of the time.[30] Striking down the federal regulation of working hours in bakeries based on the freedom of contract, the decision demonstrated a strongly formal, negative, and economic understanding of individual freedom, directed against the state but not other private parties. And though considerable national administration existed well before the twentieth century,[31] administrative law as a field of specialized judicial review of administrative action only really came into existence with the enactment of the Administrative Procedure Act (APA) in 1946.[32]

The Roosevelt administration eventually broke this early reactive spirit by threatening to 'pack' the Supreme Court with a number of additional (pro-government and New Deal-supporting) judges.[33] As a result, some typical features of a more activist conception of constitutional law slowly started to emerge in the Court's jurisprudence: One was an increasing willingness on the part of the Supreme Court to use constitutional law to interfere in relationships between private parties;[34] the other was a concern with equality in addition to liberty. Especially in the field of racial justice, the Court demonstrably ventured out of its prior classical reactive paradigm of protecting individual rights against state intervention.[35] Instead of restricting government, the Court started collaborating with it in order to change society and with it the opportunities and life offered to black people.[36] Nevertheless, the change to a more activist brand of constitutionalism was never complete.

[28] See also Ackerman, *Reconstructing American Law*, whose terminology is slightly different from mine here insofar as it focuses on legal methodology rather than the substance of legal reasoning.

[29] Cited according to Aviam Soifer, 'The Paradox of Paternalism and Laissez-Faire Constitutionalism: United States Supreme Court, 1888–1921', *Law and History Review*, 5 (1987).

[30] *Lochner v New York*, 198 US 45 (1905).

[31] Mashaw, *Creating the Administrative Constitution*.

[32] See, however, for previous forms of administrative control under the common law, Mashaw, *Creating the Administrative Constitution*, pp. 75 et seq.

[33] Bruce Ackerman, *We the People. Transformations* (Cambridge: Harvard University Press, 2000), pp. 317–24.

[34] See e.g. *Shelley v Kraemer*, 334 US 1 (1948).

[35] Ackerman, *Reconstructing American Law*.

[36] See Bruce Ackerman, *We the People. The Civil Rights Revolution* (Cambridge: Harvard University Press, 2014), for a detailed account of this cooperation between the Court and the political branches.

Contemporary US constitutionalism is truly a hybrid. While conservatives beginning with the Reagan administration made a strong case for a return to a reactive paradigm of government and law and started to roll back some features of activist statehood, the US administrative state is nevertheless alive and well today. At the same time, rights are still largely conceived of as protections of negative freedoms rather than mandates to compel specific governmental action.[37] Even progressives often understand the US constitution in reactive terms, focusing on the protection of individual rights, for example when Richard Fallon argues for the necessity of judicial review in the US:[38] According to Fallon, it is not that the judiciary will necessarily protect rights better than Congress, but that it is always better to err on the side of more rights (and less government) rather than the other way round. This attitude is, unsurprisingly, even more pronounced in conservative circles such as the Tea Party movement and the more conservative parts of the Republican Party, who sometimes argue for a return to an eighteenth-century-style reactive government. Drawing a lesson from conservative backlash against the Warren Court and being disenchanted with courts' ability to bring about change,[39] many academics even on the left now look significantly to other institutions to bring about social justice and change. In spite of the importance of the Constitution in US public discourse,[40] constitutional law is therefore mostly not understood as a roadmap to (socially engineered) justice, but rather serves as a reminder of important truths Americans must not forget. This does not rule out the possibility that the Supreme Court may use its more activist precedents as a basis to develop the law further at some point, but it means that US constitutionalism today retains considerable reactive features.

2. *Activist constitutional regimes: South Africa*

The paradigm case for activist constitutionalism today is South Africa. Its own brand of transformative constitutionalism resembles closely what I have called activist constitutionalism here[41] and exhibits all the traits we

[37] For the continued prevalence of a negative rights conception in the US, see with further examples Helen Hershkoff, 'Transforming Legal Theory in the Light of Practice: The Judicial Application of Social and Economic Rights to Private Orderings', in *Courting Social Justice: Judicial Enforcement of Social and Economic Rights in the Developing World*, ed. Varun Guri and Daniel M. Brinks (New York: Cambridge University Press, 2008).

[38] Richard H. Fallon, Jr., 'The Core of an Uneasy Case for Judicial Review', *Harvard Law Review*, 121 (2008), 1693.

[39] Following e.g. Gerald N. Rosenfeld, *The Hollow Hope. Can Courts Bring about Social Change?*, 2nd edn (Chicago: University of Chicago Press, 2008).

[40] Sanford Levinson, *Constitutional Faith* (Princeton: Princeton University Press, 2011).

[41] For a fuller argument of the German–South African similarities, see Hailbronner, 'Not Only in the Global South'.

set out as a prerequisite of an activist understanding of constitutional law: It is set in a deeply activist state with a constitution that provides a comprehensive vision of a better society and a constitutional court to help protect and realize this vision.

Like Germany, South Africa has a long history of activist government. The apartheid state's aim was to provide an enduring social, economic, and governmental structure that would promote the welfare of Afrikaners, and enforce racial segregation and the subordination of non-whites in an effective and economically sustainable way. To achieve this aim, apartheid entailed much more than enforcing existing racist social structures.[42] Keeping black people out of white and urban areas and enforcing and preserving the white monopoly on economic and political power required constant governmental intervention and oppression. But it involved more than repression; it also implied strengthening Afrikaner culture and language, and improving their economic situation vis-à-vis the English-speaking white population. Apartheid state activism, however, did not rely primarily on courts to enforce its activist agenda; instead, its legal culture remained heavily influenced by a Westminster model of parliamentary supremacy and a largely reactive legal culture that emphasized securing private rights rather than providing a mechanism for state regulation. This reactive common-law heritage initially led to clashes with the demands of the apartheid state's repressive system with its engagement in torture and indefinite detentions.[43] As in most repressive states, however, most lawyers and judges came to accommodate the government's policies; sometimes they did so by relying on formalism and the Westminster tradition of deference of legislature to argue that it was not the judiciary's place to disagree, and sometimes by adapting legal forms and rules to the demands of the political system.[44] If we seek to qualify the role of law in the apartheid state then, it is—much like German law during the Nazi time—neutral insofar as it did not stand in the way of the activist state's agenda, but also it did not play a major role in the project of social transformation. When the apartheid regime finally collapsed and South Africa

[42] See Hermann Gilliomee, *The Afrikaners: Biography of a People* (2009), pp. 340–54 and pp. 542–3.

[43] See e.g. Hugh Corder, *Judges at Work: The Role and Attitude of the South African Appellate Judiciary, 1910–1950* (Cape Town: Juta, 1984); Dennis Davis and Michelle le Roux, *Precedent and Possibility: The (Ab)use of Law in South Africa* (Cape Town: Double Storey, 2009), chapter 1.

[44] See for examples Edwin Cameron, 'Legal Chauvinism, Executive-Mindedness and Justice—LC Steyn's Impact on South African Law', *South African Law Journal*, 99 (1982), 38; David Dyzenhaus, *Hard Cases in Wicked Legal Systems: Pathologies of Legality* (New York: Oxford University Press, 2010); Stephen Ellmann, *In Time of Trouble: Law and Liberty in South Africa's State of Emergency* (New York: Oxford University Press, 1992).

emerged as a truly democratic state in 1994, social transformation—only now with very different aims—was unsurprisingly again high on the agenda. As decades of oppression had deprived people of adequate education and impoverished and radicalized them, with social and economic inequality remaining high, it was clear that the battle for equality had only just begun with granting everyone equal political rights.

This new activism was not confined to South African ideas of statehood and society. It took a distinctly legal form, with a constitution that incorporated the idea of change and a vision of a better society. The Preamble itself declares the Constitution to be a means to

> (h)eal the divisions of the past and establish a society based on democratic values, social justice and fundamental human rights; (l)ay the foundations for a democratic and open society(...); (i)mprove the quality of life of all citizens and free the potential of each person; and (b)uild a united and democratic South Africa able to take its rightful place as a sovereign state in the family of nations.

And Art. 7 (2) of the Constitution obliges the state to 'respect, protect, *promote* and *fulfill* the rights in the Bill of Rights',[45] thus taking a markedly activist position.

The South African Constitution also provides explicitly—unlike the German Basic Law—for the necessary institutional and explicit textual mechanisms to enforce its agenda of a more just and equal society:[46] It includes a long list of justiciable socio-economic rights such as a right to housing and a right to education, and obliges the state to take action; these rights can and have in the past been enforced by its constitutional court.[47] It also provides explicitly for the direct horizontal application of constitutional law between private parties (s. 8), complementing the courts' constitutional duty to develop the common law and customary law in the light of constitutional values (s. 39), thus making the Constitution the fundamental matrix of the entire legal system.[48]

[45] Emphasis added by this author.

[46] See for a good overview Lourens du Plessis, 'The Evolution of Constitutionalism and the Emergence of a Constitutional Jurisprudence in South Africa: An Evaluation of the South African Constitutional Court's Approach to Interpretation', *Saskatchewan Law Review*, 62 (1999), 299, 317 et seq.

[47] Though not always to the extent its critics have wanted it to go. For a summary of the cases and critiques of them, see e.g. Sandra Liebenberg, *Socio-Economic Rights: Adjudication under a Transformative Constitution* (Cape Town: Juta, 2010). See also for a defence of the Court's activity against some of its critics James Fowkes, *Building the Constitution: The Practice of Constitutional Interpretation in South Africa Since 1994* (Cambridge: Cambridge University Press, forthcoming 2016), chapter 8.

[48] See especially *Carmichele v Minister of Safety and Security* 2001 (4) SA 938 (CC); *Khumalo v Holomisa* 2002 (5) SA 401 (CC). The details of application remain controversial: see further Stu

Initially, these activist elements engendered some resistance in parts of the legal community accustomed to a more restrained role of law and courts. This is especially visible in the domain of private law, which many academics and judges continued to treat as an autonomous realm of its own, mostly unaffected by the shifting paradigm in constitutional law. The South African Constitutional Court, however, has mostly opposed such attempts and embraced in its own jurisprudence an activist understanding of constitutional law. On the level of constitutional theory, its approach is similar to the German: 'Our Constitution is not merely a formal document regulating public power. It also embodies, like the German Constitution, an objective, normative value system(...).'[49] Similarly, in contrast to the sometimes formalist and restrained approach taken by lower courts,[50] the constitutional court has taken its task to develop the common law increasingly seriously, building partly on the German concept of the constitution as a value system: 'The influence of the fundamental constitutional values on the common law is mandated by s. 39(2) of the Constitution. It is within the matrix of this objective normative value system that the common law must be developed.'[51]

This value-based conception already points to the importance of substantive law, which is accompanied by a high degree of legal flexibility, both procedural and substantive. South African academics in particular routinely call for procedural flexibility and more judicial intervention when it comes to realizing socio-economic rights.[52] And while judicial talk of values is frequent, only infrequently will it be spelt out in detail what these values mean. They therefore remain highly indeterminate and flexible, prompting one critic to describe the Court's style as 'rainbow jurisprudence'.[53] Often the Court will play the ball back to the government or other state institutions, when they

Woolman, 'Application', in *Constitutional Law of South Africa 2 ed.*, ed. Stu Woolman and Michael Bishop (Cape Town: Juta, 2005).

[49] *Carmichele*, para. 54.

[50] See Dennis Davis, 'Private Law after 1994: Progressive Development or Schizoid Confusion', *South African Journal on Human Rights*, 24 (2008), 318.

[51] *Carmichele*, para. 54. The influence of formalist culture and the adequacy of the Constitutional Court's approach are subjects of continuing controversy: see e.g. Davis, 'Private Law after 1994'; Dennis M. Davis and Karl Klare, 'Transformative Constitutionalism and the Common Law and Customary Law', *South African Journal of Human Rights*, 26 (2010), 403.

[52] See e.g. Brian Ray, 'Evictions, Aspirations and Avoidance', *Constitutional Court Review*, 5 (2013), 172, and Stuart Wilson and Jackie Dugard, 'Taking Poverty Seriously: The South African Constitutional Court and Socio-economic Eights', *Stellenbosch Law Review*, 22(3) (2011), 664.

[53] Alfred Cockrell, 'Rainbow Jurisprudence', *South African Journal on Human Rights*, 12 (1996), 1.

seem better equipped to deal with the task of social transformation.[54] In doing so, its conception of its function is dynamic and highly context-sensitive. As James Fowkes demonstrates in his analysis of the South African Constitutional Court's jurisprudence, the court is often engaged in institutional calculations, attempting to build up constitutional mechanisms and institutions and to collaborate with them in the common enterprise of realizing constitutional values.[55]

C. Models of Authority

As important as the distinction between reactive and activist constitutions is understanding the way in which societies organize and construct state authority.[56] Traditionally, many activist states have operated with the help of hierarchically ordered bureaucracies and sometimes highly specialized judiciaries. Conversely, in reactive states where courts carve out spheres of individual freedom from government intervention and help solve conflicts between privates in the market economy of the 'Lockean' state,[57] courts operate in a sort of intermediary space between state and society. Here, judges tend to be well-integrated members of social elites rather than official functionaries, drawing in their legal practice on the prevalent social values and norms rather than technical standards of decision-making.[58] But these matches (activist state and hierarchical authority/reactive state and coordinate authority) are not as neat today as they used to be. The global rise of constitutionalism and rights review has in many ways disturbed these old alliances. But before we consider potential matches between activist and reactive states and different concepts of authority, we need to take a closer look at the latter.

[54] See e.g. *Mazibuko and Others v City of Johannesburg and Others* 2010 (4) SA 1 (CC) (8 October 2009).

[55] See Fowkes, *Building the Constitution*. Similarly, but less convincingly, Theunis Roux has interpreted the South African Constitutional Court's activity in this regard as political strategy, see *The Politics of Principle: The First South African Constitutional Court, 1995–2005* (New York: Cambridge University Press, 2013).

[56] For the following paragraphs see Damaška, *The Faces of Justice and Authority*.

[57] John C. Reitz, 'Political Economy as a Major Architectural Principle of Public Law', *Tulane Law Review*, 75 (2001), 1121.

[58] See also Ackerman, *The Civil Rights Revolution*, and Damaška, *The Faces of Justice and Authority*.

I. Hierarchical authority

1. Professionalism

In a hierarchical system, professional expertise provides the most important source of state authority.[59] While there may exist some higher source of legitimation at the highest level (God, the king, the people), administrative offices as well as the judiciary depend on their professionalism and expertise as their main source of public authority. Separation of powers is a key element of this system, but it functions primarily not as a protection against concentrations of political power, but rather as a tool for the rational ordering of the state in order to increase efficiency. Bureaucracies consist of professionals who have undergone significant training and usually choose an entire career as government officials.

2. Division of tasks and hierarchy

The strict division between different functions guarantees that only those officials with the necessary knowledge and expertise deal with particular tasks. This applies both on the horizontal and the vertical level. The horizontal division of functions ensures greater specialization, which is reflected in the separation between different tasks within the administration. Vertical divisions of functions ensure that more abstract and broader questions are delegated to the upper echelons of the bureaucracy.

3. Technicality and de-personalization

As a result of professionalization, the exercise of state power is de-personalized and a tendency towards technical standards of decision-making prevails. Decision-making standards are divorced from the common-sense pragmatism of the well-socialized layman. As officials perform their functions, they act in the name of the institution, not their individual personalities.

4. The legal system

Legal authority is constructed along the same lines. In a system that puts a premium on expertise, law is a science whose mastery requires considerable effort. Arbitrariness and inconsistency threaten the claim to judicial authority. In order to avoid them, lawyers, scholars, and judges work towards constructing law as a logically consistent, gapless system of rules and principles.

[59] The following paragraphs on hierarchical and coordinate authority follow closely Damaška's description of hierarchical and coordinate authority (Damaška, *The Faces of Justice and Authority*, pp. 16 et seq.), with the exception of the paragraphs on constitutional review, which I have added.

The imperative of upholding this system prevails over case-to-case considerations of what seems right in individual disputes. The legal system is moreover likely to allow for specializations in order to ensure correct outcomes and efficiency; different courts will hence deal with different sorts of claims. As a science, legal interpretation must be as objective as possible: courts will therefore typically act unanimously. This means that judges will only deliberate secretly, dissents will be prohibited, and decisions will be presented to the public as those of the court, as opposed to mere opinions of a majority of individual judges.

5. Constitutional review in hierarchical systems

Constitutional review does not naturally fit into a hierarchical system of authority. Because hierarchical systems emphasize the strict separation of lawmaking and legal interpretation, they make generally no easy match with constitutional review that looks a lot like lawmaking. Interpreting the necessarily broad and reasonably vague provisions that are characteristically found in constitutions moreover makes it hard to uphold the ideal of judicial determinacy and legal certainty, and hence of legal interpretation as a non-arbitrary, rational enterprise. This applies not only, but especially to rights review, which allows courts to strike down legislation on substantive grounds.

If, however, we try to imagine what constitutional review in a hierarchical system of authority might look like once established, the famous constitutional theorist Hans Kelsen provides us with a good starting point:[60] According to Kelsen, constitutional review should first of all be entrusted only to a special constitutional court, rather than providing all courts with this power, in order to ensure the uniformity of constitutional law.[61] Judges must be appointed on the basis of their expertise in constitutional law,[62] not as elected representatives of the people or political parties. We might add that decisions should be presented to the public as decisions of the court, not those of its individual members, and therefore voting results should not be displayed and dissents prohibited. Because the strict division of functions is key in this system, judicial review should moreover best not include rights that may drag the court too far into politics, but should instead focus on the protection of the constitution's organizational norms, especially those regulating the process of ordinary lawmaking, thus enforcing the existing

[60] Hans Kelsen, *Wer soll der Hüter der Verfassung sein? Abhandlungen zur Theorie der Verfassungsgerichtsbarkeit in der pluralistischen, parlamentarischen Demokratie* (Tübingen: Mohr Siebeck, 2008), p. 8, pp. 27–8.

[61] Ibid., pp. 29 et seq.

[62] Ibid., p. 27.

hierarchical divisions between different institutions. If rights are, however, included in the constitution, the court must find a way to deal with them, either by avoiding them as a basis for striking down laws or by making sure that their interpretation is guided by a distinctly legal methodology.

II. Coordinate authority

1. Public and laymen influence

Things are different in coordinate systems of authority. Here, it is key that the state and its institutions be connected to the public and the prevailing social mores. Ideally, state officials will therefore not be specialized professionals, but generalists and sometimes laymen who represent the social elites or—in more egalitarian states—the people. Delegations of power based merely on professional expertise are generally viewed with suspicion, as they evoke the undesirable image of unaccountable technocracies. If professional expertise is indispensable to fulfilling particular state functions and delegations of tasks to particular offices therefore necessary, their competences tend to be subjected to some mechanism of surveillance, preferably one that brings the society and the people back into the administrative process.

2. Power-sharing and collaboration

Authority is not exercised on the basis of a strict separation of functions, but instead is shared among several officials or institutions whose functions are not strictly delimited. The separation of powers here becomes a system of checks and balances allowing for a blurring of functions that enable different institutions to monitor each other rather than provide for a strict exclusive allocation of tasks to specific institutions.

3. Personalization and common-sense pragmatism

The idea that decision-makers give up their social/private personality when they become part of the administration of justice would seem undesirable and contrary to their dignity. Standards for decision-making cannot be separated from the prevailing social norms and expectations or—in some cases—the elites' idea of justice. Decisions are expected to reflect this broader ethos of the community or its elites and decision-makers to justify their decisions accordingly.

4. Law in the coordinate state

Again, these features are reflected in the legal system. Law is a practice rather than a science to be studied. Key to its mastery is not the ability to imagine it as a system with first principles from which everything else can be deduced, but rather an awareness of social facts and their meanings. The life of law is here indeed not logic, but experience.[63] Key to 'good' decision-making is, then, that judges know the practice, both past and present, which is typically ensured by their education—historically in the common-law tradition by clerking for a lawyer. Where legal education takes place in universities, the study of cases instead of doctrines, often compiled at least partly in chronological order in law school textbooks, allows lawyers at the same time to historicize decisions and understand law in a broader social context that is typically ignored in the doctrine- rather than precedent-focused continental tradition. As legal practice is deeply rooted in society, attention must be paid to the facts of each case. It becomes more important to do individual justice rather than uphold an abstract principle. Moreover, judges are not specialists but generalists and their individual personalities matter greatly. Dissents and even concurring opinions are therefore key, as only they allow judges to express their different personalities and justify openly what they are doing to the public, thus making them personally accountable.

5. Constitutional review under the coordinate paradigm

The coordinate model of authority with its acceptance of blurred functions provides in many ways an easier fit for constitutional review. Since offices share responsibilities in coordinate systems, constitutional review will empower courts, but not necessarily deny other institutions the right to have their say about the constitution. As a result, the different branches of the state may often be engaged in some kind of dialogue over constitutional meaning.[64] The ambiguous character of judicial review and the shared responsibility for protecting the constitution ensure that it is ultimately open to debate if the court should really enjoy the last word on a matter. At the same time, the blurring of functions also opens up enormous scope for courts to intervene in matters that are not traditionally within their purview as long as they can justify this extension of their authority to the public.

In order to convince the public and political actors to acknowledge their authority, courts in coordinate systems cannot entirely rely on formalistic legal arguments, but will have to be more discursive, open, and rhetorical. Policy arguments pose less of a problem for them because legal autonomy is understood in less absolute terms than in hierarchical systems. As judges are supposed to act as representatives of society, with their personality being an

[63] Oliver W. Holmes, Jr., *The Common Law* (Boston: Little, Brown and Company, 1881), p. 1.

[64] Compare most famously Allison Bushell and Peter Hogg, 'The Charter Dialogue between Courts and Legislatures', *Osgoode Hall Law Journal*, 35 (1997), 75.

important asset for fulfilling their tasks, the appointment process is likely to pay more attention to their individual biographies and temperaments. This does not necessarily imply a more partisan and political appointment process, since candidates may also be chosen in more consensual procedures, but it will generate a process that is less focused on securing specialized professional expertise and more focused on other personal and political factors.

III. Examples

1. Hierarchical systems of authority: Japan

In any description of the Japanese political system or judiciary, its bureaucracy features centrally. Usually entering government directly or soon after their graduation from university as the country's top graduates, bureaucrats form a highly influential class of their own in Japanese politics. Like in Germany, they enjoy major influence in preparing new legislation, as well as considerable discretion in implementing important administrative programmes.[65] The judiciary is no exception to this rule. The requirements to become a judge or prosecutor in Japan are—even after some reforms in the 1990s—highly rigorous. In order to practise law, candidates must not only possess a (graduate-level) law school degree (a legal requirement only since 2004, though most would pursue an LLB and a year of 'cram-school' beforehand), but also have passed a bar exam with a pass rate of only 40–50 per cent[66] followed by a one-and-a-half-year training period at the Supreme Court's Institute of Legal Research and Training. The Japanese judiciary is federally organized and largely self-regulating, with senior legal bureaucrats in the General Secretariat allocating posts to their colleagues who are rotated between different courts within the country, usually after about ten years. Unlike the German judiciary, the Japanese judiciary is largely unified, with no specialized courts except family courts, which are attached to the local district courts.[67] The rigid selection process ensures that Japanese judges are nevertheless among the best educated and qualified in the world.[68] Moreover,

[65] Shigenori Matsui, *The Constitution of Japan: A Contextual Analysis* (Portland: Hart Publishing, 2011).

[66] Before the reforms, the pass rate was at around 3 per cent; Matsui, *The Constitution of Japan*, p. 125.

[67] The lowest level of courts, so-called summary courts, may not be staffed with professional judges but other bureaucrats having previously received certain legal training in administrative positions in the judiciary (and sometimes retired 'ordinary' judges).

[68] John O. Haley, 'The Japanese Judiciary: Maintaining Integrity, Autonomy, and the Public Trust', in *Law in Japan: A Turning Point*, ed. Daniel J. Foote (Seattle: University of Washington Press, 2007), pp. 9 et seq.

legal academics play a significant role in the development of Japanese law, criticizing, discussing, and interpreting court decisions and thus contributing to the uniformity and consistency of the system.

The fact that the judiciary itself exercises control over appointments and the allocation of postings contributes to the isolation of the Japanese judiciary against politics. This is, if to a lesser degree, even true for the selection of Supreme Court Justices: Though the Cabinet selects the Associate Justices, it routinely picks from a pool of one to three candidates selected by the Chief Justice (the Chief Justice himself is selected by the Prime Minister and appointed by the Emperor[69]). And while as a matter of law the Japanese second chamber (the House of Councillors) may conduct its own investigations, and once interfered in a legal case when it considered the criminal sentences received were too low,[70] such parliamentary involvement has remained an exception that is now agreed to be unacceptable behaviour.[71] Similarly, newly appointed Justices to the Supreme Court may in theory be voted out of office by the people in the first parliamentary election following their appointment, but no Justice has ever been dismissed that way. Active participation of laymen in the judicial administration is rare. While it is true that the judiciary is known to occasionally draw on the Japanese community, this involvement is merely instrumental insofar as the community contributes to fulfilling certain tasks set by the bureaucracy. Only recently (since 2004) and in very rare instances have laymen been able to take a more active role by participating as lay judges in certain criminal trials.[72]

An especially strong emphasis on the principle of *stare decisis* ensures that vertical hierarchies are strictly upheld. Though following the civil-law tradition in not recognizing legal decisions per se as a source of law, Japanese courts are nevertheless known to follow judicial precedent strictly. If lower courts diverge in their decisions from the established precedents, their decisions will routinely be dismissed at the appeals stage. It comes as no surprise then that Japanese legal culture values predictability and uniformity highly. While this has led some scholars to describe Japanese lawyers as conservative in a political sense—pointing to the long-standing political dominance of the conservative Liberal Democratic Party (LDP) in Japanese politics—better arguments suggests that their conservatism should instead be understood as a matter of professional or institutional disposition rather than referring to any particular political ideology.[73]

[69] Matsui, *The Constitution of Japan*, pp. 123–4. [70] Ibid., p. 84.

[71] Ibid., p. 123. [72] Ibid., pp. 130–1.

[73] See especially Haley, *The Japanese Judiciary*, who shows convincingly that there is no evidence for any kind of political pressure involving judicial appointments or for influence in concrete cases, with the single exception regarding the fate of the members of the left-leaning Young Jurists

Judicial review was only introduced in Japan after the Second World War. Unlike many continental European states that followed the Kelsenian model by establishing a separate Constitutional Court, Japan followed the US model of diffuse review. But if diffuse review may classically appear less suitable to guarantee uniformity throughout the system, in Japan the strong hold of the judicial administration over appointment as well as the *stare decisis* principle leave little room for worry of this sort and illustrate the importance and persistence of legal culture even where institutional settings suggest a different course. Unlike in the United States or Germany, constitutional review in Japan never assumed great importance. The number of statutes declared unconstitutional by the Court—eight as of 2013—is low, with the Court backing down from one of its more expansive decisions after governmental criticism.[74]

This restraint has been the subject of much scholarly interest. While some have sought to explain it in terms of purely political control—conservative LDP politicians appointing conservative judges—this explanation has been largely disproved by the more recent developments: In spite of the change in political leadership from 2009 to 2012 and a number of new appointments to the Court, neither has the Court more aggressively invalidated the policies of the new government nor have the new appointments led to any shift in the Court's jurisprudence towards more liberal ideas.[75] Scholars largely agree that Japanese courts treat statutory and constitutional law differently. Dealing with ordinary statutory law, Japanese judges have in the past not infrequently been expansionist and creative in their interpretation. This has prompted Matsui to argue that the Justices simply do not understand the Constitution in terms of ordinary justiciable law.[76] Similarly, Itoh claims that Japanese judges do not want to engage in lawmaking.[77] Other scholars (Ginsburg and Matsudaira) put more emphasis on Japan's nineteenth-century Prussian heritage that conceives of the state as an organic whole.[78] In this picture, the state's

League, one of whose members (Assistant Judge Yasuaki Miyamoto) was not reappointed after refusing to give up membership and others were being allocated to undesirable and partly less lucrative posts (p. 24). However, the Miyamoto incident caused widespread protests among the Japanese judiciary and in the Japanese media, with the effect that no other judge has since been denied re-appointment (p. 28).

[74] Matsui, *The Constitution of Japan*, pp. 145–8.

[75] See especially Tom Ginsburg and Tokujin Matsudaira, 'The Judicialization of Japanese Politics', in *The Japanese Legal System: An Era of Transition*, ed. Tom Ginsburg and Harry Schreiber (Berkeley: The Robbins Collection, 2013), pp. 36 et seq.

[76] Matsui, *The Constitution of Japan*, pp. 148–9.

[77] Hiroshi Itoh, 'Judicial Review and Judicial Activism in Japan', *Law and Contemporary Problems*, 53(1) (1990), 177.

[78] Ginsburg and Matsudaira, 'Judicialization of Japanese Politics', pp. 28 et seq.

different organs must contribute to the well-being of the whole, but—in doing so—take care not to interfere with the tasks of others. Because the judiciary is traditionally allocated a comparatively narrowly circumscribed function, Ginsburg and Matsudaira argue that this has inhibited the development on constitutional activism until today. Finally, Haley emphasizes the importance of legal stability and community sense as entailing respect for political decisions that are seen to represent social consensus rather than mere majority preferences.[79]

Whichever of these explanations captures the Japanese Supreme Court's restraint best, they share a broadly hierarchical approach to judicial authority that emphasizes a strict division between judging and lawmaking. Whether the constitution is not really understood as law or judges do not want to intrude into the political domain or preserve stability, all of these explanations are concerned with preserving the respective autonomy of both legal and political actors. The responsibilities of judges and politicians are conceptualized as distinct, and the Japanese approach ensures that they remain so. Within a hierarchical system, the Japanese reaction seems indeed consequent: Since constitutional review tends to blur judicial and political functions insofar as it engages judges in lawmaking, the easiest way out for a court is to engage as little as possible in constitutional review. And while a separate constitutional court such as the German Constitutional Court would not have been able to avoid this challenge to the same degree, the Japanese Supreme Court can easily focus on interpreting statutory law, the traditional province of judges, which is well accepted in the community, and bears little risk. It also fits with our hierarchical model that the Japanese Justices, like their German colleagues, tend to avoid both dissents and concurring opinions to a much greater degree than their Anglo-Saxon counterparts.[80] Voting results in the Supreme Court are not usually disclosed, and decisions are written in the deductive style of continental law. Moreover, the Justices' usually high age at their appointment means they will only sit for a comparatively short period of around five years (because they are automatically retired when they turn 70).[81] This gives them little time to leave their personal imprint on the Court's jurisprudence. In addition, the workload at the Court is high, and clerks who are themselves judges serving the Court in general rather than any

[79] John O. Haley, 'Constitutional Adjudication in Japan: Context, Structures, and Values', *Washington University Law Review*, 88 (2011), 1467.

[80] David M. O'Brien, with Yasuo Ohkoshi, *To Dream of Dreams: Religious Freedom and Constitutional Politics in Postwar Japan* (Hawaii: University of Hawaii Press, 1996), pp. 82 et seq.; see also David S. Law, 'The Anatomy of a Conservative Court: Judicial Review in Japan', *Texas Law Review*, 87 (2009), 1584.

[81] Haley, 'Constitutional Adjudication in Japan', p. 1488.

particular judge are not required to help with the drafting of individual opinions. This ensures that the influence of individual personalities will remain marginal in favour of upholding established constitutional doctrine and thus contributing to the ultimate goals of internal consistency and legal predictability—typical hallmarks of any hierarchical system.

2. Coordinate systems of authority: the United States

A good example of a still largely coordinate system is the United States. As in other common-law jurisdictions, law in the US held for a long time the status of a valuable social practice requiring considerable experience and assumed only slowly the character of a profession to be studied at university. The authority of office-holders was connected to their high social standing and their familiarity with the prevailing social mores, rather than their expertise in any specific task: Until today, judges in the United States are not career bureaucrats recruited after they have done well in some exam, but instead are professionals with considerable prior expertise and a certain social and political standing.[82] Their appointment is at least partly political and sometimes they are directly elected—something that also holds true for many US prosecutors or sheriffs. For a long time, the jury as the people's representation played a significant role in US criminal trials.

Since the New Deal and the increase in federal administrative activity in the beginning of the twentieth century in the United States, however, professionalism has been on the rise here, too. Civil service appointments had long been an important part of the spoils system that distributed offices as a form of political patronage. A tedious process of reforms, however, ultimately replaced this system with a more rationalized mechanism that includes entry exams and internal advancement based on performance criteria.[83] Nevertheless, the delegation of authority to officials who were not directly elected has never stopped raising suspicions. Administrative agencies were subjected to judicial review as a means of ensuring that they did not stray too far from their congressional mandate and the notice and comment procedure provided for in the APA ensured transparency and dialogue between administrative agencies and citizens.

The Supreme Court is no exception to this coordinate culture of authority.[84] Especially during the eighteenth century, its claim to final authority has

[82] See Damaška, *The Faces of Justice and Authority*, p. 45.

[83] Stephen Skowronek, *Building a New American State: The Expansion of National Administrative Capacities, 1877–1920* (Cambridge: Cambridge University Press, 1982).

[84] Samuel Huntington similarly points to this coordinate nature of the US political system, which he describes as a remnant of the Tudorian political institutions imported from England, ibid., *Political Order in Changing Societies* (New Haven: Yale University Press, 1986), chapter 2.

repeatedly been contested by other political actors, most notably by various presidents. These presidents insisted that they were not bound by the Supreme Court's interpretation of the Constitution and could act on their own understanding of the Constitution. Departmentalism, as this approach to the separation of powers is called, forms a significant part of the US constitutional tradition.[85] The list of departmentalist presidents begins early on with Thomas Jefferson, who insisted repeatedly on its own authority to interpret the Constitution and refused to execute the Alien and Sedition Act passed by the Federalist Congress. Andrew Jackson built on this Jeffersonian approach when he vetoed rechartering the Second Bank of America in spite of the Supreme Court's ruling in McCulloch, and affirmed this position in dealing with the Cherokee cases.[86] Lincoln's administration undermined the Court's infamous Dred Scott ruling by granting passports and patents to blacks based on a similar departmentalist position,[87] and Roosevelt defended his Court-packing plan as legitimate in pointing to the coordinate nature of US government where all three branches together, not just one of them, were responsible for the well-being of the people.[88] Traces of departmentalist rhetoric then surfaced again in the Reagan administration.[89]

Even if we put these past instances of departmentalism aside, however, and concentrate on the more recent decades of US constitutionalism when judicial supremacy has broadly been accepted, we find a very different vision of constitutionalism than the one prevailing in hierarchical systems. It encapsulates a strong belief that it is the people and all three branches together who elaborate the constitutional meaning. Sanford Levinson has for this reason described US Constitutional Faith as Protestant rather than Catholic.[90] Bruce Ackerman presents in *We the People* another coordinate model of US constitutionalism, focusing on constitutional change.[91] Even though, strictly speaking, Ackerman does not challenge the idea of judicial supremacy in constitutional interpretation, his account of US constitutional history is nevertheless strongly coordinate in its emphasis on the need for collaboration between all three branches to bring about constitutional change. In order to overcome institutional hurdles, transformative presidents (and sometimes other institutions) seek to mobilize the people, who then approve or deny in a 'moment' of heightened political and constitutional awareness the proposed changes. While Ackerman presents these changes

[85] Keith E. Whittington, *Political Foundations of Judicial Supremacy: The Presidency, the Supreme Court, and Constitutional Leadership in U.S. History* (Princeton: Princeton University Press, 2007).

[86] Ibid., pp. 33–4. [87] Ibid., p. 35. [88] Ibid., p. 36. [89] Ibid., p. 39.

[90] Sanford Levinson, *Constitutional Faith* (Princeton: Princeton University Press, 2011).

[91] Bruce Ackerman, *We the People. Foundations* (Cambridge: Harvard University Press, 1991) and Ackerman, *Transformations*.

as constitutional amendments rather than merely changes in constitutional interpretation, they happen outside the procedure provided for in Art. 5 of the US Constitution.

Whittington, Levinson, and Ackerman are moreover hardly alone in emphasizing the role of the political branches and the people in elaborating the constitutional meaning. The idea is alive and well in the more recent scholarship of Robert Post and Reva Siegel,[92] Bill Eskridge and John Ferejohn,[93] Barry Friedman,[94] and many others. Whatever the differences between these authors, they agree in according certain traditionally non-constitutional events or texts constitutional significance. In doing so, they go beyond what is commonly understood as dynamic interpretation, i.e. reading constitutional norms in the light of political and cultural changes, and instead present us with a normative as well as a descriptive account of US constitutionalism. Underlying Post and Siegel's account as well as Friedman's is the idea that it is ultimately a good thing when law and courts are responsive to citizens and their beliefs. Eskridge and Ferejohn not only point to the significance of entrenched statutory regimes called super-statutes for constitutional interpretation, but also argue that the evolution of (formal) constitutional law should be guided by such statutes. In pointing to both the normative and empirical importance of these other actors for constitutional interpretation, these theories elaborate in their core a coordinate ideal of constitutional interpretation. More radical, anti-court positions are taken by another group of scholars, including for example Larry Kramer,[95] Marc Tushnet,[96] and Jeremy Waldron,[97] who have been championing the idea of popular constitutionalism as a counterweight to the concept of judicial supremacy.[98] Popular constitutionalism represents in many ways an expanded version of departmentalism that treats non-state actors alongside political institutions as legitimate constitutional interpreters that may or may

[92] Robert C. Post and Reva B. Siegel, 'Roe Rage: Democratic Constitutionalism and Backlash', *Harvard Civil Rights–Civil Liberties Law Review*, 42 (2007), 373.

[93] William N. Eskridge, Jr. and John Ferejohn, *A Republic of Statues: The New American Constitution* (New Haven: Yale University Press, 2013).

[94] Barry Friedman, *The Will of the People: How Public Opinion Has Influenced the Supreme Court and Shaped the Meaning of the Constitution* (London: Macmillan, 2010).

[95] Larry Kramer, *The People Themselves: Popular Constitutionalism and Judicial Review* (Oxford: Oxford University Press, 2004).

[96] Mark Tushnet, *Taking the Constitution Away from the Courts* (Princeton: Princeton University Press, 1999).

[97] Jeremy Waldron, *Law and Disagreement* (Oxford: Oxford University Press, 2001).

[98] For an overview of the different positions, including the ones considered here, see James E. Fleming, 'Judicial Review without Judicial Supremacy: Taking the Constitution Seriously Outside the Courts', *Fordham Law Review*, 73 (2005), 1378.

not endorse the interpretation chosen by the courts. Of course, critics of these approaches are not amiss, among them notably Laurence Tribe.[99] Nevertheless, theories that seek to displace courts as the ultimate constitutional interpreters have a significant following.

This tradition is accompanied by a rhetorical and policy-oriented style of many US Supreme Court decisions, which openly engage in discussions about the legitimacy of judicial involvement (see more in Chapter 5), the politicization of the appointment of Justices, and a high frequency of both dissenting and concurring opinions. Together, they shape the coordinate culture of US law.

It fits with this picture that the preservation of legal autonomy is less important to US lawyers than their German counterparts. This is especially manifest in US legal education, where law is taught only as a graduate subject and law students usually have a background of three or more years of prior academic education when they enrol in law. Moreover, legal education is usually completed in three years, only one year of which is typically dedicated to mandatory black letter law courses (compared to six years in Germany, if one includes the mandatory two-year clerkship period necessary to become a practising lawyer, judge, etc.). Finally, US Law Schools, especially those in the upper echelons that later produce Supreme Court Justices, are strongly interdisciplinary. In short, 'pure law' is not high on their agenda.[100]

This interdisciplinarity of US law becomes also apparent in its legal scholarship and, if to a lesser degree, in the jurisprudence of US courts, with the law and economics movement as its perhaps most well-known example. As Bruce Ackerman points out, this new kind of legal discourse reflected a shift from an emphasis on social mores and common sense to a new, more professional idea of jurisprudence that often requires lawyers to draw additionally on scientific research.[101] This emerging professionalism has, however, been

[99] Laurence H. Tribe, 'The People's Court', *New York Times*, 24 October 2004, <http://query.nytimes.com/gst/fullpage.html?res=9C06EEDE163AF937A15753C1A9629C8B63>.

[100] Of course, US-style legal education has much to do with the success of legal realism and an emerging different specific style of professionalism. One of early legal realism's favourite aims of attack was the Langdellian method of legal education and doctrinal scholarship. Langdell, Dean and re-inventor of the Harvard Law School, propagated the 'scientific' study of law that sought to approach common law in a more systematic way. Though Legal Realism was influenced by the German Free Law School, its success was nevertheless highly dependent on the already prevalent legal culture at the time. As Brian Tamanaha demonstrates, US legal discourse was already before the advent of Legal Realism often realist in acknowledging judicial indeterminacy, the lawmaking role of judges and the fact that judges would sometimes ex-post rationalize their decisions in legal terms. Perhaps unsurprisingly, Tamanaha also notes that many of the examples quoted by the early Realists for a formalist, mechanical model of jurisprudence were in fact German; Brian Tamanaha, *Beyond the Formalist–Realist Divide: The Role of Politics in Judging* (Princeton: Princeton University Press, 2009).

[101] Ackerman, *Reconstructing American Law*, pp. 20 et seq.

very different to what we encounter in hierarchical systems. There, professional expertise is tied to specialization in one very particular task and does not usually venture out of disciplinary boundaries. In contrast, even the new professionalism now propagated by many of the best US Law Schools is strongly social-context related. Where statues mandate social engineering, lawyers often work alongside professionals of other disciplines to give effect to them. In doing so, they open themselves up to the prevailing discourses in US political culture with their transition to a more scientific style of administration.[102] What has changed is, then, not so much the degree to which lawyers draw on professional knowledge, but instead the culture surrounding them, which has itself become more professional. As a result, judicial claims to expert authority are not as stable as in hierarchical systems: after all, judges share and borrow their expertise from and with many other social science professionals.

D. A good match?

Different legal paradigms come with different ideas about the legitimacy of constitutional law and constitutional jurisprudence. Any one of them can provide legitimation to a constitutional court, but they also can and often are combined. Though all combinations between different systems of authority and legal paradigms are in general feasible, some fits are easier than others.

Tensions arise, for example, between activist constitutional regimes and hierarchical systems of authority. Because of the breadth of activist systems' vision of justice and the scope of change they envisage, courts may not always be able to stick to established doctrine in deciding cases. Realizing a transformative constitution will involve adjudication of many traditionally non-legal questions. Courts, therefore, will have a hard time defending that what they do is still interpretation and not lawmaking—a key division in hierarchical systems. Moreover, they often may not have the necessary expertise to deal with many of the new questions that arise. They will thus have to cooperate closely with other bodies and institutions, and/or judges themselves will have to be familiar with other disciplines than law in order to grapple with the challenge of social engineering. Most of this is hard to reconcile with the hierarchical model's emphasis on legal autonomy and its tendency towards specialization. Lawyers in hierarchical systems are only qualified to deal with legal as opposed to other social problems. And a court, even if endowed with

[102] Ackerman, *The Civil Rights Revolution*, pp. 32–3.

the power of constitutional review, must first and foremost seek to remain a court and mark its difference to political bodies if it does not want to risk the basis for its authority. The flexible legal frameworks that the activist state requires threaten judicial determinacy because their openness increases the risk of inconsistent application. The resulting seeming arbitrariness of legal interpretation poses a huge threat to the judges' claim to special expertise.

As a matter of institutional design, one of the most common ways of constructing a court's authority as a professional institution is to emphasize its difference to political institutions. It is therefore important to preserve at least some features that are traditionally associated with the judiciary and courts, for example, by adhering to procedures that will typically be characterized as judicial. Judicial robes or the non-disclosure of the judges' votes in individual cases are other attributes that may contribute to creating authority in line with the expectations in a hierarchical system.

E. Looking Forward

As we now venture out to take a closer look at German constitutionalism, we should be able to finally pick out the forest from the trees. The German state is and has been for a long time strongly activist, but its constitutional law has only more recently really turned so with its conceptualization of the Basic Law as an objective order of values. Initially introduced as part of a concept of transitional justice, the basic doctrinal tools and creations the German Constitutional Court developed along this line have become entrenched over time: Indirect effect of constitutional rights, state duties, and an emphasis on substantive law are hallmarks of contemporary German constitutionalism. With the transition passed, however, the Court's authority no longer rests on the shared agreement that German society needs to change, in other words on the Basic Law's appeal as a tool for social transformation. Rather, it can rely on a long-standing culture of hierarchical legal authority, which required the Court to assume a legal rather than a political character. If we are looking for catchwords to describe the differences between US and German constitutionalism today, it will hence not be popular sovereignty vs distrust in popular sovereignty and/or internationalism.[103] Rather, it is popular sovereignty vs expertise.

[103] Jed Rubenfeld, 'Unilateralism and Constitutionalism', *New York University Law Review*, 79 (2004), 2003.

2

Transitions and Transformations: towards Activist Constitutionalism

The success of the German Constitutional Court has in the past attracted little scholarly attention. Though often admired and sometimes even described as one of the most powerful courts in the world, few scholars have set out to investigate this success more closely and they have not usually done so from a comparative perspective. German lawyers in particular have only reluctantly addressed this question, often in a couple of stray sentences in work dedicated mainly to other subjects. This may come as a surprise to foreign observers; yet, the things German law may rightly be admired for—a comparatively high degree of precision, clarity, and nuance in complex questions—also explain why many scholars may avoid engaging in this kind of broad, non-legal inquiry. If we turn nevertheless to the existing paragraphs and passages in the legal literature that touch on this question, we will be able to make out the traces of two different approaches to the German Court's authority: one emphasizing newness and the break with the past, the other continuity.

Among those who emphasize change is Frieder Günther, who describes the post-war development of German constitutionalism as a process of 'Westernization':[1] Germans replaced the state at the centre of public law thinking with the individual, so Frieder Günther argues, and thereby opened up and pluralized German society and the state. In particular, German lawyers came to accept that the state was no longer the objective arbiter between different factional interests, the only protector of the public good, but that a common good was itself plural, a process of negotiation and argument between different parties. This process entailed the revolutionary shift from what used to be 'state theory' (*Staatsrechtslehre*) to constitutional theory.[2]

[1] Frieder Günther, *Denken vom Staat her: Die bundesdeutsche Staatsrechtslehre zwischen Dezision und Integration 1949–1970* (München: Oldenbourg, 2004).

[2] Ibid.

In a slightly different key but with a similar emphasis on change, foreign observers often explain the German Court's extensive authority as a reaction to National-Socialism: Because the Nazis came to power with the support of the German people, the standard argument runs, the people (and their representatives) could after 1945 no longer be trusted to protect fundamental human rights. It was hence inevitable that a strong counter-majoritarian institution, the Court, would arise to play this role. This idea is often not articulated in detail, but one encounters it frequently in conversations about the German Constitutional Court and its traces can be found both in international and German scholarship on German constitutionalism.[3]

Others adopt a different story that is less about rupture and change and more about continuity. In their eyes, German constitutionalism broadly follows existing nineteenth-century public-law paradigms, in particular the idea of the *Rechtsstaat*. National-Socialism here marks mostly an interruption of an existing trend towards juridification—a trend that is afterwards taken up again with renewed emphasis. Proponents of this approach can point to numerous examples: the existence of the *Staatsgerichtshof* in the Weimar Republic (a federal court with its powers of constitutional review on organizational matters and questions of federal law) and the fact that rights review was already debated in the Weimar Republic. Beyond that, some scholars argue that the nineteenth-century paradigm of constitutional law remains key to understanding contemporary German constitutionalism: Like in Britain, Christoph Möllers argues, public law in Germany had long not been directed towards establishing a new order, but rather been understood as a means to limit an already existing one. Because of the failure of the *Paulskirche* in 1848 and with it German democratization, the German *Rechtsstaat* idea developed as a means of protecting private freedom against incursions by the non-democratic state, a tendency further exacerbated as

[3] Versions of it can be found, for example, in the works of Bruce Ackerman, 'The Rise of World Constitutionalism', *Virginia Law Review*, 83 (1997), 771, 779–80 (arguing that the Constitutional Court enjoyed special legitimacy because the judges were, unlike other parts of the German government, not former Nazi collaborators); Douglas P. Kommers and Russell Miller, *The Constitutional Jurisprudence of the Federal Republic of Germany*, 3rd edn (Durham: Duke University Press, 2012), p. 1; Jed Rubenfeld, 'Unilateralism and Constitutionalism', *New York University of Law Review*, 79 (2004), 2003 (arguing that European internationalism constituted a reaction to bad experiences with both nationalism and democracy (since Hitler and Mussolini were both elected leaders) and that current international institutions are for this reason both antinationalist and antidemocratic); Kim Scheppele, 'Constitutional Interpretation after Regimes of Horror', *University of Pennsylvania Law School, Public Law Working Paper*, 5(3), available at SSRN: <http://ssrn.com/abstract=236219> (2000); however, more recently in a modified and somewhat toned-down version, Kim Scheppele, 'Jack Balkin is an American', *Yale Journal of Law and Humanities*, 25 (2013), 23; in this direction also Friederike Lange, *Grundrechtsbindung des Gesetzgebers: Eine rechtsvergleichende Studie zu Deutschland, Frankreich und den USA* (Tübingen: Mohr Siebeck, 2010), p. 40.

a result of Nazi totalitarianism.[4] And while the state lost its position as a focus point of German public-law thinking after 1945, post-war German constitutional law still understands itself primarily as a means to restrain the state, some argue.[5] As a consequence, it emphasizes individual rights rather than institutional and organizational questions, which have up to this point remained comparatively under-theorized in German constitutional doctrine.[6] This then in turn drives the German Constitutional Court's expansive rights' jurisprudence and its broader acceptance in the legal and political community.

For both accounts, the 'negative', limiting function of German constitutionalism is therefore key. Both emphasize the German Court's role as a guardian of negative individual rights against infringements by executive or legislative action. They disagree mainly when it comes to evaluating the weight of National-Socialism for contemporary German public law and the relationship of German constitutionalism to other Western systems, in particular, its US counterpart. Those who emphasize change tend to see the German Court broadly following the footsteps of US constitutionalism—if perhaps in a slightly more aggressive key. As a matter of comparative methodology, they therefore emphasize similarity. In turn, those who emphasize continuity with nineteenth-century ideas, emphasize difference. To them, US constitutionalism diverges from its German counterpart in that its primary concern seems to be with democracy, the separation of powers, and federalism—that is, with institutional and organizational matters—rather than individual rights as in the German case.

Both accounts entail important insights. As we will see, there are indeed considerable differences between German and US constitutionalism, and there is in turn a tendency to overemphasize the role of National-Socialism as a basis for the Court's authority. What neither of the two narratives captures adequately, however, is the turn to an activist model of constitutionalism, related to its counterparts in the Global South. Yet, this is not only important when we place Germany in a broader global framework of constitutionalism, but it is also a distinctive difference of the German model to the US one. Germans may not have adopted a full-blown transformative concept of constitutionalism such as South Africa, but German constitutionalism

[4] Christoph Möllers, 'Pouvoir Constitution—Constitution—Constitutionalisation', in *Principles of European Constitutional Law*, ed. Armin von Bogdandy and Jürgen Bast (Oxford/München: Hart Publishing/C. H. Beck, 2009), pp. 169–204, p. 174. See also Oliver Lepsius, 'Rezension von: Frieder Günther: Denken vom Staat her. Die bundesdeutsche Staatsrechtslehre zwischen Dezision und Integration 1949–1970', *Sehepunkte*, 4 (2004), <http://www.sehepunkte.de/2004/05/5714.html>. In this direction also Justin Collings, *Democracy's Guardians: A History of the German Federal Constitutional Court 1951–2001* (Oxford: Oxford University Press, forthcoming 2015), in particular introduction and conclusion.

[5] Ibid. [6] See Lepsius, 'Rezension Günther'.

represents at least a prototype of this brand, as I will argue. The current German Court is hence best understood not so much as a guardian of individual rights against state infringement, but rather as the public protector of a more comprehensive idea of a just society. National-Socialism plays a role in this story, as a driver towards this new model of activist constitutionalism, but its role is much more limited than often assumed.[7]

In this chapter, I seek to trace this turn towards transformative constitutionalism and thereby show what the existing narratives have missed. Because transformative constitutionalism entails in its core the idea of an activist state, I begin in the nineteenth century with the rise of the German welfare state. Around this time, too, courts assume the classical liberal role of guardians of individual rights against state action, a trend that continues during the Weimar Republic and in the debates of the German framers in post-war Western Germany. Yet, in spite of the framers' emphasis on providing justiciable individual rights, they did not attempt to create the kind of strong counter-majoritarian court the German Court has become today—contrary to what those who emphasize the role of National-Socialism tend to assume. National-Socialism did play a role, however, in the Court's conceptualization of the Basic Law as a comprehensive 'objective order of values' in the *Lüth* case. In deciding *Lüth*, the Court displaced the traditional reactive constitutional paradigm with an early form of transformative constitutionalism that understood the German Basic Law as a roadmap for a new state and society, rather than a mere charter of restraints.

A. Foundations

As most legal systems, German public law in the nineteenth century was broadly reactive. Over the course of the nineteenth century, individual rights were becoming increasingly important as a means of protecting society against interference by the undemocratic feudal states. Yet, even then, German public law was considerably less radical in this reactive spirit than its US counterpart. Unlike much late nineteenth- and early twentieth-century US constitutional theory, which the Lochner jurisprudence epitomizes, German public law generally embraced the idea of activist statehood. Earlier German feudal states had with 'police decrees' ('*Policeyverordnungen*')

[7] This chapter uses in part the same material as my paper 'Rethinking the Rise of the German Constitutional Court: From Anti-Nazism to Value Formalism', *International Journal of Constitutional Law*, 12(3) (2014), 626, which, however, presents a somewhat fuller version of my argument on the influence of National-Socialism on the Court's authority.

regulated wide spheres of their citizens' private and public lives, extending to prohibitions of luxury and rules on proper clothing. Certainly, this kind of activism did not pursue any overarching purpose of social transformation, but instead sought to realize the monarch's paternalist role within the divine arrangement of social order.[8] The advent of Enlightenment and the French and American Revolutions did not bring about major changes in this general acceptance of a strong state. While demands for more liberty became part of the political agenda of the rising middle class during the nineteenth century, for the most part their idea of freedom focused less on the idea of a limited than a rationalized and sometimes democratized government.[9] The famous Stein–Hardenberg reforms in Prussia introduced a number of measures aiming to liberate citizens from existing restrictions; ultimately, however, they intended to increase citizens' energy and their support for the state in the longer term in order to be able to compete with Napoleon's France and its armies.[10] Slowly, citizens were liberated from restrictions attached to their social standing and equality before the law was increasingly realized, causing a nearly unprecedented surge of state activity: As old feudal structures were being abolished, new state institutions had to be established to take over their functions.[11] State activism grew further after the formation of a unified German state in 1871. Industrialization and the social question gave rise to increasing levels of regulation in social and economic matters. Massive urban growth caused problems of hygiene and land distribution that required the intervention of municipalities, sometimes called 'municipal socialism'.[12] On the federal level, new agencies were founded, among them the federal judicial agency, a treasury, and the federal post office.[13] The number of civil servants between 1875 and 1907 tripled, with a parallel increase in the general population of only 50 per cent.[14] It was the hour of birth for the German welfare state with the introduction of pension schemes and health and casualty insurances for workers.

But even though the state's general role in ordering society remained largely unchallenged, individual rights became increasingly important as protections of a private sphere in which the state was not allowed to interfere. This development was partly a reaction to the *Paulskirche* failure to expand

[8] Michael Stolleis, *Geschichte des öffentlichen Rechts in Deutschland: Erster Band 1600–1800* (München: C. H. Beck, 1988), pp. 246 et seq.

[9] Michael Stolleis, *Geschichte des öffentlichen Rechts in Deutschland: Zweiter Band 1800–1914* (München: C. H. Beck, 1992), pp. 60 et seq.

[10] Ibid.

[11] Bernd Wunder, *Geschichte der Bürokratie in Deutschland* (Frankfurt am Main: Suhrkamp, 1986), p. 24.

[12] Ibid., p. 84. [13] Ibid., p. 70. [14] Ibid., p. 72.

parliamentary powers and establish a truly democratic German state.[15] German parliaments could only exercise limited powers during the nineteenth century and the growing realm of administration remained closed off against any kind of democratic or laymen participation. This isolation of the administration from society was justified as a means to preserve the state's function as a neutral mediator between opposing forces of society and a guardian of the public good against factional interests. Indeed, parliament itself was within this intellectual paradigm seen as a part of society rather than the state because it represented the different societal interests and factions.[16]

As a result, individual rights were primarily understood as rights against (monarchical) *executive* interference, granted, enforced, and guaranteed as statutory rights by parliament. They were not, in other words, conceptualized as pre-existing natural rights to freedom against *all* kinds of state action, including legislative.[17] Requiring a statutory basis as a prerequisite for limitations of individual freedom, the principle of legality became one of the most important legal concepts of the time. For a statute was, of course, not just any decree, but a rule formulated in abstract and general terms. Because this rule would be abstract and general, it provided a first barrier against arbitrary and discriminatory exercises of feudal power. Once a statute gave a citizen a so-called 'subjektives öffentliches Recht' (individual right),[18] she could access courts to demand her rights against the state. German public law in the nineteenth century thus secured the division between state and society, and with it a realm of private freedom against the monarchical executive.

[15] Stolleis, *Zweiter Band 1800–1914*, pp. 274 et seq.

[16] Christoph Schönberger, *Das Parlament im Anstaltsstaat: Zur Theorie parlamentarischer Repräsentation in der Staatsrechtslehre des Kaiserreichs (1871–1918)* (Frankfurt am Main: Vittorio Klostermann, 1997); see also Christoph Möllers, *Der vermisste Leviathan: Staatstheorie in der Bundesrepublik* (Frankfurt am Main: Suhrkamp, 2008), p. 16.

[17] Stolleis, *Zweiter Band 1800–1914*, p. 115.

[18] For an explanation of the concept of the 'subjective individual right' see Michael S. Greve, 'The Non-Reformation of Administrative Law: Standing to Sue and Public Interest Litigation in West German Environmental Law', *Cornell International Law Journal*, 22 (1989), 197–243, fn. 15: 'In German law, legal claims individuals possess against the state are called subjektive öffentliche Rechte ("subjective public rights"): "subjektive," so as to distinguish the "subjective" sense of the word Recht (a right) from its "objective" sense (law); "öffentliche," because these rights exist under public (as opposed to private, i.e., civil) law and against the state (as opposed to other private parties). "Subjektive öffentliche Rechte" are uniformly understood to be individual rights. A literal translation ("public rights") might be mistakenly understood as referring to (presumptive) rights held not by individuals but by the public qua public. This is exactly the opposite of the intended meaning. The translation "individual rights" or "private rights" captures the substantive meaning of "subjektive öffentliche Rechte." '

German nineteenth-century constitutions were therefore rightly understood as acts of monarchical self-limitation and tools to restrain state action. Yet, it is doubtful how much these early constitutions influenced the contemporary focus of German constitutional law on individual rights. To start with, it is not entirely clear why a conception of constitutional law that emphasizes restraining state power would prioritize rights questions over institutional issues. After all, both federal and horizontal separations of powers often function as limits on state action, as the US example illustrates. Second, German public law before 1945—more than later—was hardly disinterested in institutional questions. The Prussian constitutional crisis over the proposed budget for military reforms between 1859 and 1862 in particular prompted heated debates among politicians and scholars over the question of where sovereign power ultimately resided, in the monarch or the parliament. In some German states moreover, first constitutional courts were established with the competence to decide on organizational and institutional questions. In the Weimar Republic, discussions about the Federal President's power to govern via emergency decrees or judicial review represented just the tip of a lively debate about institutional issues. The federal *Staatsgerichtshof* also played an increasingly important role in deciding institutional questions such as the debate between Preussen and the Reich in 1932—a tradition in which many saw the German Constitutional Court after 1945, as we will see shortly.

And for all its faults, the Weimar Constitution represented for the first time in German history a constitution fully and unequivocally based on the people's sovereign will. In doing so, it went considerably beyond establishing further limits to the existing state. Including an extensive catalogue of socio-economic 'rights' and individual and state duties, the Weimar Constitution even had some early transformative elements.[19] Yet, neither traditional liberal nor progressive socio-economic rights were considered justiciable. Socio-economic rights in particular were understood as mere directive principles for state action, which citizens would not be able to invoke in courts. For the more traditional liberal rights, this was contested. Weimar courts made a few tentative steps in the direction of rights' review and scholars increasingly applauded this move, many of them because they sought a way of restraining the social-democrat majorities that were now in charge.[20] But it was *because* the Weimar Constitution established a new

[19] Christoph Gusy, *Die Weimarer Reichsverfassung* (Tübingen: Mohr Siebeck, 1997).

[20] See e.g. RGZ 111, 320, decision of 4 November 1925. See also for the major trends in this debate, Stolleis, *Zweiter Band 1800–1914*, pp. 100 et seq. and Christian Bumke, *Der Grundrechtsvorbehalt. Untersuchungen über die Begrenzung und Ausgestaltung der Grundrechte* (Baden-Baden: C. H. Beck, 1998), p. 110.

democratic state after a period of revolutionary upheaval and did not simply continue the tradition of self-limitation by the state that many started to argue for justiciable liberal rights.[21]

B. Transitions

The post-war period saw both continuity and change. But it was neither just the change towards a Western system of rights protection nor merely the continuity with the traditional concept of constitutionalism as a limit on state power. Continuity was mostly to be found in the deeper layers of German legal culture and legal methodology, as I will show in the next chapter. And what changed was not merely that liberal rights were now finally 'activated' by the judiciary—this was an important step, but it was indeed in keeping with previous trends—but rather that the Constitutional Court went in its jurisprudence considerably beyond that, towards a more transformative model of constitutionalism. These changes were partly influenced by the reaction to National-Socialism and Communism. However, key for the expansion of the Court's jurisdiction and its later robust authority, they went considerably beyond what the framers of the German Basic Law had anticipated and wanted.

I. Drafting the Basic Law

The German framers started out cautiously; this was perhaps not surprising. After the war, the Allies and the newly emerging German elites shared a goal: to build a new democratic state that would never again wage war on Europe and commit the kind of atrocities the Nazis had committed. To do so, they relied on law—and establishing the rule of law formed an important part of their programme. But at the same time, the legal profession had acquired a bad reputation during the Nazi era. Lawyers had participated significantly in the administration of Nazi injustice whether within the administration, the academy, or the judiciary. Nine out of the fifteen participants in the infamous Wannsee conference, which organized

[21] Paradigmatic for this new, often conservative expansionism is a series of famous cases decided by the German Supreme Court (*Reichsgericht*) during the inflation that proscribed that debts had to be adapted to the level before inflation. This was widely viewed as a conservative ingression into legislative territory in the interest of creditors; see Richard Scholz, *Analyse der Entstehungsbedingungen der reichsgerichtlichen Aufwertungsrechtsprechung: Untersuchung unter besonderer Berücksichtigung der konservativen Geldpolitik der Reichsbank und der Inflationspolitik der Reichsregierung* (Frankfurt am Main: Lang, 2001), pp. 69–95.

the deportation and systematic mass murder of European Jews in concentration camps, were lawyers.[22] If there was one lesson to draw from the legal profession's behaviour during the Nazi era, it was certainly not that courts would be the institutions that could be trusted with safeguarding individual rights and justice.

What seemed key to the framers at the time was first of all to establish a state whose institutional structure would be better suited to resist a takeover by totalitarian and antidemocratic forces. The Basic Law's institutional arrangements thus reflect the attempt to avoid those institutional arrangements that had enabled the Nazis to take power in the Weimar Republic: Most importantly, the presidentialist system, with its strong role for the Federal President, was abandoned in favour of a strongly representative conception of parliamentary democracy. And individual rights meant to signal that the new state would serve the individual rather than the other way around as the Nazis had captured it most famously in their slogan for the Hitler Youth: You are nothing, your people everything![23] The framers hence placed a catalogue of fundamental rights at the beginning of the Basic Law, in conscious contrast to the Weimar Constitution that had started with the basic organizational and structural provisions and only listed rights later on.

It was nevertheless a cautious beginning. To many, this new constitution seemed a disappointment. One constitutional theorist complained: 'In it, you won't find any risky fresh ideas, no forward-looking willingness to take up a challenge and no courageous decision' (Weber, 1949).[24] In contrast to the Allies' wishes, the Basic Law was supposed to be a transitory solution—the word '*Verfassung*' (constitution) was to be avoided until the Reunification of Eastern and Western Germany. If it was a prosaic and realistic document, this merely reflected that its main purpose was to avoid the mistakes of Weimar and provide a workable framework for the time being. Law and rights were conceptualized in the Basic Law primarily along classical reactive lines, as safeguards for individual liberty. The framers wanted to establish effective mechanisms for rights' review and therefore chose to frame rights narrowly to ensure that courts would

[22] They were Josef Bühler, Roland Freisler, Gerhard Klopfer, Friedrich Wilhelm Kritzingen, Rudolf Lange, Alfred Meyer, Erich Neumann, Karl Eberhardt Schöngarth, and Wilhelm Stuckart; see online documentation on the participants and their curricula vitae of the Haus der Wannsee-Konferenz, available at <http://www.ghwk.de/fileadmin/user_upload/pdf-wannsee/allgemein/viten-dt.pdf>.

[23] Quoted according to Peter Kohrs, *Kindheit und Jugend unter dem Hakenkreuz. Nationalsozialistische Erziehung in Familie, Schule und Hitlerjugend* (Stuttgart: Metzler, 1983), p. 10 (translation by this author).

[24] Werner Weber, *Weimarer Verfassung und Bonner Grundgesetz* (Göttingen: Karl-Friedrich Fleischer, 1949), p. 12.

actually be willing to protect them.[25] This meant first and foremost leaving aside socio-economic rights that were widely seen as non-justiciable.

But the framers could not agree which courts should enforce these rights, or how. Christian Democrats in particular refused to provide for an individual complaint mechanism in the constitution itself, which is today responsible for 95 per cent of all cases in the Constitutional Court's docket.[26] Such a mechanism would allow individual citizens to challenge the state and thus, so some imagined, have a democratizing effect on the German tradition of a strong, unchallengeable state. The Christian Democrats, however, who were in power at the time, managed to block its introduction. They feared that it would endanger the sovereignty of the German state by allowing individual troublemakers to challenge the state on their own account and lead to a juridification of politics.[27] As a result, the individual complaint procedure was initially only established on a statutory basis, mostly with the support of the Social Democrats.[28]

The framers also worried about granting courts too much power.[29] Mostly, however, they paid little attention to the new Constitutional Court or to rights review.[30] Certainly, they did not envisage a strong court along the lines of the current German Constitutional Court that would frequently interfere in democratic politics. If they had, the Constitutional Court would have played a much more important role in their debates. Instead, the Constitutional Court constituted at best a matter of secondary importance for the delegates at the Herrenchiemsee Convention, who spent most of their time discussing questions of federal relations, the allocation of taxes, and budgetary authority.[31] While the Convention already attributed a significant number

[25] Deutscher Bundestag und Bundesarchiv, under guidance from Rubert Schick and Friedrich Kahlenberg (eds), *Der Parlamentarische Rat 1948–1949. Akten und Protokolle. Band 5: Ausschuss für Grundsatzfragen, Teilband 1* (1993), pp. 33 ff., p. 43.

[26] See official statistics for the years 1951–2012, <http://www.bundesverfassungsgericht.de/DE/Verfahren/Jahresstatistiken/2013/gb2013/A-I-1.html>.

[27] Michael Stolleis, *Geschichte des öffentlichen Rechts in Deutschland: Vierter Band 1945–1990* (München: C. H. Beck, 2012), p. 212.

[28] A constitutional complaint procedure was, however, provided for in ordinary statutory law, and in 1969 the Basic Law was finally amended in this regard, adding Art. 93 para. 1 Nr. 4a Basic Law. I am using constitutional complaint and individual complaint in this book interchangeably.

[29] See *Der Parlamentarische Rat 1948–1949. Akten und Protokolle. Band 5, Teilband 1*, p. 67: Dr Schmid: 'The judge can veto such a law and claim that the legislature has not acted in accordance with the constitution.' Zinn: 'But this power of constitutional review cannot without boundaries' (translated by myself), also at p. 68 (Dr V. Mangoldt).

[30] See Chapter 1; generally on the framers' lack of interest in the new Court: Heinz Laufer, *Verfassungsgerichtsbarkeit und politischer Prozess: Studien zum Bundesverfassungsgericht der Bundesrepublik Deutschland* (Tübingen: Mohr Siebeck, 1968), pp. 52 et seq.

[31] Ibid., p. 38.

of functions to the new institution, no one seemed to notice or care about this resulting assembly of competences.[32] In the Parliamentary Council, matters were no different. Heinz Laufer concludes that the majority of its members showed no special interest in the question of constitutional review.[33] In fact, things even got worse for the Court. The Herrenchiemsee drafters had at least inserted a specific section titled 'the Federal Constitutional Court' into their draft to ensure the Court's equal status with other constitutional organs, all of whom had been accorded their own, specifically titled section in the Basic Law. The Parliamentary Assembly, however, exchanged this specific title with a more general one, 'the judiciary', and thus lumped the Constitutional Court in with all other courts.[34]

The framers' foremost attention in the drafting process was ultimately not with rights or courts, but rather with institutional design. What mattered was how one could build the new state and *all* its institutions in a way that would be less susceptible to a descent into authoritarianism than the Weimar Republic. For this purpose, the framers declared in the so-called eternity clause, Art. 79 of the Basic Law, that a number of constitutional principles could not be amended. This often-cited clause contains the basis of what Bruce Ackerman has described as German foundationalism:[35] the idea that the German state and society are based on a number of key values or principles that are beyond the reach of democratic majorities. Together with a number of other provisions, this clause provides the legal backbone of German militant democracy, a concept introduced by Karl Loewenstein. A German (and Jewish) political scientist and émigré, Loewenstein had famously argued that democracies needed to guard themselves against their enemies by making participation in democratic processes conditional upon the acceptance of basic principles of democracy.[36] But again, this idea—developed against the background of the National-Socialists' rise to power—was not primarily concerned with rights, but rather with the basic structures of the democratic state requiring protection against non-democratic forces. This was also visible in Art. 79 para. 3 itself, which stated that '[a]mendments to this Basic Law affecting the division of the Federation into Länder, their participation on principle in the legislative process, or the principles laid down in Articles 1 and 20 shall be inadmissible'. Only Art. 1 therefore, the right to human dignity, was to be protected against amendments. And while some other fundamental

[32] Ibid., p. 45. [33] Ibid., p. 52. [34] Ibid., p. 57.

[35] Bruce Ackerman, *We the People: Foundations* (Cambridge: Harvard University Press, 1991), p. 15.

[36] Karl Loewenstein, 'Militant Democracy and Fundamental Rights', in *Militant Democracy*, ed. András Sájo (Utrecht: Eleven International Publishing, 2004), pp. 231 et seq.

rights may possess a substantive core that would be protected as part of the right to dignity insofar as they are necessary to guarantee a democratic order that respects dignity, both scholars and the Court have taken a narrow view on what might hold up against amendment.[37] In contrast to a widespread understanding, the Basic Law hence neither 'explicitly precludes amending provisions that establish rights (and federalism)'[38] nor 'declare(s) that a long list of fundamental rights cannot constitutionally be revised'.[39]

Insofar as the framers did consider the Constitutional Court and its role, legislators both in the Parliamentary Council and later the German Bundestag (responsible for drafting the Court's organizational statute) were mainly concerned with the traditional questions of how to separate law and politics, what kind of institution (judicial or political) should exercise constitutional review (only a specialized court or all courts), and how this new institution should be staffed (lawyers or laymen).[40] Broadly speaking, the Social Democratic Party (SPD) delegates stressed both the Court's political and rights-protecting function and argued for the introduction of an individual complaint procedure in the Basic Law. In contrast, Christian Democrats paid very little attention to rights review, but focused on the Court's competences in adjudicating conflicts between different institutions. This had been the traditional function of the Weimar *Staatsgerichtshof* in whose tradition they saw the new Court. Consequently, they pushed successfully for a majority of their own nominees in the Court's Second Senate, then mostly charged with organizational and federal questions. In doing so, they accepted that the First Senate, charged with rights review, would be staffed with a majority of Social Democrat appointees. The Social Democrats, who seem to have had a better sense of the things to come, were quite pleased about this.[41]

If we think about it, this should not surprise us. After all, the framers could not actually draw on any positive example of a strong individual rights-oriented court at the time. In the 1940s the US Supreme Court, the Germans' primary model for rights' review, had not yet decided *Brown v. Board of Education* (1954), and its famous civil rights jurisprudence would develop only much later in the 1960s and 1970s. Before then, the Supreme

[37] BVerfGE 94, 49, pp. 209 et seq.; BVerfGE 84, 90, pp. 120–1; BVerfGE 30, 1, p. 24; see also Hans D. Jarass and Bodo Pieroth, 'Art. 79', in *Grundgesetz für die Bundesrepublik Deutschland. Kommentar* (München: C. H. Beck, 2012), para. 6 with further references.

[38] Alec Stone-Sweet, *Governing with Judges. Constitutional Politics in Europe* (New York: Oxford University Press, 2000).

[39] Ackerman, *Foundations*, p. 15.

[40] Laufer, *Verfassungsgerichtsbarkeit*, pp. 52 et seq.

[41] Udo Wengst, *Staatsaufbau und Regierungspraxis 1948–1953: Zur Geschichte der Verfassungsorgane der Bundesrepublik Deutschland* (Düsseldorf: Droste-Verlag, 1984), p. 241.

Court had, if anything, a reputation in both the United States and Germany as a defender of economic liberties, such as the freedom of contract. But the Lochner jurisprudence, of which the German framers were roughly aware,[42] hardly provided a model towards which Germans would aspire considering that the US Supreme Court had spent much of its time in the late 1930s and 1940s rolling this very jurisprudence back. In other words: A strong human rights tribunal along the lines of current constitutional courts simply did not exist when the Basic Law was drafted.

II. First steps

When the new Constitutional Court took up its work in 1951, it seemed initially to continue along the *Staatsgerichtshof*'s lines. As a matter of institutional design, it was mainly governmental institutions, which benefited from the Court's assembly of competences. They enjoyed privileged access to the new Court, not only to safeguard their own constitutional rights towards other institutions and check the competences of others, but abstract review also allowed the federal and state governments as well as a third[43] of all members of parliament to challenge the constitutionality of laws without being affected in their own rights. It thus involved the Court quite directly in high politics.

Rights review in contrast took off slowly, and only after the Court had already acquired a reputation and some political standing in other cases. This, too, suggests that the reaction against National-Socialism played a more limited role in establishing the Court's authority than is often assumed. For if it had been a key idea the German Court was acting upon, we would expect to see a stronger counter-majoritarian rights jurisprudence earlier on. This is, however, not the picture we get from the German Court in the 1950s. Proceeding rather cautiously, many of its most important cases concerned organizational disputes rather than rights issues, and never before the 1960s did the Court declare a major project of the federal government unconstitutional.[44]

At the same time, the Court signalled early on that it would not shy away from exercising its jurisdiction even in politically highly charged questions.

[42] See Deutscher Bundestag und Bundesarchiv, under guidance from Horst Risse and Hartmut Weber (eds), *Der Parlamentarische Rat 1948–1949. Akten und Protokolle. Band 14: Hauptausschuß, Teilband 1* (München: Oldenbourg, 2009), p. 697.

[43] This was later amended to only require a quorum of a quarter of all Members of Parliament.

[44] Collings, *Democracy's Guardians*, chapter 1 (conclusion).

Indeed, its first ever case involved a politically charged debate about the unification of two states into one, Baden-Württemberg.[45] The Court dealt with the question in Marbury-style—not challenging those parts of the proposed federal law that mattered to the federal government, but nevertheless prescribing minor changes and thus indicating its willingness to take on such highly political questions. While the decision hence drew attention to the new Court—the *Frankfurter Allgemeine Zeitung* trumpeted 'We have a Court'[46]—it was nevertheless very modest in its demands towards the government.

Then the Rearmament Case brought the Court its first conflict and victory against the government.[47] The Adenauer administration sought to realize a defence-union between Germany and France, which would have required German rearmament. The union marked a cornerstone in Adenauer's strategy of political and military alliance with the West (*Westbindung*). However, worrying about the implications of this policy for reunification, the Social Democrats objected to rearmament, bringing the issue before the Constitutional Court. Because the Court's position was unclear, its involvement constituted a serious risk to the government. The administration reacted by undertaking a series of attempts to manipulate the Court's proceedings in order to increase the chances of a favourable decision, first attempting to bring the issue before the entire Court sitting in one bench. But when rumours were spread that this did not guarantee success, they launched another application in the matter, this time before the so-called 'black' senate, i.e. the senate staffed with a majority of Christian Democratic Union (CDU) appointees. The Court, however, did not yield to the government's attempts at procedural

[45] The case concerned a federal law regulating the creation of a new state (Baden-Württemberg) out of what had been three separate military administrative zones and later three separate states. The new German federal government had—based on Art. 118 GG, which suggested that the matter could be regulated by federal law, requiring a referendum in the states concerned—assumed control after some failed attempts by the states themselves. It had provided a law for the formation of a new state, pending a referendum in all three states that, however, would not require the population of each of the states to agree separately, but instead treated their population as one. Unlike a separate referendum it would therefore likely pass, as prior polls suggested. Before this compromise had been worked out, the federal government had moreover sought to postpone two upcoming state elections until the questions concerning the formation of a new state had been settled and new elections would have to be called in any event.

[46] Hans Baumgarten, Wir haben ein Verfassungsgericht, *Frankfurter Allgemeine*, 11 September 1951.

[47] Oliver Lembcke, 'Das Bundesverfassungsgericht und die Regierung Adenauer—vom Streit um den Status zur Anerkennung der Autorität', in *Das Bundesverfassungsgericht im politischen System*, ed. Robert C. Ooyen and Martin Möllers (Wiesbaden: Verlag für Sozialwissenschaften, 2006), pp. 163 et seq.; see also Collings, *Democracy's Guardians*, chapter 1 (II. A.), and Richard Häußler, *Der Konflikt zwischen Bundesverfassungsgericht und politischer Führung* (Berlin: Duncker & Humblot, 1994), p. 22.

manipulation and instead confronted it with a show of near unanimity and (party–)political neutrality. For this, it incurred sharp, insulting criticism and even threats from politicians, most notably from then Minister of Justice, Thomas Dehler. The Court, however, fought back, again nearly unanimously, attracting much applause from the media.[48] Shortly afterwards, Adenauer publicly distanced himself from Dehler. The Court had won its first battle. As the French parliament eventually declined to ratify the treaty, the substantive question of rearmament eventually became moot—no doubt to the relief of the Justices themselves who could therefore avoid answering the substantive questions involved.

Only after these successes did the Court start to take its first important decisions in rights cases—and it took much longer for it to establish itself as a strong rights tribunal and to be noticed as such by the public. The reaction to National-Socialism played a small part in this development, but in a different way than is often assumed. In particular, it did not drive a countermajoritarian judicial activism in rights cases—in contrast to what we can observe after the fall of Communism in some parts of Central and Eastern Europe.[49] In the 1950s and 1960s German elites sought to rebuild a new state and society that would be different not only from the Nazi past, but also from the Communist regimes in its East.[50] The Constitutional Court participated in these efforts, which in turn provided impetus and authority for many of its early landmark judgments. The Court was, however, by no means *specifically* entrusted with the task of preventing a backslide into fascism. Though a majority of the judges at the Court in the 1950s had been opponents of the Nazis or had even been persecuted by them, and some had emigrated during the war,[51] the same was true for most members of

[48] See Collings, *Democracy's Guardians*, chapter 1 (I. B.) with further references; Häußler, *Der Konflikt zwischen Bundesverfassungsgericht und politischer Führung*, p. 34.

[49] Ruti G. Teitel, *Transitional Justice* (Oxford: Oxford University Press, 2000), pp. 204 et seq., and Ruti G. Teitel, 'Post-Communist Constitutionalism: A Transitional Perspective', *Columbia Human Rights Law Review*, 26 (1994), 167. See also more critically Wojcjech Sadurski, *Rights Before Courts: A Study of Constitutional Courts in Postcommunist States of Central and Eastern Europe* (The Netherlands: Springer, 2005), pp. 223 et seq.

[50] Scheppele, 'Constitutional Interpretation after Regimes of Horror', acknowledging the role of keeping a distance from the Communist regimes.

[51] Those who were critics of the Nazi regime or were persecuted by it included Martin Drath, Wilhelm Ellinghaus, Julius Federer, Ernst Friesenhahn, Georg Fröhlich, Gerhard R. Heiland, Rudolf Katz, Gerhard Leibholz, Erna Scheffler, Egon Schunck, Erwin Stein Franz Wessel, and Bernhard Wolff, and most of the other judges had kept their distance from the Nazis (see Stolleis, *Vierter Band 1945–1990*, pp. 148–52). The most prominent exception was probably Willi Geiger, who had made an impressive Nazi career, acting among other things as a prosecutor at one of the specialist courts and participating in a number of death sentences there (Stolleis, *Vierter Band 1945–1990*, pp. 152–3).

Adenauer's first federal government.[52] Its make-up was insofar typical of a general attempt to avoid placing former Nazis in publicly highly exposed offices, partly in order to placate the Allies and partly out of a genuine desire for moral reformation. In this regard, the Court was hardly unique.

Between 1957 and 1961 the Court decided three landmark cases that still provide the basis for much of its expansive rights jurisprudence today. However, only one of them, *Lüth*, addressed the past experiences of National-Socialism. In contrast, both the *Elfes* and the *Pharmacies* cases were set against the background of an intensifying Cold War. Both were concerned to make a point about individual freedom, although in different ways. In *Elfes*, the Court adopted a broad and generous reading of individual freedom as a residual right to liberty, thus greatly increasing its own jurisdiction and the justificatory burden on the government.[53] This generous abstract conception, however, did not cash out on the individual level: The Court upheld the government's refusal to provide the plaintiff, Elfes, with a passport to travel outside of Germany where he planned speak out at a conference against the West German military alliance with the West and for a peaceful solution in dealing with the German Democratic Republic (GDR).[54] Coming as it did shortly after the 1956 Soviet intervention in Hungary, this kind of politics had lost its former attraction for most West Germans.[55] In affirming the government's restrictive stance, the Court continued its tough line on left dissidents following its prohibition of the German Communist party in the previous year.[56]

If the Court in *Elfes* demonstrated its support for the fight against communism by upholding repressive measures, it turned liberal in the *Pharmacies* case.[57] The plaintiff in that case had originally settled in the GDR where he

[52] The members in Adenauer's first government who had been opposition to the Nazi regime were Thomas Dehler (Justice), Gustav Heinemann and Robert Lehr (Interior), Heinrich Hellwege (Relations with the Bundesrat), Jakob Kaiser (Unification), Hans Lukaschek (Resettlement), Wilhelm Niklas (Agriculture), Fritz Schäffer (Finances), Hans Schuberth (Telecommunication), and Eberhardt Wildermuth (Housing) (source: Internationales Biographisches Archiv, available online under <http://www.munzinger.de/search/query?query.id=query-00> (18 August 2013)).

[53] BVerfGE 6, 32.

[54] See Gunter Rojahn, 'Elfes—Mehr als ein Urteil. Aufladung und Entladung eines Politikums' (Doctoral thesis, Freie Universität Berlin, 2009), pp. 117 et seq., <http://www.diss.fu-berlin.de/diss/servlets/MCRFileNodeServlet/FUDISS_derivate_000000008674/Dissertation_-_ohne_Lebenslauf.pdf;jsessionid=DA083A32675851772A975F5297A571A9?hosts=>.

[55] Rojahn, 'Elfes', p. 184.

[56] BVerfGE 5, 85. The prohibition of parties is also one of the rare instances where the Court was granted a power directly in response to Nazi history as part of the Basic Law's conception of militant democracy.

[57] BVerfGE 7, 377.

had managed a pharmacy as a state-appointed tenant. In 1955 he left the GDR and moved to Bavaria, where, after working under the supervision of a local pharmacist, he applied for a licence to open a new pharmacy. The Bavarian authorities, however, refused to grant him such a licence on the grounds that the geographic area in question was already supplied with one pharmacy and there was no need for another. Arguing on the basis of the right to freely choose one's profession, the Court found for the pharmacist and struck down the Bavarian law that provided the basis for refusing the licence. It argued that the statute's only legitimate purpose could be the protection of public health, not protection against economic competition, and that this goal could be achieved by different, less restrictive means. Though the decision is silent about the political context of the time, elaborating instead on the pre-war German paternalist history of regulation, the discussion about public health was, as in any other field of policy, heavily shaped by the constant need for self-assertion in relation to the GDR and the opposition to socialism.[58] In light of this context, the irony of the facts at hand was hard to overlook: The plaintiff after all had already achieved his aim of having his 'own' pharmacy within the limits of the GDR economic system, but had later left and chosen the supposedly free Germany where he had now been refused a licence for a pharmacy on grounds of extensive state planning. Sanctioning this rejection by means of constitutional law would therefore have sent a rather odd political signal.

C. Transformations

On their own, both the *Elfes* and the *Pharmacies* cases suggest that what we see is the Court shifting towards a more aggressive protection of liberal individual rights—thus fulfilling the role sketched out for it in the Basic Law, albeit in a more expansive way. On their own, they seem to validate the claim that the German Constitutional Court was following the established US model of liberal constitutionalism by finally taking individual freedom seriously.

Transformative constitutionalism seems a long way from this kind of jurisprudence—and the Constitutional Court moreover demonstrated early scepticism towards justiciable socio-economic rights: When a widowed mother asked it to declare that the welfare grants she was receiving were insufficient

[58] See Philip Manow, 'Entwicklungslinien ost-und westdeutscher Gesundheitspolitik zwischen doppelter Staatsgründung, deutscher Einigung und europäischer Integration', *Zeitschrift für Sozialreform*, 43 (1997), 101.

as a matter of constitutional law and that the government had to remedy this situation, the Court dismissed the case on all grounds. Arguing that the role of the legislature under the Basic Law would be weakened in an unconstitutional manner if citizens could make positive, justiciable demands for legislative action, the Court firmly rejected a transformative vision of the Basic Law:

> To bring about law that is in accordance with the ideals of social justice, liberty, equality and equity is an eternal task of the legislator in which the individual citizen only participates by exercising his right to vote. The Constitutional Court is not a legislating body and it is not its function to put itself in the shoes of the legislator. (...) Whether a law must be made depends on economic, political and ideological considerations that are beyond judicial scrutiny.[59]

In a second step, the Court then read the widow's request for legislative action as a mere request for invalidating the existing statutory regulations, but without prescribing positive action. Again, however, it dismissed the request. While the idea of a welfare state had become increasingly accepted in public discourse, it was nevertheless only marginally reflected in the Basic Law, the Court argued. Drawing on the drafters' original intent, who had decided against including an explicit right to a material subsistence minimum in the Basic Law, the Court concluded that neither the obligation to protect human dignity nor the right to life and physical integrity implied a right to protection against poverty. While this did not mean that there existed no individual right to welfare of any kind due to the Basic Law's social state principle, the government nevertheless enjoyed wide discretion in fulfilling its task, subject only to an arbitrariness standard that had not been met in the case at hand.[60]

This rather reactive vision of constitutional review would not survive long. The Court's contemporary jurisprudence on welfare rights stands in sharp contrast to its early decision.[61] Indeed, only a few years later, the federal German administrative court would embrace the idea of a positive right to welfare,[62] as would most German constitutional lawyers. But it was only in 1957 that it became clear that a shift towards a new, transformative paradigm of constitutional law was truly occurring.

The *Lüth* case had already attracted much attention in the media, as it concerned one of the most precarious and sensitive topics of the post-war years:[63] how to deal with the past and those who had been involved in Nazi

[59] BVerfGE 1, 97. [60] BVerfGE 1, 97.

[61] See BVerfGE 125, 175; also see Chapter 5. [62] BVerwGE 1, 159.

[63] At the time, the media hardly reported the decision at all and it certainly did not stir much public interest. See Collings, *Democracy's Guardians*, chapter 1 (V. C.).

injustice. Lüth, a politician and administrator in the state of Hamburg, had called for the boycott of a movie directed by Veith Harlan. Harlan had notoriously collaborated with Goebbels some years earlier in the making of the anti-Semitic propaganda movie '*Jud Süß*'. Lüth's call for a boycott stirred up a heated public debate about whether the time had come to draw a line on discussions of the uncomfortable past.[64] Harlan's production company sought and gained an injunction against Lüth based on established German doctrine that the incitement of boycotts constituted an act against public morale and was thus illegal under the German civil code. With the help of the Social Democrat parliamentarian Adolf Arndt, Lüth eventually turned to the Constitutional Court. He argued that the civil courts had infringed on his right to free speech under the Basic Law, thus raising the question if fundamental rights could be applied in disputes between two private individuals. The Court answered 'yes' and justified its decision by reading the Basic Law as an 'objective order of values' that had to be taken into account when interpreting general statutory clauses.[65]

This turn to values reflected a widespread conviction at the time that the moral catastrophe of the Third Reich had been brought about by a lack of (Christian and humanist) values in German society. The fact that value jurisprudence methodologically resembled the techniques of the Nazi jurists was initially only noticed by few.[66] In any case, different values were now rediscovered, be it in the writings of Goethe and Lessing or the Bible. This came with a strong role for the Christian churches, which offered redemption and often acquittal from the responsibility for past injustices.[67] In the legal realm, natural law theories surfaced again for a brief time, partly as a way of dealing with Nazi era statutes, some of which were still legally valid,[68] providing a justification for refusing to apply these statutes. Beyond such practical utility, it also seemed to offer a moral anchor for law and the legal profession, which

[64] Thomas Henne, 'Erich Lüth vs. Veit Harlan—Sechs Göttinger Beiträge zum Lüth-Urteil des Bundesverfassungsgerichts von 1958', in *Kontinuitäten und Zäsuren: Rechtswissenschaft und Justiz im 'Dritten Reich' und in der Nachkriegszeit*, ed. Eva Schumann (Göttingen: Wallstein, 2008), p. 225.

[65] BVerfGE 7, 198. [66] Stolleis, *Vierter Band 1945–1990*, p. 243.

[67] See 'Erstes gemeinsames Hirtenwort nach dem Krieg, Eichstätt, 28. Juni 1945', in Wolfgang Löhr (ed.), *Dokumente deutscher Bischöfe, Bd. 1: Hirtenbriefe und Ansprachen zu Gesellschaft und Politik, 1945–1949*, 2nd edn (Würzburg: Echter, 1985), pp. 29 et seq. and 'Erster gemeinsamer Hirtenbrief nach dem Krieg, Fulda, 23. August 1945', Wolfgang Löhr (ed.), *Dokumente deutscher Bischöfe, Bd. 1: Hirtenbriefe und Ansprachen zu Gesellschaft und Politik, 1945–1949*, 2nd edn (Würzburg: Echter, 1985), pp. 40 et seq.

[68] Michael Stolleis, *The Law Under the Swastika: Studies on Legal History in Nazi Germany*, trans. Thomas Dunlap (Chicago: University of Chicago Press, 1998), p. 181.

had been deeply corrupted during the Third Reich and were now in dire need of rehabilitation.

The *Lüth* decision implied, however, no counter-majoritarian activism. On the contrary, the judgment explicitly mentioned that the remark of a German parliamentarian calling the showing of Harlan's new film a 'disgrace' for Germans had earned applause from both the government and the opposition in the parliament as a supporting argument in its decision.[69] Moreover, *Lüth* fit in nicely not only with the prevalent value-talk, but also with an emerging willingness among political leaders to take past injustice and its perpetrators more seriously, reflected, for example, in the founding of a central prosecutorial agency for Nazi crimes in Ludwigsburg in 1958.[70] This second dimension, how to grapple with the past, was also what caught the judges' primary attention rather than the implications of the new concept of values: As a participant in the case later admitted, the judges were not fully aware of the scope of the decision they had taken at the time.[71] The reaction against National-Socialism hence influenced the development of the Court's concept of the Basic Law as an order of values, but it does not support the bigger claim that this history provided the basis for the Court's subsequent authority.

Nevertheless, *Lüth* is rightfully remembered as one of the, if not *the* most important decision of the German Court of all time. With *Lüth*, the Court marked its departure from a classical liberal understanding of rights as mere protections of certain spheres of private life against governmental intervention and of private law as a mere framework to settle conflicts between private individuals. It converted constitutional law into a fundamental matrix of the whole legal system and thus enabled the jurisprudential development of governmental duties to protect the Basic Law's values (*Schutzpflichten*). Fundamental rights became 'objective law', decoupled from the violation of individual 'subjective' rights.[72] And *Lüth* signalled that the Court was moving beyond the established reactive paradigm of rights protection towards a more transformative model of constitutionalism. This new kind of constitutional thinking would view the constitution as a comprehensive vision for a better

[69] Henne, 'Erich Lüth vs. Veit Harlan', p. 225. [70] Ibid.

[71] Uwe Kranepohl, *Hinter dem Schleier des Beratungsgeheimnisses: Der Willensbildungs- und Entscheidungsprozess des Bundesverfassungsgerichts* (Wiesbaden: Verlag für Sozialwissenschaften, 2010).

[72] For examples and critique see Christoph Möllers, 'Legalität, Legitimität und Legitimation des Bundesverfassungsgerichts', in *Das entgrenzte Gericht: Eine kritische Bilanz nach sechzig Jahren Bundesverfassungsgericht*, ed. Matthias Jestaedt, Oliver Lepsius, Christoph Möllers, and Christoph Schönberger (Berlin: Suhrkamp, 2011), pp. 279–419, p. 398.

and more just society that would require not only considerable state-driven change but also intervention in formerly sacrosanct private relationships.

None of this implied of course that classical liberal rights and individual freedom were not an important part of the new transformative paradigm. Indeed, the *Lüth* decision itself began by stating that 'fundamental rights are first and foremost negative rights against the state', before explaining that the Constitution also expressed broader objective values. The new transformative paradigm of constitutional law therefore had a distinctly liberal character, and the Court contributed much to the liberalization of the German state and society in the following years.[73] Gender equality in particular had become a hot topic in the Court's jurisprudence and an important reason for judicial intervention.[74] Similarly, the rights of criminal defendants increasingly attracted the Court's attention.[75] As Adenauer's popularity started to decrease in the 1960s, this opened up more political space for the Constitutional Court. In 1961 the Court for the first time thwarted a major governmental initiative. The Second Senate, consisting in its majority of Christian Democrat nominees, declared Adenauer's project to create a federal (government-controlled) TV channel unconstitutional for violating the freedom of broadcasting, which had to be organized in a way that ensured that a plurality of voices would be represented and it was not entirely subject to governmental control.[76] While Adenauer publicly stated that the government considered the case wrongly decided, this time he refrained from threatening non-implementation.[77] And with good reason: The press again ran headlines favouring the Court, and opinion polls demonstrated that even among Adenauer's own party members, support for his project was in fact rather low.[78] Another setback for his government came in 1962 with the so-called Spiegel scandal. In response to the publication of military information revealing weaknesses in the German defence by the news magazine *Der Spiegel*, the government arrested two journalists, and confiscated documents after searching the publisher's premises. This highly contested move was sharply criticized by the public and further weakened Adenauer's leadership, and he resigned in 1963. In 1966 political winds eventually turned and the first (grand) coalition government between the CDU and the SPD came into operation. Ultimately, the Constitutional Court upheld

[73] See also Werner Heun, *The Constitution of Germany, A Contextual Analysis* (Oxford: Hart Publishing, 2011), p. 1.

[74] Collings, *Democracy's Guardians*, chapter 1 (V. B.) for an overview of the Court's jurisprudence on gender equality.

[75] Stolleis, *Vierter Band 1945–1990*, pp. 232 et seq.

[76] BVerfGE 12, 205.

[77] Häußler, *Der Konflikt zwischen Bundesverfassungsgericht und politischer Führung*, p. 51.

[78] Ibid., p. 32.

the search of the rooms and confiscation of documents in the Spiegel case as constitutional in 1966, but it did so only with the narrowest possible margin of four votes against four dissenting votes. With this, the decision reflected a general trend to subject increasing fields of classical state prerogative to judicial review. A long-standing doctrine of public law that had exempted certain hierarchical relationships (*Sonderrechtsverhältnisse*) between individuals and the state from judicial scrutiny such as prisoners, schoolchildren, or civil servants crumbled in the wake of this trend.[79] Alongside the Court, legal academics, but also administrators and politicians, contributed to the changes.[80] Ultimately, they led to the 'perfection' of the German *Rechtsstaat*, where every state measure relevant to individual rights, both statutory and constitutional, could be challenged before the courts.[81]

But the new judicial activism would soon go beyond the classical liberal paradigm. With the increasing number of fundamental rights cases came the development of proportionality analysis and the end of a conception of rights as absolute trumps. Proportionality had been outlined in bits and pieces in the Court's earlier jurisprudence, but it now started to assume structure and substance. Though during the 1960s it was often still used as a relatively meaningless catch-all phrase, but over time it acquired its later four-pronged structure and more bite.[82] In its 1960s jurisprudence, the Court increasingly relied on proportionality, particularly when dealing with violations of physical integrity, where the Court employed this doctrine as a tool against excessive state action. Allowing the judges to carefully weigh individual and community interests, its use indicated that the Court would not follow a formalist reading of individual rights as absolute spheres of individual freedom against government intervention. Almost every right could now be limited—within proportionality analysis rights shrank to valuable considerations that had to be taken into account, but without a real substantive core that would resist infringements at whatever cost. For even though Art. 19 para. 2 Basic Law protects the core of constitutional rights, this requirement was in practice absorbed by proportionality analysis. Only once so far has the Court found a violation of the

[79] Christoph Schönberger, 'Verwaltungsrecht als konkretisiertes Verfassungsrecht', in *Das Bonner Grundgesetz: Altes Recht und neue Verfassung in den ersten Jahrzehnten der Bundesrepublik Deutschland (1949–1969)*, ed. Michael Stolleis (Berlin: Berliner Wissenschafts-Verlag, 2006).

[80] Stolleis, *Vierter Band 1945–1990*, pp. 232–4.

[81] Rainer Wahl, *Herausforderungen und Antworten: Das öffentliche Recht der letzten fünf Jahrzehnte* (Berlin: De Gruyter, 2006).

[82] The first question is if a legitimate governmental purpose for the limitation of a right exists, second, if the means employed to achieve this purpose are generally suitable, third, if they represent the less restrictive means possible, and finally, if the good achieved is on the whole proportional to the harm done to the right (see for more on proportionality Chapter 4).

Basic Law's core guarantee and this is not surprising.[83] Proportionality precedes the assessment whether a right has been violated in its core, and because disproportionate rights' limitations are already unconstitutional and conversely proportional rights limitations cannot violate the core guarantee, the core guarantee has become largely superfluous.[84] But then again, neither the possibility to limit rights nor the application of proportionality analysis implies a weak protection against governmental restrictions of freedom as we will see in Chapter 4.[85]

In other respects, too, the Court has often emphasized that the Basic Law's idea of liberty is not to be understood in a strict, formal sense of restraining state action, but that it is bound up in a broader vision of a just society: 'its (the Basic Law's) idea of man is not one of the autocratic individual, but of a person standing in the community and being obliged to it in multiple ways'.[86] In its jurisprudence, the Court made clear that its transformative task required a broad, substantive understanding of liberty that would reach far into the private domain. In *Blinkfuer*, for example, an early follow-up case to *Lüth*, the Court assumed a substantive rather than formal understanding of freedom of speech when it clarified that freedom of speech did not include the freedom to exercise massive economic pressure in order to suppress the opinions of others.[87] The case involved one of the country's biggest publishing houses, Springer, which had for political reasons announced a boycott of print media retailers that would continue to distribute the East German radio and TV programme guide 'Blinkfuer' which the Court refused to protect as free speech.

For a while, the idea of the Basic Law as a promise for a better state and society seemed attractive to many. Especially in the 1960s, politicians and academics emphasized the Basic Law's transformative dimension as never before. The political and academic catchwords were '*Verfassung and Verfassungswirklichkeit*'—constitution and constitutional reality—they could be found in the title of numerous speeches, essays, and academic publications.[88] Much like in current

[83] BVerfGE 22, 180, p. 219; Barbara Remmert, 'Art. 19 Abs. 2', in *Maunz/Dürig: Grundgesetz Kommentar*, ed. Matthias Herdegen, Roman Herzog, Hans H. Klein, and Rupert Scholz. (München: C. H. Beck, 2013), para. 38; Dreier, 'Art. 19 II', in *Grundgesetz. Kommentar*, 3rd edn, ed. Horst Dreier (2013), para. 8, fn. 29.

[84] BVerfGE 58, 300, p. 348.

[85] See also Alec Stone-Sweet and Jud Matthews, 'Proportionality Balancing and Global Constitutionalism', *Columbia Journal of Transnational Law*, 47 (2008), 111.

[86] BVerfGE 12, 45. [87] BVerfGE 25, 256.

[88] See Collings, *Democracy's Guardians*, chapter 2 (conclusion) referring to Adolf Arndt, *Das Nicht erfüllte Grundgesetz. Ein Vortrag* (Tübingen: Mohr, 1960). The antagonism between the two terms has been described as typically German; see Wilhelm Hennis, 'Verfassung und Verfassungswirklichkeit—ein deutsches Problem', in *Regieren im modernen Staat* (Tübingen: Mohr

South African legal discourse, this comparison between constitutional promise and reality sought to emphasize how the social and political realities in Western Germany still differed from their constitutional ideal. While mainly a political task, law and the Constitutional Court also had an important role to play in this enterprise. And under Adenauer's paternalist and conservative reign, the Court held for some time a position as a progressive frontrunner.

This started to change, however, towards the end of the 1960s and the beginning of the 1970s. The newly elected SPD government's campaign slogan 'Dare more Democracy' ('*mehr Demokratie wagen*') stood in sharp contrast to Adenauer's previous motto 'no experiments' (with socialism). Chancellor Willie Brandt's call for a new beginning and political reforms increasingly displaced the Court and the Basic Law as focal points of national transformation. As a result, the Court suddenly became the conservative branch. As it could not and would not keep up with the government's plans for reform, the two branches increasingly clashed with each other. It invalidated important parts of the Social Democrat policy agenda such as the decriminalization of abortion, the restructuring of German universities, and a reform of military service that benefitted conscientious objectors.[89] Social Democrats who had previously been the Court's biggest defenders reacted with harsh criticism. Especially on the left, scholars started to wonder if the Court's previous expansive jurisprudence had not been a mistake and began to argue for a more narrow conception of constitutional rights as negative rights against the state.[90] Eventually though, these conflicts died down again when the Court upheld one of the government's most contested reforms introducing labour co-determination in certain company boards.[91] The era of Social Democrat reforms ended shortly thereafter.

Yet, the 1970s had brought considerable changes in German society; the reformers had taken up and challenged—justly and unjustly—many established German traditions that were seen to have contributed to the rise of National-Socialism. Perhaps unsurprisingly, their drive for reform was not universally shared. By the 1970s the earlier post-war consensus that there was a need for political and social change had crumbled: As the new West

Siebeck, 1999). See also for the 'aspirational' character of German constitutionalism, but with a somewhat different approach, Jacco Bomhoff, *Balancing Constitutional Rights. The Origins and Meanings of Postwar Legal Discourse* (Cambridge: Cambridge University Press, 2013), in particular chapters 3 and 5.

[89] See for an overview Häußler, *Der Konflikt zwischen Bundesverfassungsgericht und politischer Führung*, pp. 52 et seq., and Collings, *Democracy's Guardians*, chapter 2.

[90] See Dieter Grimm, 'Reformalisierung des Rechtsstaats als Demokratiepostulat?', *Juristische Schulung*, 20 (1980), 704.

[91] BVerfGE 50, 290.

German state had finally evolved into a stable and economically successful democracy, the need for change seemed much less urgent. Conservatives now expected citizens to be proud of what they had already achieved, rather than constantly think about what else needed to be done.[92] Germany had finally joined ranks with other Western democracies, or so it seemed, and its Basic Law became a prime object of German pride.[93] Calling for change hence again became a partisan affair rather than a shared commitment of both conservatives and Social Democrats. The Basic Law, too, was in this atmosphere no longer understood by all to provide a roadmap to further change. As Stolleis points out, changing society through fundamental rights provided a mainstream framework when it was directed against outdated legal frameworks as a means of modernization.[94] But with the push for social reform from the left, conservative scholars started to worry that the very instruments that had brought the once desirable modernization might now be used to drive a different, unwelcome kind of social change. As a result, some sought to return to more traditional conceptions of constitutional law that emphasized negative rights. And after the judicial expansionism in the 1970s, even on the left some started to sympathize with proposals for a more modest understanding of rights.[95] But their criticism came too late. By this time, many of the Court's tools of transformative law—indirect effect, positive rights, etc.—had already become so entrenched in its jurisprudence and constitutional doctrine that abandoning them was no longer feasible.

Yet, with the Basic Law losing its transformative appeal, talk of values became increasingly rare.[96] Nevertheless, rights preserved their 'objective' function, which now increasingly served as a basis for the development of justiciable so-called protective duties (*Schutzpflichten*) that required the state to provide certain organizational and institutional frameworks to safeguard constitutional rights. This new institutional and organizational dimension of rights sought to ensure that rights existed not merely on paper, but also that individuals would be able to exercise them in practice. Much like in

[92] See e.g. Dolf Sternberger, 'Rede zur Hundertjahrfeier der Sozialdemokratischen Partei Deutschlands', in *Schriften Bd. 4: Staatsfreundschaft* (Frankfurt am Main: Insel, 1990), pp. 17 et seq.

[93] For more on this see Chapter 6.

[94] Stolleis, *Vierter Band 1945–1990*, pp. 475–6.

[95] Grimm, 'Reformalisierung des Rechtsstaats als Demokratiepostulat?'.

[96] See e.g. Dominik Rennert, 'Die verdrängte Werttheorie und ihre Historisierung. Zu "Lüth" und den Eigenheiten bundesrepublikanischer Grundrechtstheorie', *Der Staat*, 53(1) (2014), pp. 31–59, doi: 10.3790/staa.53.1.31; also see Thilo Rensmann, *Wertordnung und Verfassung: Das Grundgesetz im Kontext grenzüberschreitender Konstitutionalisierung* (Tübingen: Mohr Siebeck, 2007).

many Global South jurisdictions today,[97] this new understanding of rights only rarely generated new entitlements to any concrete state measure or action, but prompted adjustments on the margins, emphasizing in Germany in particular control of procedures and legislative reasoning. Nevertheless, this approach provided the basis for a number of expansive judgments and sometimes even yielded concrete benefits.[98]

Terrorist threats by the Red Army Fraction during the 1970s on one side of the political spectrum and increasing concern for environmental issues on the other moreover strengthened demands for a strong activist state among both progressives and conservatives.[99] Unlike in the Weimar Republic, however, state action could now no longer be imagined in a legal vacuum. With its increasing emphasis on the protective aspects of individual rights, German constitutional theory accompanied the expansion of state regulation; a return to a more liberal understanding of constitutional law was in this situation simply not on the table.

D. Conclusion

Post-war German constitutionalism could build on a rich nineteenth-century tradition of rights as limitations of state power. Yet, the German Constitutional Court did more than merely take liberal rights seriously. By conceptualizing constitutional norms as 'objective' values (or later, principles), the Court read the Basic Law not just as a charter of individual rights and restraints on state power, but also as a more comprehensive framework to bring about broader social change. And though the Basic Law lost its early transformative appeal over time, its transformative precedents became entrenched and were further expanded in its later jurisprudence.

National-Socialism and Communism, the past and present 'regimes of evil',[100] initially helped to furnish the Court with an ideological basis on which it could then develop its expansive reading of fundamental rights. The transition away from them did not, however, entail a robust idea of counter-majoritarian judicial activism, as the standard narrative implies. Moreover, as concepts of transitional justice, National-Socialism and Communism

[97] See Daniel M. Brinks and Varun Gauri (eds), 'Transforming Legal Theory in the Light of Practice: The Judicial Application of Social and Economic Rights to Private Orderings', in *Courting Social Justice: Judicial Enforcement of Social and Economic Rights in the Developing World* (Cambridge: Cambridge University Press, 2010).

[98] See for details Chapter 4.

[99] Stolleis, *Vierter Band 1945–1990*, p. 505.

[100] Scheppele, 'Constitutional Interpretation after Regimes of Horror'.

have become less and less relevant as the distance to the transition grows.[101] National-Socialism in particular certainly remains an important political symbol of what Germany today seeks to avoid repeating. But while this is important, it does not support the bigger claim that it provided the basis for the Court's subsequent authority. Not only did the framers pay little attention to the new Court in general and even less to rights review in particular, but the Court's jurisprudence also developed only slowly and over time, initially deferring often to the supposedly discredited German parliament. By the time the Court finally did make more expansive use of the possibilities of the value jurisprudence created in *Lüth*, it had already built its legitimacy on a different, more traditional legal basis, as we will see.

[101] See Teitel, *Transitional Justice*.

3

Hierarchical Authority in German Constitutional Law: the Constitutional Court between Law and Politics

The history of German constitutionalism is a story of change, but it is also a story of preserving traditions. Whatever its forays into the realm of transformative law, German constitutionalism is built on a centuries-old continental legal culture in which law has become a science to be studied at university and legal practice become rooted in an ethic of professionalism of its own.

That the German Court would be able to draw legitimacy from this cultural heritage was perhaps surprising. The introduction of constitutional review already constituted an innovation and, to some degree, a break with the legal culture. Worse still, transformative constitutionalism brought further challenges to the traditional continental emphasis on a scientific approach to law and legal autonomy. Transformative law demanded legal answers to a host of new questions previously not considered legal questions at all. It also went far beyond the established nineteenth-century German idea of a *Rechtsstaat* with its reactive understanding of constitutional law as a mere restraint on state action. Becoming entrenched over time, this reactive understanding of law appeared—and still appears to some—as the only properly 'legal' conception. The reason for this is simple: Scholars and judges had already worked out the content and meaning of core concepts associated with the *Rechtsstaat*, as Stolleis rightly points out,[1] and this assured both lawyers and laymen that courts were doing law rather than politics. With the turn to transformative constitutionalism and its demand

[1] Michael Stolleis, *Geschichte des öffentlichen Rechts in Deutschland: Vierter Band 1945–1990* (München: C. H. Beck, 2012), p. 214.

for legal answers to questions that had never previously been explored in legal writing, this changed.[2]

In this situation, there were two ways the new German Court could respond. One, more political response would have been to openly acknowledge the existing challenge, to emphasize dialogue with other institutions, and to bring new voices into the judicial process to find common solutions to the cases at hand. The alternative was to work hard at reducing the challenges of newness by building up doctrines and jurisprudence, keep legal interpretation technical, and insist on legal autonomy. Unlike their Indian colleagues in the 1980s, Germans followed the second path. The German Justices did little to open up judicial processes to new, non-traditional stakeholders, nor did they engage in negotiation to bring about just results rather than legally correct ones. Instead, they worked on formalizing the Court's value jurisprudence, while emphasizing legal autonomy and the need for expertise in constitutional interpretation. This fit with the traditional hierarchical legal culture and its emphasis on professionalism, technicality, and de-personalization.

That this was going to be a successful strategy was not initially clear. The Court's character as a political or as a legal institution was contested among the framers and in the early 1950s. With its turn to value jurisprudence, it seemed hard to defend the Court's jurisprudence in terms of traditional continental law—its decisions did not sound technical, nor did values lend themselves to produce legally certain and consistent results. Building a bridge between transformative constitutionalism and continental legal tradition was no easy task. Sometimes more open and pragmatic approaches dominated, as is typical for transformative legal systems. More recently though, more traditional legal and even positivist approaches have dominated; the Court's authority has become more firmly entrenched and so has its particular style of jurisprudence, Value Formalism, a synthesis of transformative and hierarchical elements.

This chapter provides a short overview of this development, which forms the basis of the Court's current authority, beginning with important features of German legal culture as it emerged in the nineteenth century. In doing so, I am drawing on the work of others before me—most notably Michael Stolleis[3]—who have provided us with a more comprehensive historical account. If I nevertheless re-tell parts of their stories here, it is to draw

[2] For the importance of newness in constitutional review see James Fowkes, 'Socio-economic Rights and the Newness Hypothesis', Max Planck Lecture, delivered 29 January 2014; and James Fowkes, *Building the Constitution: The Practice of Constitutional Interpretation in South Africa since 1994* (Cambridge: Cambridge University Press, forthcoming 2016).

[3] See, in particular, Michael Stolleis, *Geschichte des öffentlichen Rechts in Deutschland: Zweiter Band 1800–1914* (München: C. H. Beck, 1992), and Stolleis, *Vierter Band 1945–1990*.

out a particular point the straightforwardly historical accounts are not interested in: the reconciliation of a transformative understanding of law with the older German legal culture, with its emphasis on professionalism and legal certainty. As I have mentioned, the establishment of rights review already represented a challenge to the traditional hierarchical German legal culture, which was then further exacerbated by the Court's turn to value jurisprudence. The ensuing debate about where the Court belonged—to the realm of law or the realm of politics—was fought on multiple fronts: first, in the Court's self-presentation to the public; and second, and perhaps more importantly, in the debates over the appropriate methodology for constitutional interpretation. Perhaps surprisingly, the Court eventually managed to have the best of both worlds: a flexible, teleological methodology and a hierarchical approach to its own role and function.

A. Beginnings

Over the course of the nineteenth century, Prussia and other German feudal states increasingly started to abolish existing feudal structures of governance and create modern bureaucracies. Oriented towards providing efficient and professional governance, reformers introduced merit-based access and promotion schemes for many state offices that subsequently came to be administered by a specific class of professionally trained and educated career bureaucrats, many of them lawyers.[4] Strict hierarchical divisions, both horizontally, between different tasks, and vertically, between the lower and upper echelons of the administrative apparatus, were established to provide rational and efficient administration. Following reformer Stein's suggestions, the Prussian Cabinet (encompassing the consultants of the monarch) was in 1807 for the first time divided and organized according to different policy fields.[5] Increasingly, passing formal exams became a requirement for the exercise of certain state functions. As a result of these changes, the middle classes increasingly gained access to the bureaucracy, which remained for a long time an important gateway for social advancement. Bureaucratization also extended to the organization of the German judiciary, where feudal

[4] Bernd Wunder, *Geschichte der Bürokratie in Deutschland* (Frankfurt am Main: Suhrkamp, 1986), p. 28, pp. 36 et seq.

[5] Freiherr von Stein published his reform suggestions for the cabinet in a short essay, titled 'Darstellung der fehlerhaften Organisation des Kabinetts und der Notwendigkeit der Bildung einer Ministerialkonferenz', re-printed in Freiherr von Stein, *Lebenserinnerungen und Denkschriften* (Altenmünster: Jazzybee-Verlag, 2011).

jurisdiction was abolished and the exercise of judicial functions handed over to legal professionals. The judiciary itself was organized in differently specialized high- and low-level courts. With the creation of the German Reich, legal professionals became increasingly important as civil servants in the growing administrative state, with many upper echelon posts being reserved exclusively for them.[6]

Though a break with existing feudal structures, these innovations could nevertheless build on a long-standing continental legal culture. Continental law had since the twelfth and thirteenth centuries been understood and taught as a systematically organized subject at universities.[7] With the codification movements in the nineteenth century, some had expected that the newly drafted comprehensive codes would make law more approachable to laymen and do away with professional lawyering. Efforts were made to increase legal determinacy in order to minimize judicial discretion. In this vein, the famous Prussian General Land Law from 1794 sought to regulate virtually every possible situation and close existing legal gaps. Prussia's Frederick the Great issued a prohibition on the use of legal analogies. He established a commission to which judges could appeal in cases of doubt, which was, however, soon overworked due to persistent queries from lower courts and had to be abandoned.[8] The Prussian Land Law itself was eventually regarded as overambitious and a failure. The drafters of the later German Civil Code from 1891 therefore took a very different approach, based from the outset on a scientific understanding of law, which was to be handled and dealt with by legal professionals.

What codification achieved, then, was not the abandonment of lawyers, but rather the centrality of the positive statute for legal science, which became a science of interpretation. For most of the nineteenth century, the prevailing school of legal interpretation in Germany was *Begriffsjurisprudenz*.[9] Its aim was to construct law as an internally consistent and logical system of norms and principles that would be able to provide right answers to any potential legal question. This school of thought significantly shaped not only private law, but was also adopted by famous public law scholars and constitutional theorists, most notably the influential Paul Laband.[10] Though sometimes

[6] Wunder, *Geschichte der Bürokratie*, pp. 78 et seq.

[7] For more, see Harold Berman, *Law and Revolution: The Formation of the Western Legal Tradition* (Cambridge: Harvard University Press, 1983).

[8] Johanna Höltl, *Die Lückenfüllung der klassisch-europäischen Kodifikationen: Zur Analogie im ALR, Code Civil und ABGB* (Wien: LIT-Verlag, 2005), p. 110.

[9] Stolleis, *Zweiter Band 1800–1914*, pp. 330 et seq.

[10] Laband's most influential work in this regard was his widely read and re-edited textbook *Das Staatsrecht des Deutschen Reichs*, in three volumes (Tübingen: Laupp, 1876–82).

characterized as a caricature of Laband's actual work, his much-quoted foreword gives us an idea of the trust that nineteenth-century public lawyers placed in doctrine (*Dogmatik*[11]) as a means of determining the law:

Dogmatics is not the sole dimension but is certainly one of the dimensions of legal science. The scientific task of the dogmatics of a particular body of positive law lies in the construction of legal institutes (Rechtsinstitute), in tracing individual legal norms back to more general concepts and, on the other hand, in deriving from these concepts the consequences that follow. Except for research into prevailing positive-law norms, arriving at a thorough knowledge and mastery of the material at hand, the task of dogmatics is a purely logical, intellectual activity. In order to carry out this task, there is no other means than logic, nothing can replace logic toward this end. As valuable as historical, political, and philosophical considerations in and of themselves may be, they are all insignificant for the dogmatics of concrete legal material, serving only too often to conceal the paucity of constructivist work.[12]

As we will see later on, while *Begriffsjurisprudenz* has been abandoned, Laband's emphasis on legal autonomy and on *Dogmatik* is still a feature of current German legal scholarship.

Laband's influence did not go unchallenged. His most radical opponents would be the advocates of the German Free Law School (*Freirechtsschule*), a predecessor and model for American Legal Realism.[13] With its fundamental challenge to the determinacy of legal interpretation, the Free Law School threatened German lawyers' self-understanding as professional experts. Prominent Free Law Scholars would call upon lawyers to be more policy-oriented and less focused on the text.[14] Ultimately, however, the Free Law School would not gain any lasting influence. It functioned as a gate-opener for other less formalistic schools of interpretation, but never managed to shake sufficiently

[11] To translate *Dogmatik* as doctrine is somewhat inadequate insofar as *Dogmatik* incorporates both judicial decisions and scholarship of a kind that is strongly linked to judicial practice in a way that is rare in most places and inconceivable in the United States. For an excellent overview of what *Dogmatik* is and can or cannot do, see Gregor Kirchhof, Stefan Magen, and Karsten Schneider (eds), *Was weiß Dogmatik? Was leistet und wie steuert die Dogmatik des Öffentlichen Rechts?* (Tübingen: Mohr Siebeck, 2012).

[12] Laband, *Staatsrecht*, Introduction to the Second Edition, English translation quoted after Stanley L. Paulson, 'The Theory of Public Law in Germany 1914–1945', *Oxford Journal of Legal Studies*, 25(3) (2005), 525–6.

[13] See James E. Herget and Stephen Wallace, 'The German Free Law Movement as the Source of American Legal Realism', *Virginia Law Review*, 73 (1987), 399–456. See also William Twining, *Karl Llewellyn and the Realist Movement* (Cambridge: Cambridge University Press, 2012), p. 107 et seq. for Llewellyn's acquaintance with the German Free Law movement.

[14] See most famously Hermann Kantorowicz, *Der Kampf um die Rechtswissenschaft* (Berlin: Berliner Wissenschaftsverlag, reprinted 2003).

German lawyers' trust in their capability to correctly interpret the law.[15] Since the *Freirechtsschule* was furthermore often (incorrectly) associated with moral nihilism and relativism, the general intellectual climate after the Second World War was not favourable to its revival. The so-called interest jurisprudence (*Interessenjurisprudenz*), itself a close relative of the Free Law movement, took over its heritage. Interest jurisprudence shared many of the Free Law School's criticisms of more formalist approaches to legal interpretation. In particular, it successfully managed to shift the emphasis in legal interpretation from an analysis of logic and semantics to an analysis of the underlying facts and the different interests involved. Importantly, however, it ultimately preserved the attachment to the legal norm itself as the key consideration.[16]

In the Weimar Republic, German scholars debated fundamental questions of legal methodology from a wide range of different perspectives in the famous debate on methods (*Methodenstreit*).[17] Among them were positivist democrats such as Kelsen[18] and Anschütz,[19] who argued against the more conservative democracy-sceptics like Schmitt[20] and Smend,[21] who drew on what was called the *geisteswissenschaftliche Methode* (liberal arts/humanities method). The *geisteswissenschaftliche Methode* encompassed the introduction of more open and flexible approaches to legal interpretation, sometimes drawing, for example, on half-digested philosophical arguments about the supposed nature of things.[22] Though some of these approaches were less than

[15] Kristoffel R. Grechenig and Martin Gelter, 'The Transatlantic Divergence in Legal Thought: American Law and Economics vs. German Doctrinalism', *Hastings International and Comparative Law Review*, 31(1) (2008), 295, 352.

[16] Grechenig and Gelter, 'The Transatlantic Divergence', 353–6.

[17] For many, see Stolleis, *Vierter Band 1945–1990*, pp. 153 et seq.

[18] Hans Kelsen's famous arguments for democracy were published in *Vom Wesen und Wert der Demokratie* (Tübingen: Mohr Siebeck, 1920). The clearest elaboration of his theoretical approach is contained in Hans Kelsen, *Reine Rechtslehre: Einleitung in die rechtswissenschaftliche Problematik* (Leipzig/Wien: Deuticke, 1934).

[19] Gerhard Anschütz, a student of Paul Laband, became most famous for his commentary of the Weimar Constitution, *Die Verfassung des Deutschen Reiches vom 11. August 1919. Ein Kommentar für Wissenschaft und Praxis*, 14th edn (Berlin, 1933).

[20] Schmitt's key work in this regard is his *Verfassungslehre* (München: Duncker & Humblot, 1928).

[21] Rudolf Smend, *Verfassung und Verfassungsrecht* (Berlin: Duncker & Humblot, 1928).

[22] For a detailed review and critique, see Oliver Lepsius, *Die gegensatzaufhebende Begriffsbildung* (München: C.H. Beck, 1994), pp. 219 et seq. However, the lines were not always so clearly aligned between legal methodology and ideological convictions: Most famously, Social Democrat Hermann Heller was on the Smend/Schmitt side in the methodological debate, as was Erich Kantorowicz, advocate of the German Free Law School. See also Klaus Rennert, *Die geisteswissenschaftliche Richtung in der Staatsrechtslehre der Weimarer Republik: Untersuchungen zu Erich Kaufmann, Günther Holstein und Rudolf Smend*, vol. 518 (Berlin: Duncker & Humblot, 1987).

convincing, it is sometimes claimed that the richness of the debates on constitutional theory in the Weimar Republic has been unmatched ever since.[23] At the same time, the wide array of possible methods and positions to choose from and the lack of clarity (and maybe rationality) of some of these methods prepared the ground for the later National-Socialist reinterpretation of statutes in light of Nazi ideology.[24]

Under National-Socialist rule, law partly lost its normative force in restraining state action. The disempowerment of the German Parliament in 1933 led to a rule by administrative decrees issued by the government, i.e. by Hitler himself. National-Socialists pursued a gigantic project of social transformation that affected all areas of life: the family, art, literature, work, and leisure activities.[25] But while state activism peaked, law did not keep up with the changes and became increasingly irrelevant to a new regime that was proud of its defiance of the liberal idea of the *Rechtsstaat* and the Weimar Constitution. Existing laws and hierarchical divisions of functions that obstructed the planned transformation were either discarded or adapted to the new transformative agenda. Legal scholars like Carl Schmitt[26] or (in private law matters) Karl Larenz[27] furnished the theoretical tools to overcome these obstacles by interpreting existing statutes in light of new National-Socialist concepts.[28] The *Führerprinzip* ensured that functional divisions of tasks were only acceptable insofar as the regime allowed it—authority hence came to be seen not as based on expertise and specialized knowledge, but first and foremost as derived from the Führer as the nation's caretaker. Among the earliest measures introduced by the Nazis was a law that purged the bureaucracy of regime critics as well as Jews.[29] While the ordinary 'normative state' (*Fraenkel*[30]) with its reliance on the established institutions and laws was allowed to coexist with the 'prerogative state' responsible for the explicit pursuance of the National-Socialist agenda, it was constantly threatened, its rules having to cede in case of a conflict to the goals set by the ruling elite.

[23] Christoph Möllers, *Der vermisste Leviathan: Staatstheorie in der Bundesrepublik* (Frankfurt am Main: Suhrkamp, 2008), p. 24.

[24] Lepsius, *Begriffsbildung*, pp. 365 et seq.

[25] For a recent historical account see Ulrich Herbert, *Geschichte Deutschlands im 20. Jahrhundert* (München: Beck, 2014), Dritter Teil 1933–45.

[26] See e.g. Carl Schmitt, 'Nationalsozialistisches Rechtsdenken', *Deutsches Recht*, 4(10) (1934), 225.

[27] See e.g. Karl Larenz, *Deutsche Rechtserneuerung und Rechtsphilosophie* (Tübingen: J. C. B. Mohr, 1934).

[28] Bernd Rüthers, *Die unbegrenzte Auslegung* (Tübingen: Mohr Siebeck, 1986), pp. 322 et seq.

[29] Wunder, *Geschichte der Bürokratie*, pp. 138 et seq.

[30] Ernst Fraenkel, *The Dual State* (Oxford: Oxford University Press, 1941).

B. Recovering the *Rechtsstaat*

After the war and the moral catastrophe of the Holocaust, the role of law and lawyers had to be redefined. This was not an easy task. Not only were different explanations offered of what precisely had gone wrong during the years of National-Socialism, but many legal scholars also rejected any attempt at analysis to avoid confronting their personal guilt. For many of those who did attempt to analyse what had gone wrong, like Gustav Radbruch, National-Socialism exemplified where law without morality would lead.[31] As a result, legal positivism became widely discredited—unfairly so as we know today.[32] Many therefore subscribed at least rhetorically to a somewhat undefined anti-positivism, even though the renaissance of natural law eventually turned out to be short-lived.[33] By blaming positivism, lawyers could shift responsibility to existing structures rather than accept their individual guilt.[34] They were not alone in this endeavour. In order to gain re-employment and their pensions, dismissed civil servants argued that the German bureaucrat had been an apolitical expert, who had taken up a life-long career as a loyal servant of the state, whatever the political regime in question.[35] Bureaucrats should not, therefore, lose their time-honoured status and employment as a result of injustices committed by political leaders. Many of these bureaucrats had of course been lawyers and they found a sympathetic response in many legal circles, including the German Supreme Court,[36] even though their demands were ultimately rejected by the Constitutional Court[37]—a matter of considerable outrage to many.[38]

At the same time, even those who had been firm supporters of the regime were often concerned about the breakdown of the rule of law during the

[31] Gustav Radbruch, 'Statutory Lawlessness and Supra-Statutory Law (1946)', *Oxford Journal of Legal Studies*, 26(1) (2006), 1–11.

[32] Rüthers, *Die unbegrenzte Auslegung*, pp. 293 et seq.

[33] Michael Stolleis, *The Law Under the Swastika: Studies on Legal History in Nazi Germany*, trans. Thomas Dunlap (Chicago: University of Chicago Press, 1998), p. 186 and p. 200.

[34] See the argument in Radbruch, 'Statutory Lawlessness'; for further background see also Stolleis, 'Verwaltungsrechtswissenschaft in der Bundesrepublik Deutschland', in *Rechtswissenschaft in der Bonner Republik. Studien zur Wissenschaftsgeschichte der Jurisprudenz*, ed. Dieter Simon (Frankfurt am Main: Suhrkamp, 1994), p. 238.

[35] BVerfGE 3, 58 (and follow-up decisions, BVerfGE 3, 208 and 288).

[36] See BGHZ 2, 117 and BGHZ 10, 30.

[37] BVerfGE 3, 58.

[38] See e.g. Ernst Forsthoff, 'Das Bundesverfassungsgericht und das Berufsbeamtentum', *Deutsche Verwaltungsblätter* (1954), 69; Ernst Kern, 'Probleme der Rechtsprechung des Bundesverfassungsgerichts', *Deutsche Verwaltungsblätter* (1954), 211; Arnold Köttgen, 'Das Beamtenurteil des Bundesverfassungsgerichts', *Archiv des öffentlichen Rechts*, 79 (1954), 351.

later years of the Nazi regime.[39] It was hence important to emphasize law's *normative* force in post-war constitutional discourse: Law should once again serve as a guideline for politics rather than merely its handmaiden. Legal interpretation during the war had in many ways seemed merely to reconstruct and retrace political events without providing any guidance of its own. This was now supposed to change as German lawyers and politicians set out to rebuild the German *Rechtsstaat* with an emphasis on an adequate separation of powers, an independent judiciary, habeas corpus rights, and broader access to courts for citizens seeking to defend themselves against arbitrary state action.[40] All this implied a strong distinction between law and politics.

Such a separation was further supported by the establishment of a number of political science chairs in German universities by the American Allies. With its increasing emancipation in the 1960s, political science began to develop a somewhat competitive relationship with public law.[41] That two different disciplines now existed where there had previously only been state theory, located in the law faculties, generated the need to find ways and means of institutional and personal cooperation, but also the need for distinction. Eventually, this led to an increasing division between the more normative and social science components of institutional scholarship and a consequent decline of social science-oriented scholarship in law faculties.[42]

Coupled with the value-laden rhetoric of the time, this increasing institutional and rhetorical separation of law and politics provided the basis for the reconciliation of transformative law with the traditional German legal culture, ultimately combining a flexible and open style of constitutional interpretation with an emphasis on legal autonomy. Rejecting a return to the more formalist methods associated with legal positivism, many lawyers continued to work with the open legal methodology developed during the Weimar Republic and National-Socialism, often replacing National-Socialist ideology with natural-law thinking and later with constitutional values.[43] Given the fact that these open methodological approaches had just failed to isolate law

[39] Ernst Forsthoff, *Recht und Sprache* (Halle: M. Niemeyer, 1940); Arnold Köttgen, *Deutsche Verwaltung*, 3rd edn (Berlin: V. Fahlen, 1944); for a discussion see Stolleis, 'Verwaltungsrechtswissenschaft', p. 229.

[40] Stolleis, 'Verwaltungsrechtswissenschaft', p. 214.

[41] Frieder Günther, *Denken vom Staat her: Die deutsche Staatsrechtslehre zwischen Dezision und Integration 1949–1970* (München: Oldenbourg, 2004), pp. 232–4.

[42] Ibid., p. 234.

[43] For the comprehensive argument regarding the continuity of National-Socialist and post-war legal methodology in German law (going beyond the post-war years) see Bernd Rüthers, *Die heimliche Revolution. Vom Rechtsstaat zum Richterstaat* (Tübingen: Mohr Siebeck, 2014).

from politics, this was perhaps surprising. It may explain, however, why there was little in-depth or theoretical work in the early years of the Bonn Republic, for it would have been hard to reconcile these different trends.[44] The lack of grand theory was also helped by the fact that for those who sought to avoid confronting their past explicitly by publicly declaring a change of heart—a difficult move that could easily appear hypocritical or ridiculous[45]—the best tactic often consisted in ignoring the larger legal and political narratives.

The Constitutional Court benefitted from these differing constraints and conceptual inconsistencies. To conceptualize the Basic Law as an 'order of values' sounded like natural-law thinking and thus seemed not too far from the mainstream legal and political rhetoric of the time. It was, however, in fact the nemesis of natural law. By making clear that the relevant values were now present in the Basic Law itself, the Constitutional Court ended the era of natural law.[46] This entailed also an important strategic move. For other courts, too, had been able to decide competently, and in the last instance, on natural law. As constitutional values replaced natural law, the Constitutional Court could trump them. And in dealing with the new values, National-Socialist methodology came in handy: To realize the Basic Law's transformative vision, it was important not to get bogged down by narrow formalities. The persistence of open approaches to legal interpretation from the Weimar and Nazi era thus furnished the Court with the necessary flexibility to further its transformative agenda. The Court was also remarkably pragmatic in its first years. In its decision on the Saar Statute, for example, the Constitutional Court explained that, while the treaty posed constitutional problems, the Court would nevertheless refrain from declaring its invalidity because the 'state of affairs created by the treaty is "closer to the Basic Law" than the status quo ante'.[47] Taking an approach that would have only accepted a state of affairs exactly in accordance with the Basic Law, the Court explained, implied advocating a 'constitutional rigorism that can be summed up in the sentence: The bad may not cede to the better because the better (...) is unattainable'.[48]

[44] Möllers, *Leviathan*, p. 24.

[45] The letters exchanged after the war between Carl Schmitt and Ernst Forsthoff provide a good sense of the psychological obstacles of mentioning the subject of the past and one's role as well as the potential incriminations those who did—for whatever reasons—turn around after the war might face; see Angelika Reinthal and Reinhard Mußgnug (eds), *Briefwechsel Ernst Forsthoff—Carl Schmitt 1926–1974* (Berlin: Akademie Verlag, 2007).

[46] Schönberger, 'Anmerkungen zu Karlsruhe', in *Das entgrenzte Gericht: Eine kritische Bilanz nach sechzig Jahren Bundesverfassungsgericht*, ed. Matthias Jestaedt, Oliver Lepsius, Christoph Möllers, and Christoph Schönberger (Berlin: Suhrkamp, 2011), p. 34, and Oliver Lepsius, 'Die maßstabsetzende Gewalt', in *Das entgrenzte Gericht*, p. 192.

[47] BVerfGE 4, 157.

[48] BVerfGE 4, 157 (para. 38).

Yet, ultimately the German Court would build its authority not primarily on its role in improving state and society (unlike the Indian Supreme Court), but on a more traditional *legal* basis. This distinctly legal nature of the Court, however, was not always as comfortably accepted as it is today. Particularly in the early 1950s, it was by no means a foregone conclusion. Chances were that the Court might have turned into a more political institution, in the style of the French Conseil Constitutionnel, staffed with prominent former politicians. Or it might have become a court in the Kelsenian/Austrian tradition, following its Kelsenian design and adhering to what was—if partly wrongly[49]—associated with legal positivism: a narrow textualist approach to legal interpretation, a focus on the Basic Law's procedural/institutional provisions, and caution in the field of constitutional rights. Eventually, the Court was to be neither of these things, but would instead reconcile what seemed to many at the time irreconcilable: a Court that frequently engaged highly political questions while grounding its authority on a traditional judicial and distinctly hierarchical basis of legitimacy.

Among the framers, it had been contested whether the new Constitutional Court should be a more political or legal institution. Christian Democrats championed a more traditionally judicial vision for the new Court, which they sought to staff exclusively with legal professionals and understood the Court as a similar kind of institution as the *Staatsgerichtshof*, which had decided questions of organizational law and federal disputes in the Weimar Republic.[50] In contrast, Social Democrats saw the new institution as a counterweight to the traditional German judiciary, which had discredited itself by its cooperation with the Nazi regime. They suggested appointing at least a certain number of laymen to the new Court—unsuccessfully, as all judges were eventually required by law to have completed both State Exams and hence the full six- to seven-year training all German lawyers undergo.[51]

The two perspectives came with different approaches to legal interpretation. Those who emphasized the Court's legal nature and function as a *court* broadly argued in favour of more restrained approaches to constitutional review to keep it sufficiently legal. This entailed drawing a sharp distinction between law and politics, even if it was contested how exactly this distinction must be drawn. Some, like Ernst Forsthoff, a former disciple and friend of Carl Schmitt, relied on the Basic Law's invocation of the *Rechtsstaat* principle

[49] Kelsen actually said very little about legal interpretation and, insofar as he did, was rather legal realist about it; see Horst Dreier, *Rechtslehre, Staatssoziologie und Demokratietheorie bei Hans Kelsen* (Baden-Baden: Nomos, 1990), pp. 145 et seq.

[50] Michael Stolleis, *Geschichte des Öffentlichen Rechts in Deutschland: Dritter Band 1914–1945* (München: C. H. Beck, 1999), pp. 117 f.

[51] See s. 3 II Bundesverfassungsgerichtsgesetz (BVerfGG).

and distinguished between justiciable and non-justiciable elements in the Basic Law: According to Forsthoff, liberal fundamental rights were justiciable, but not, for example, the social state principle (*Sozialstaatsprinzip*).[52] In this manner, Forsthoff sought to preserve traditional state prerogatives from judicial intervention and thereby leave room for a strong state.[53]

Another way of drawing the line between legal and political questions was proposed by Erich Kaufmann in his presentation at the 1951 *Staatsrechtslehrertagung*[54]—an important annual conference established during the Weimar Republic to which only German, Austrian, and Swiss law professors were (and still are) invited to participate. Kaufmann was a law professor and legal advisor to the diplomatic service who had been forced to emigrate during the Nazi era because of his Jewish descent, and who now argued for what would became the mainstream position. According to him, legal questions differed from political questions merely in that they could be answered with legal arguments, as opposed to moral or political considerations.[55] However, for Kaufmann and his contemporaries this did not yet imply the justification for judicial expansionism it later became. Rather, he seemed to assume that the new Court's primary function would continue to be that of a *Staatsgerichtshof*, dealing mostly with institutional questions about the delimitation of state and federal powers and different state organs. While acknowledging the role of rights review, Kaufmann thought it would imply controlling merely the 'outer limits' of legislative discretion on the basis of an arbitrariness standard. And even though he was sympathetic to demands for staffing the Court with personalities with political experience, he ultimately imagined the Court as a thoroughly judicial institution that would only address legal questions.

Others saw the Court in a different, more political role: as an organ of governance. They were, however, in a minority. Their most important advocate was Martin Drath, who presented together with Kaufmann at the 1951 *Staatsrechtslehrertagung*. Martin Drath was a former student of the eminent Weimar constitutional theorist Herrmann Heller,[56] who had been one

[52] See Forsthoff's presentation at the *Staatsrechtslehrertagung* in 1954, printed in 'Begriff und Wesen des sozialen Rechtsstaats', *Veröffentlichungen der Vereinigung der deutschen Staatsrechtslehrer*, 12 (Berlin: de Gruyter, 1966).

[53] For an excellent, more detailed account of the shifting debates around the social state principle see John Philipp Thurn, *Welcher Sozialstaat? Ideologie und Wissenschaftsverständnis in den Debatten der bundesdeutschen Staatsrechtslehre 1949–1990* (Tübingen: Mohr Siebeck, 2013).

[54] Erich Kaufmann, 'Die Grenzen der Verfassungsgerichtsbarkeit', *Vereinigung der Deutschen Staatsrechtslehrer*, 9 (Berlin: De Gruyter, 1950), pp. 1–133.

[55] Ibid.

[56] For a more detailed biographical and intellectual account of Martin Drath, see Michael Henkel and Oliver Lembcke, 'Staat als Lebensaufgabe: Martin Drath', *Kritische Justiz*, 36(4) (2003), 445.

of the few Social Democrat anti-positivists in Weimar and died in exile in Madrid during the Nazi regime. Drath shared not only his teacher's political affiliations, but also a keen sense for the socio-political realities behind legal doctrine. His presentation provided a brilliant and—in German scholarship—rare example of a legal realist conception of German constitutionalism.[57] Drath started by explicitly admitting that constitutional norms lacked determinacy. From this he drew the conclusion that the Court had to be understood as a special kind of governmental institution rather than as a court in the original sense of the word. Nevertheless, it was—in Drath's eyes somewhat unfortunately—publicly legitimated as a court even though it differed in many important respects from ordinary courts. Constitutional court judges would have to consider to a much greater degree than ordinary judges the future implications of their work (including the reactions of the other branches) and should not shy away from taking pragmatic decisions. In other words, they had to engage in politics. Their job might involve the realization of justice—especially in the field of fundamental rights—but it also involved much more than that. Drath pointed out that the division between the legality and the expediency of a political act would often be less than clear and that arguments which might under normal circumstances count as merely political (such as the expediency of a particular measure) may well count as legal under exceptional conditions. Unlike Kaufmann, who—though agreeing with the necessity of bringing political expertise to the Court—worried a great deal about the implications for judicial independence, Drath wholeheartedly endorsed the influence of parties on the selection of judges. At the same time, he exhorted the future judges not only to avoid active (party-)political engagement, but also to engage in critical self-reflection of their own ideological pre-dispositions. Their most important task and constraint upon their activity, according to Drath, would be to realize a free democratic society. This task was considerable and required the Court to function—similarly to the first state administrations—at times even as a provisional dictator and educator of the German people about democracy.[58] Nevertheless, Drath emphasized that in this enterprise of democratization the Court had to exercise its function in cooperation with the political forces and the other branches. Only by realizing the limitations of narrow legal analysis and the necessity of a political conception of liberal democracy, he

[57] Martin Drath, 'Die Grenzen der Verfassungsgerichtsbarkeit'.

[58] For a different, and in this author's opinion one-dimensional, account of Drath's presentation, see Birgit von Bülow, who overemphasizes Drath's description of the Court as a provisional dictator and on the whole misrepresents his account of the Court's role: Birgit von Bülow, *Die Staatsrechtslehre der Nachkriegszeit (1945–1952)* (Berlin: Berlin Verlag Arno Spitz GmbH, 1996), pp. 74 et seq.

argued, would the judges be able to respect the boundaries of constitutional jurisprudence.

In the discussion following the two presentations, other scholars similarly voiced doubts regarding the determinacy of constitutional norms, but no one went as far as Drath in his assessment of the Court as a political institution. In general, scepticism towards the new institution prevailed and most argued for a restrained idea of constitutional jurisprudence. Unlike most of his colleagues, however, Drath was appointed a Justice in the new Constitutional Court (on an SPD ticket) in the same year and thus had the opportunity in the Court's First Senate to shape the new Court's jurisprudence. And he did, as one of the authors of the Court's 1957 *Lüth* decision in which the Court declared its allegiance to an activist paradigm of constitutional law.

Yet, what finally came to be adopted by both the Court and mainstream scholarship was the schizophrenic middle position: Though often taking a broad activist approach to constitutional interpretation, the Court nevertheless followed in its official pronouncements and in its judgments the established hierarchical line. In its own words:

> The work of the Federal Constitutional Court also has political effect. This becomes particularly clear when the Court declares a law to be unconstitutional. However, the Court is not a political body. Its sole standard of review is the Basic Law. Questions of political expediency may not be taken into account by the Court. It merely determines the constitutional framework within which politics may develop. The delimitation of state power is a feature of modern democratic constitutionalised states.[59]

That this, rather than a more political approach, became the mainstream position was partly the work of one of the Justices, Gerhard Leibholz,[60] and partly a result of political contingencies in the Court's first years. In particular, the government's strategic manoeuvring in the debate about rearmament to bring the case before the 'right' senate, which was staffed with a majority of its own appointees, demonstrated the need for judicial independence from party-politics. It was not hard to see that the Justices would gain little respect and authority if their decisions seemed predisposed by the political tickets on which they had been selected. If the 'black' (CDU) senate was merely going to provide whitewash for the government, this would hurt the Court's authority. Establishing independence from politics further meant that the Court

[59] Homepage of the Federal Constitutional Court, description of its task, <http://www.bundesverfassungsgericht.de/EN/Das-Gericht/Aufgaben/aufgaben_node.html>.

[60] For more on Leibholz's conception of the Constitutional Court and his influence, see Oliver Lembcke, *Hüter der Verfassung. Eine institutionentheoretische Studie zur Autorität des Bundesverfassungsgerichts* (Tübingen: Mohr Siebeck, 2007).

had to become institutionally independent. During its first years, its budget was overseen by the Department of Justice, which was headed by Thomas Dehler, the Court's main critic in the rearmament debate. On this matter, the Court issued a so-called report on its status (*Statusbericht*), written by Gerhard Leibholz, in which it claimed to be a constitutional organ of its own. As the drafters of the Basic Law had omitted to accord the Court a specific chapter and title in the constitution that would have put it on an equal footing with other constitutional organs such as the Bundestag, this was by no means a foregone conclusion.[61] The Justices, however, argued that the Court's constitutional role nevertheless implied its institutional independence and its equality with other constitutional branches.[62] In order to realize this institutionally, they asked to be allocated their own budget and to be removed from the supervision of the Ministry of Justice. And in spite of strong political protest, they eventually got their way.[63]

At the same time, even the Status Report included a long section on judicial self-restraint, emphasizing again the wide discretion the legislature enjoyed in the exercise of its function and the promise that the Court would only scrutinize laws with regard to their legality, and not as to their quality as good or bad laws.[64] Only if legislators abused their discretion and a measure could be characterized as arbitrary would the Court interfere. The Status Report also stated that the Court was political insofar as its decisions affected politics, but that its methodology was going to be purely legal.

This surprises perhaps, given that neither then nor now have German scholars actually thought or claimed that constitutional norms are determinate. On a second glance, however, it should not, for German scholars have always reacted differently to legal indeterminacy than their American colleagues. Rather than using this insight to provide external accounts of how law gets made or to criticize existing frameworks, Germans have worked to overcome indeterminacy by attempting to provide more systematic and detailed accounts of the existing law. In other words, what drives American scholars to turn away from law and doctrine is for Germans a reason to work harder on these things. And not only that, but they also tend to emphasize different things—rather than seeking to design strict, content-neutral tests, thick conceptual analysis dominates German constitutional analysis.[65]

[61] Laufer, *Verfassungsgerichtsbarkeit und politischer Prozess*, pp. 57–8. For more on this, see also Hailbronner, 'Rethinking the Rise of the German Constitutional Court, 626.

[62] Statusbericht, reprinted in *Jahrbuch des Öffentlichen Rechts*, 6 (1957), 144.

[63] Richard Häußler, *Der Konflikt zwischen Bundesverfassungsgericht und politischer Führung* (Berlin: Duncker & Humblot, 1994), p. 28.

[64] Statusbericht, p. 144.

[65] See for a poignant comparison of German constitutional reasoning with the US Jacco Bomhoff, *Balancing Constitutional Rights. The Origins and Meanings of Postwar Legal Discourse*

Yet, most scholars and judges understand their work as perfectly legal, and attempts to conceptualize constitutional interpretation as a more political or dialogic enterprise, more akin to US constitutional theory, have largely failed. As we have seen, Drath's call for a context-sensitive analysis of socio-political realities was not taken up by the mainstream. And most scholars reacted with similar scepticism to Ehmke's 1961 arguments for an avowedly common-law, pragmatic, problem-oriented approach to constitutional interpretation, the so-called topic method.[66] Though many agreed that a return to the legal formalism of the nineteenth century was not desirable and the topic method in fact became influential both in constitutional scholarship and the Court's jurisprudence,[67] Ehmke's suggestion to draw on the professional and socio-political consensus as an interpretative guideline seemed too open-ended to most legal scholars to provide a suitable yardstick for interpretation. Peter Häberle's concept of an 'open society of constitutional interpreters'[68] that emphasized the role of other institutions and citizens in constitutional interpretation suffered a similar fate. Unlike in Latin America, in Germany, Häberle's idea did not come to play a major role in contemporary constitutional theory.[69] Unsurprisingly then, as Stolleis points out, outsiders to the German system often noted that German constitutional theory involved 'a high degree of metaphysics, ignored realist analysis of political power and (showed) weakness in the field of comparative constitutional law'.[70]

Instead, it was Rudolf Smend's concept of integration through constitutional values which became influential in German constitutional theory after the war.[71] According to Smend's 1928 treatise, the constitution's main

(Cambridge: Cambridge University Press, 2013), in particular chapter 5. See also for a broader analysis of the German Constitutional Court's style of reasoning Michaela Hailbronner and Stefan Martini, 'German Report', in *Comparative Constitutional Reasoning*, ed. A. Jakab, A. Dyevre, and G. Itzcovich (eds) (Cambridge: Cambridge University Press, forthcoming).

66 See Horst Ehmke, 'Prinzipien der Verfassungsinterpretation', *Vereinigung der Deutschen Staatsrechtslehrer*, 20 (Berlin: de Gruyter, 1963), 74 et seq. and the following discussion in reaction to his presentation.

67 See Ernst-Wolfgang Böckenförde, 'Die Methoden der Verfassungsinterpretation-Bestandsaufnahme und Kritik', *Neue Juristische Wochenschrift*, 46 (1976), 2089–99. For the influence of the topic method on constitutional scholarship see Bomhoff, *Balancing Constitutional Rights*, p. 89.

68 Peter Häberle, 'Die offene Gesellschaft der Verfassungsinterpreten', *Juristenzeitung* (1975), 297.

69 See remarks by Joseph Kaiser and Roman Herzog in 'Grundrechte im Leistungsstaat', *Vereinigung der Deutschen Staatsrechtslehrer*, 30 (Berlin: de Gruyter, 1972), pp. 148 and 157.

70 Stolleis, *Vierter Band 1945*–1990, p. 200.

71 See BVerfGE 7, 198 and for a more detailed analysis Rensmann, *Wertordnung and Verfassung*, pp. 81 et seq.

purpose was the integration of all forces of the political life and constitutional law entailed first and foremost a set of values[72]—thus providing the background for the Court's later reading of the Basic Law as an 'objective order of values'.[73] Consequently, constitutional interpretation was, according to Smend, not to be bound by 'the letter of the law', but a means to discover the spirit of the Constitution that commanded 'fulfillment of the goal of integration'.[74] Something similar applied to the Court's own understanding of constitutional law as an objective order of values: Recourse to broader ethical and historical considerations, sometimes in addition to structural arguments, rather than a narrow focus on text, characterized its reasoning in the first decades.[75] With this approach, the Court could draw not only on Smend, but increasingly also on more recent German scholarship, in particular the first commentary on the Basic Law by Günter Dürig and Theodor Maunz, which made human dignity the central cornerstone of his constitutional theory[76]—a move not only appealing to Kantians, but also to Catholics and many others, including the Constitutional Court Justices.[77] Dürig's broad approach to constitutional interpretation with its idea of the human being and its dignity in the centre brought considerable flexibility to constitutional interpretation, while not running the risk of questioning the legal nature of constitutional interpretation.

The emerging synthesis of value jurisprudence and an insistence on legal autonomy might not have lasted forever, though, for it was a precarious balance to strike, vulnerable to scholarly and political criticism. Yet, over time, the idea of law as a science became partly of a self-fulfilling prophecy: The more cases the Court would decide and the more scholars would elaborate vague constitutional terms, the more was there to know about constitutional law and the more 'scientific' constitutional interpretation became. Broad terms were now filled with legal doctrine, sub-doctrines were developed to deal with particular arguments, and sub-sub-arguments would take care of the

[72] Smend, *Verfassung und Verfassungsrecht*.

[73] See BVerfGE 7, 198; also Dominik Rennert, 'Die verdrängte Werttheorie und ihre Historisierung', *Der Staat*, 53 (2014), 31–59.

[74] Excerpt from Rudolf Smend, *Verfassung und Verfassungsrecht* (1928), translation quoted from Arthur J. Jacobson and Bernhard Schlink, *Weimar: a Jurisprudence of Crisis* (Berkeley: University of California Press, 2000), p. 241.

[75] See e.g. many of the early landmark cases such as *Lüth* and *Elfes*, or the *Pharmacies* decision (for more, see Chapter 2).

[76] Günter Dürig, 'Art. 1 Abs. I', in *Kommentar zum Grundgesetz*, ed. Theodor Maunz and Günter Dürig (München: Beck, 1958); also Günter Dürig, 'Der Grundrechtssatz der Menschenwürde. Entwurf eines praktikablen Wertsystems der Grundrechte aus Art. 1 Abs. I in Verbindung mit Art. 19 Abs. II des Grundgesetzes', *Archiv für öffentliches Recht*, 81 (1956), 117.

[77] Stolleis, *Vierter Band 1945–1990*, p. 220.

exceptions. This did not, of course, do away with indeterminacy, but it at least narrowed down what counted as a permissible argument.

Legal scholars played an important role in this development. Even though many of them had initially shown scepticism towards the Basic Law and the new Constitutional Court, in the long run they had no choice but to cooperate. If law professors wanted to be relevant, total opposition was not a sensible solution. By constructing and elaborating the new doctrines of constitutional law, scholars could and did support the Court while at the same time strengthening the idea that constitutional law could only be reliably entrusted to legal experts. In this new relationship, both parties won: The Justices gained the approval of their peers, who provided valuable support for the justification of their opinions, and scholars gained real influence and a small share in the Court's authority. Nevertheless, unlike in previous times, the Court was the stronger member in this relationship.[78] In 1962 Rudolf Smend could famously state in his speech celebrating the tenth anniversary of the Court in 1962 that 'the Basic Law now meant, what the Court interpreted it to be'.[79]

C. The 1970s—Challenging Hierarchical Authority

In the 1970s the Court was confronted with new challenges to its authority when it was for the first time confronted with a Social Democrat government, headed by the charismatic Chancellor Willie Brandt. Invalidating a number of Social Democrat reform projects, the Court increasingly became the conservative branch and to some on the left an unaccountable elite institution whose power had to be restrained. By then, however, the Court had sufficiently entrenched and formalized its authority to withstand what soon became the most serious post-war challenge to the German hierarchical culture of authority. This challenge was initially not directed against the Court, but in withstanding the government's reforms, it made itself vulnerable.

Brandt's call for democracy had a broader basis in the 1968 student movement that attacked the foundations of West Germany's hierarchical culture.

[78] Bernhard Schlink famously characterized the lack of critical scholarly engagement with the Court as 'Verfassungsgerichtspositivismus', see Bernhard Schlink, 'Die Entthronung der Staatsrechtswissenschaft durch die Verfassungsgerichtsbarkeit', *Der Staat*, 28 (1989), 161 and 163. For a more nuanced approach, but one that ultimately confirms the Court's key role, see Günther, *Denken vom Staat her*, pp. 109 et seq.

[79] Quoted according to Oliver W. Lembcke, *Über das Ansehen des Bundesverfassungsgerichts. Ansichten und Meinungen in der Öffentlichkeit 1951–2001* (Berlin: Berliner Wissenschafts-Verlag, 2006), p. 53 (translation by myself).

Power relationships, especially when they were not built on popular consent but were the result of property rights (in the economy) or tradition (in families), appeared to many as pillars of an oppressive social system. In the university, students chanting 'under the academic robes, the mustiness of a thousand years' ('*Unter den Talaren, der Muff von tausend Jahren*') rebelled against professorial authority.[80] Brandt's reform agenda incorporated many of the younger generation's demands—albeit often in a more moderate key than those out protesting on the streets would have liked.

The Court itself was initially not entirely unaffected by the challenge to traditional structures of authority and even opened itself up to one important reform: the introduction of dissents in 1971. The first step in this direction had been the publication of voting results by the Court's Second Senate in 1967.[81] Open voting and individualized opinion-writing broke with the traditional continental idea of a court as a unified institution whose individual office-holders did not matter. In 1968 the German all-lawyers conference (*Deutscher Juristentag*) put the issue of dissenting votes on its agenda and issued recommendations to introduce dissents in all federal German Courts, i.e. only the highest courts.[82] A number of scholars openly discussed the relative truth of judicial opinions and argued for more transparency in judicial decision-making, based on the consideration that in any democratic society the people must be able to control the exercise of state power, including the courts.[83] When dissents were finally introduced in 1971, they were, however, restricted to the Constitutional Court. And ultimately, even here they remained rare compared to other constitutional courts: Of the Court's 2,107 decisions between 1971 and 2013, in only 151 cases, or 8 per cent of all decisions, did judges write separate opinions.[84]

Progressives also wanted to reform German legal education. Within the universities, some sought to integrate broader and sometimes critical perspectives on law into law school curricula such as legal sociology. Often, these new approaches explicitly acknowledged judicial indeterminacy and

[80] Heinrich A. Winkler, *Der lange Weg nach Westen. Deutsche Geschichte vom 'Dritten Reich' bis zur Wiedervereinigung* (München: C. H. Beck, 2000), pp. 248 et seq.

[81] Hans Spanner, 'Zur Praxis des Sondervotums beim Bundesverfassungsgericht', in *Festschrift Geiger* (1974), 893.

[82] Deutscher Juristentag (ed.), *Deutscher Juristentag. Sitzungsbericht R. zum 47. Deutschen Juristentag* (München: C. H. Beck, 1968).

[83] For a more comprehensive account of the debates, see Hans J. Lietzmann, 'Kontingenz und Geheimnis. Die Veröffentlichung der Sondervoten beim Bundesverfassungsgericht', in *Das Bundesverfassungsgericht im politischen System*, ed. Robert van Ooyen and Martin Möllers (Wiesbaden: Verlag für Sozialwissenschaften, 2006), pp. 269–82.

[84] See official Court statistics, <http://www.bundesverfassungsgericht.de/DE/Verfahren/Jahresstatistiken/2013/gb2013/A-I-7.html>.

challenged lawyers to take a broader, more socially conscious perspective in their work, rather than trying to find a 'right' answer that did not exist anyway. All this came with a push to shorten legal education and orient it more towards legal practice.

The new awareness of social context also raised interest in and drew attention to other social actors such as the public or parliaments. Taking their inspiration from this literature, legal scholars began to discuss 'participation' as a central new category both in constitutional and administrative law.[85] Unsurprisingly, however, most scholars distanced themselves from the more radical claims for direct democracy voiced on the streets. At the same time, interest groups and factions were now increasingly considered as an enrichment of political culture rather than a threat to a state-defined and static public good. In the wake of this ideological turn, Smend's theory of integration was increasingly re-framed as a theory of societal pluralism.[86]

Taking its cue from politics, the public law professors' conference in 1970 for the first time discussed democracy and shortly afterwards the parliamentary system (1974). The presentations and discussions showed that German public lawyers had finally come to terms with societal pluralism and parliamentary democracy.[87] The contrast to Weimar with its polarizing discussions and tendency towards highly theorized political concepts was striking: The discussion had become much more pragmatic and concerned with the details of specific legal regimes rather than the basics of the political system. This general consensus also included the Court's role as the final interpreter of the Basic Law. A 'counter-majoritarian' difficulty only became apparent again when the Court invalidated a series of the government's reforms in the 1970s.[88]

This Court itself had by now developed a robust, but also inflexible concept of democracy, reflecting fear of modes of popular decision-making

[85] Anna-Bettina Kaiser, *Die Kommunikation der Verwaltung: Diskurse zu den Kommunikationsbeziehungen zwischen staatlicher Verwaltung und Privaten in der Verwaltungsrechtswissenschaft der Bundesrepublik Deutschland* (Baden-Baden: Nomos, 2007), pp. 136 et seq.

[86] Günther, *Denken vom Staat her*, p. 163; see also Stolleis, *Vierter Band 1945–1990*, pp. 350 et seq.

[87] See the presentations and discussion in *Vereinigung der deutschen Staatsrechtslehrer*, 29 (1970) on the topic 'Das demokratische Prinzip im Grundgesetz', and in *Vereinigung der deutschen Staatsrechtslehrer*, 33 (1974) on the topic 'Das parlamentarische Regierungssystem des Grundgesetzes: Anlage—Erfahrungen—Zukunftseignung. Organisierte Einwirkungen auf die Verwaltung—Zur Lage der 2. Gewalt'.

[88] Stolleis, *Vierter Band 1945–1990*, pp. 354–5.

reminiscent of Socialist and National-Socialist ideas of government.[89] Its main instrument for protecting parliamentary power was the so-called *Wesentlichkeitstheorie* (principle of essentiality), which prohibits the delegation of 'essential' questions to the executive branch.[90] Derived from the rule of law and democracy principles, the *Wesentlichkeitstheorie* served as a means of forcing parliament to regulate certain issues by itself, but also to subject administrative rule-making to increasing judicial scrutiny.[91] This protection and strengthening of parliamentary powers became a key feature of German constitutional jurisprudence, textually supported by references to democracy[92] or the constitutional allocation of competences.[93] Indeed, the federal German parliament came to be central to the Court's understanding of political legitimacy in its jurisprudence, much more so than other German and European institutions.[94] Social Democrats' attempts to 'democratise' German universities by increasing the influence of students and administrative staff were defeated in the Constitutional Court, on the basis of the academic freedom of professors.[95] The Court also struck down a state law allowing for a consultative referendum on the possession and stationing of nuclear weapons. It argued that the political pressure such a referendum would exercise on state institutions constituted an unconstitutional transgression on federal competences. However pro-democratic and pluralist, this line of jurisprudence still understands state authority as hierarchically ordered insofar as each branch and each institution has to fulfil its and only its own particular tasks.

The same is true for the Court's increasingly robust approach to its own role. Its hierarchical conception of the boundaries between law and politics became a shield against political criticism of expansive judicial opinions. Its first decision on abortion in particular demonstrated how transformative

[89] See also Günter Frankenberg, 'Vorsicht Demokratie! Kritik der juridischen Versicherung einer Gesellschaft gegen die Risiken der Selbstregierung', in *Demokratie und Grundgesetz*, ed. Redaktion Kritische Justiz (Baden-Baden: Nomos, 2000), pp. 177 et seq.

[90] The definition of 'essential' is unsurprisingly vague and contested; criteria include e.g. the effects of fundamental rights, the number of affected persons, significant financial implications, the timeframe concerned, etc., see Bernd Grzeszick, 'Art. 20 GG', *Maunz/Dürig: Grundgesetz Kommentar*, ed. Matthias Herdegen, Roman Herzog, Hans H. Klein, and Rupert Scholz (München: C. H. Beck, 2013), para. 107.

[91] Christoph Schönberger, 'Verwaltungsrecht als konkretisiertes Verfassungsrecht', in *Das Bonner Grundgesetz: altes Recht und neue Verfassung in den ersten Jahrzehnten der Bundesrepublik Deutschland (1949–1969)*, ed. Michael Stolleis (Berlin: Berliner Wissenschafts-Verlag, 2006), pp. 76 et seq.

[92] BVerfGE 89, 155; BVerfGE 123, 267.

[93] BVerfGE 8, 122.

[94] Daniel Halberstam and Christoph Möllers, 'The German Constitutional Court says Ja Zu Deutschland', *German Law Journal*, 10 (2009), 1241.

[95] BVerfGE 35, 79.

constitutionalism combined with a hierarchical understanding of the Court's own role could easily lend itself to assumptions of unprecedented judicial power (discussed further in Chapter 4).[96] Together with some other judgments, this decision represented what was by many seen as an increasingly politicized and aggressive line of jurisprudence by the Constitutional Court.[97] Social Democrats had up until then looked to the Court as an ally and were surprised when it came to play the role of a staunch defender of conservative values in the 1970s. Quantitative studies, however, suggest that the Court did not in fact invalidate more laws than in the 1960s and 1980s;[98] yet, it seems that the pieces of legislation that the Court did invalidate in the 1970s were more important, at least in the public's eyes. From a global perspective, this conservative expansionism was surprising at a time when many other constitutional courts went through an era of judicial progressivism.

The Court was now better prepared to stand up to its critics than in its early years. The pillars of its transformative jurisprudence had already become entrenched. And it could build on a wealth of scholarly writing to bolster its credibility. No longer a new institution, it had become harder to challenge its previously established authority as an impartial and apolitical judicial arbiter. With an increasing number of justices who had at least partly worked in the judiciary before their appointment to the Court,[99] the Court appeared altogether more like a court. Thus when Social Democrat Chancellor Schmidt in a televised debate called upon the Constitutional Court to exercise judicial self-restraint, the Court's then-president Benda could reply with the now standard mantra, that the Court would be doing its job, interpreting the constitution, and nothing more, but also nothing less.[100]

D. Consolidation

With its long-awaited restrained decision on labour co-determination, the Court finally won much applause and the political debate over its authority

[96] BVerfGE 39, 1.

[97] See for the discussion around the decision Justin Collings, *Democracy's Guardians: A History of the German Federal Constitutional Court 1951–2001* (Oxford: Oxford University Press, forthcoming 2015), chapter 3 (E.).

[98] André Brodocz, *Die Macht der Judikative* (Heidelberg: Springer, 2009), pp. 193–4; Uwe Kranenpohl, *Hinter dem Schleier des Beratungsgeheimnisses: Der Willensbildungs- und Entscheidungsprozess des Bundesverfassungsgerichts* (Wiesbaden: Verlag für Sozialwissenschaften, 2010), p. 33.

[99] Based on my own count. Short biographies of the judges are available online.

[100] Häußler, *Der Konflikt zwischen Bundesverfassungsgericht und politischer Führung*, pp. 35–6.

died down again. No government would subsequently challenge the core of the Court's authority as much as in the 1970s.[101] A political crisis involving corruption charges implicating a number of different parties in the early 1980s did its part by making the Court look good by comparison.[102] Only in the 1990s, the Court's liberal rulings banning crucifixes in public classrooms provoked again public outcry,[103] backed by veiled threats not to implement the decision, which were partly realized.[104] Criticism further increased when the Court shortly afterwards protected the Tucholsky quote 'soldiers are murderers'[105] as free speech, invalidating the criminal conviction of a lower court. In doing so, it caused massive popular protests and a significant decrease in its public approval rates, but only for a short time.[106]

Yet, as a result of the Court's earlier expansionism during the 1970s, the idea of functional restraints on constitutional jurisprudence was more widely debated in the 1980s. Left-leaning political scientists and philosophers like Ingeborg Maus[107] and Jürgen Habermas[108] contributed to this trend by criticizing the Court for the irrationality of its value-jurisprudence and its lack of judicial self-restraint. Unlike many legal critiques that primarily sought to improve the quality and consistency of legal argument, theirs was more concerned with the effects of constitutional review on democracy. But as the 1980s passed and memory of the 1970s faded, the topic soon became again less urgent and therefore appeared less relevant.

The high time of German Value Formalism had now begun. While the Court had early on developed the key tools of German transformative constitutionalism, only now did they become firmly entrenched and formalized. In the 1950s and 1960s, the fact that everything was new led to much debate and insecurity about what to make of the new precedents. The 1970s in turn brought more critical and often US-influenced perspectives to bear that were not suited to stabilize traditional legal authority. By the 1980s,

[101] Collings, *Democracy's Guardians*, chapter 3 (conclusion). [102] Ibid.

[103] Gary S. Schaal, '"Crisis! What Crisis? Der" Kruzifix-Beschluss "und seine Folgen"', in *Das Bundesverfassungsgericht im politischen System*, pp. 175–86.

[104] Georg Vanberg, *The Politics of Constitutional Review in Germany* (Cambridge: Cambridge University Press, 2005), p. 4.

[105] In one of the original cases which were jointly dealt with by the Court, the demonstrator had in fact watched a NATO exercise and reacted to a manoeuvre of US tanks by posting a sign, saying literally: 'A soldier is a murder' (see Tade Spranger, 'Soldaten sind Mörder', in *Verfassungsrechtspre chung: Hundert Entscheidungen des Bundesverfassungsgerichts in Retrospektive*, ed. Jörg Menzel and Thomas Ackermann (Tübingen: Mohr Siebeck, 2000), p. 595).

[106] Lembcke, *Über das Ansehen des Bundesverfassungsgerichts*, p. 19.

[107] Ingeborg Maus, 'Liberties and Popular Sovereignty: On Jürgen Habermas' Reconstruction of the System of Rights', *Cardozo Law Review*, 17 (1995), 825–82.

[108] Jürgen Habermas, *Faktizität und Geltung: Beiträge zur Diskurstheorie des Rechts und des Demokratischen Rechtsstaats* (Frankfurt am Main: Suhrkamp, 1998), pp. 309 et seq.

however, German constitutional law had fully emancipated itself. This was partly a result of the newly gained political and legal self-confidence, but also a response to the fact that there was now much doctrine and case-law available. As Michael Stolleis points out, much more suggests that longer-established comfortable systems can take a more positivist approach to legal interpretation.[109] For German law, this was certainly true. The initial metaphysical foundations such as the concept of values had by now largely disappeared,[110] but their doctrinal offspring remained. Constitutional reasoning remained strongly teleological, but the Court could now refer back to its previous decisions and legal scholarship to determine the telos of a particular provision and its function within the larger constitutional framework without needing to reinvent and justify what it was doing each time. Constitutional reasoning thus became more formalist. A multitude of commentaries on the Basic Law brought order and structure to constitutional interpretation. Rights review had by now been streamlined into one general test that incorporated the different limitation requirements of rights provided for in the constitutional text. The rise in student numbers further contributed to this development. Increasing competition for good jobs strengthened the need for adequate exam preparation and hence for more education-oriented scholarship. '*Lehrbücher*', textbooks for students, multiplied.[111] As a result of the increase of jurisprudence and doctrine over time, exams also became harder, further raising the demand for exam-preparation materials. In response, authors were encouraged to reduce the presented material to the essentials, leaving aside any deeper theoretical perspectives or other kinds of background information.[112] Textbooks were competing on the market with so-called '*Skripten*', exercise material prepared by professional exam prep-schools (*Repetitorien*). This increasing focus on exam preparation largely drowned out the '*Grundlagenfächer*', broader foundational subjects like legal methodology, history, sociology, or philosophy, in legal education. Since exam grades strongly determined students' later career prospects, they often found little time to study things not relevant to these exams. And the more

[109] Stolleis, *Vierter Band 1945–1990*, pp. 548–9.

[110] Rennert, 'Die verdrängte Werttheorie und ihre Historisierung'.

[111] Stolleis, *Vierter Band 1945–1990*, p. 535.

[112] Christoph Möllers and Hannah Birkenkötter, 'Towards a New Conceptualism in Comparative Constitutional Law or: Reviving the German Tradition of the Lehrbuch', *International Journal of Constitutional Law*, 12(3) (2014), 603, 612 et seq. For a practical illustration, take any of the recent German textbooks on constitutional law such as Friedhelm Hufen, *Staatsrecht II Grundrechte* (München: Beck, 2014); Jörn Ipsen, *Staatsrecht II Grundrechte* (Neuwied: Luchterhand, 2014); Gerrit Mannsen, *Staatsrecht II Grundrechte* (München: Beck, 2014); Bodo Pieroth, Bernhard Schlink, Thorsten Kingreen, and Ralf Poscher, *Grundrechte Staatsrecht II* (Heidelberg: C. F. Müller, 2014).

important exam preparation became, the more law schools looked to hire candidates who would first of all be qualified to teach exam-related black-letter subjects.

Legal sociology suffered in particular. While the subject remained in curricula, its teaching was increasingly adapted to the prevailing textbook style that provided excellent well-structured summaries of the existing literature, but little more than that. Students hence 'learned' what the existing concepts of legal sociology were, but they were not encouraged to take up their own legal sociological research. More critical perspectives on law existed only on the margins of the political left where they typically focused on rather specific legal problems and fields such as immigration law and gender issues.[113] As such, they rarely provide a broader critical perspective on German law. Consequently, there are very few empirical studies that would, for example, attempt to trace the influence of social movements or the judges' political affiliations on judicial decision-making. From the position of the academic mainstream, which sees its function in improving legal determinacy and certainty rather than in criticizing it, this made sense.

Legal philosophy and legal theory attracted a somewhat better fate—perhaps because they had a longer pedigree in German legal scholarship. Yet, maybe in response to the increasing politicization of constitutional questions in the 1970s, this new interest took a decidedly apolitical and anti-ideological stance that emphasized legal autonomy and distanced itself from the metaphysical and natural law ideas of the 1950s as well as from value jurisprudence.[114] Unlike the first generation of critics such as Schmitt and Forsthoff, the second generation framed their critique increasingly in positivist terms. Kelsen's work experienced a sudden revival after a long period of neglect in the early post-war decades.[115] But the most important and famous (sociological) theory of law became Niklas Luhmann's system theory, which described law an autopoietic system that operates in its own code, distinct and separated from other social systems.[116] Though sociological and not normative, his emphasis on legal autonomy and law as a specific code, and hence as a way of communicating reserved for professionally trained elites, made Luhmann's theory especially attractive in the

[113] This is reflected in the contributions to the main critical journal on the left, the 'Kritische Justiz'; see Stolleis, *Vierter Band 1945–1990*, pp. 383–4.

[114] See Rennert, 'Die verdrängte Werttheorie und ihre Historisierung' for the distance to value jurisprudence; and more broadly Stolleis, *Vierter Band 1945–1990*, pp. 386 et seq.

[115] See Matthias Jestaedt (ed.), *Hans Kelsen und die deutsche Staatsrechtslehre, Stationen eines wechselvollen Verhältnisses* (Tübingen: Mohr Siebeck, 2013).

[116] Niklas Luhmann, *Law As a Social System*, trans. Klaus Ziegert, ed. Fatima Kastner et al. (Oxford: Oxford University Press, 2004).

hierarchical German legal culture—which perhaps also explains why it has been largely ignored in Common Law countries.[117]

All of this does not mean that the Court does not take popular opinion or social movements into account in its decision-making. Stephan Jaggi, for example, provides us with an impressive study of the Court's post-reunification jurisprudence and demonstrates how the Court has taken up a number of the revolutionary demands of the opposition movement in the former GDR and the Round Tables founded in the wake of the regime's downfall.[118] Jaggi argues that the Court changed its jurisprudence on women's rights and the right to property in a way that reflects the East German attempts to preserve some of the achievements of socialism, an effort which had failed in the political negotiations. Yet this is not too surprising; indeed, the German Court has never shied away from dynamic interpretation that takes social change into account. What is important and typical of the German academic reaction to such changes, however, is that they receive so little attention. Existing German scholarship largely considers these changes as consistent developments of previous jurisprudence;[119] indeed, even where scholars do recognize that the Court may have acted strategically, such as in its second abortion decision,[120] this does not usually provoke more general discussions about the relationship of law and politics.

E. Conclusion

That the Court could reconcile not only its mandate of rights review, but also its turn to transformative constitutionalism with the existing hierarchical legal culture remains its greatest achievement to date. It certainly helped that German public law had already during the Weimar Republic and National-Socialism opened itself up to a more flexible legal methodology that went beyond the formalism present during much of the nineteenth century. Yet, in the early 1950s a chorus of critical voices warned against value jurisprudence as a path to a politicized court and juristocracy. If the Court could nevertheless establish its authority as an independent, apolitical court, it was because it could tap into the deeper resources of judicial legitimacy present in German legal and political culture. Some of the conditions necessary to

[117] Moritz Renner, 'Kontingenz, Redundanz, Transzendenz? Zum Gerechtigkeitsbegriff Niklas Luhmanns', *Ancilla Juris* (2008), 62.

[118] Stephan Jaggi, 'The Forgotten Revolution? Rediscovering the 1989 Revolution in the GDR and Its Impact on Unified Germany's Constitutional Law" (PhD thesis, Yale University, 2012).

[119] Ibid.

[120] BVerfGE 88, 203.

make this a successful enterprise were present at the beginning: its Kelsenian design as a specialized constitutional court at the top of the judicial hierarchy and the requirement that judges be legal professionals. Others would only be acquired over time. Most importantly, it took time to formalize value jurisprudence and build a body of constitutional doctrine that would provide guidance for future decision-making and guarantee at least a semblance of rational decision-making and consistency across cases.

4

Value Formalism

In the previous chapters, we have observed the evolution of German constitutional jurisprudence. We have seen how the Court slowly developed its rights jurisprudence and its self-confidence. We have begun to understand how its turn to rights as values entailed the change to an activist paradigm of constitutional law, but also how the imperative of social change became less important over time and talk of values subsided. This development corresponded with a stronger entrenchment of traditional features of continental law in the realm of constitutional justice.

It is now time to get back to the analytical model developed in the first chapter of this book, and to examine more closely how activist law and hierarchical authority shape the German Court's jurisprudence and how exactly their synthesis, Value Formalism, works.

A. Changes and Challenges

The Court's success depended on its ability to reconcile activist constitutionalism with a hierarchical culture of authority. This was no small challenge: As we have seen in the last chapter, German law started out with a broadly reactive conception of individual rights, leading many scholars initially to denounce the new activist conception of law as 'political' and 'non-legal'. They were not entirely wrong, of course. Transformative constitutionalism is more prone to creating new legal questions than reactive constitutionalism, because it cherishes a comprehensive vision of social justice. Compared to such a vision, real society will always appear lacking and change therefore indispensable.

And the more comprehensive our idea of justice is and the more inadequate real society, the harder it becomes to reconcile transformative ideas of law with traditional ideas of law and judging. This applies especially in Global South societies such as India, where social inequality is high and some people lack the means to fulfil their most basic human needs and where law has consequently become more than in many other places a tool for social upliftment.[1] In order to realize the constitutional ideal there is still so much to be done that has not been done before that it becomes difficult for judges and lawyers to establish consistent a priori standards to deal with cases. Rights adjudication can easily turn here into a difficult managerial exercise where it is unclear and bitterly contested who is responsible for rights' violations and what can be done to remedy them. When, for example, workers suffer injury to their health as a result of the work they have undertaken, it may be difficult to determine who has to bear the blame for this.[2] In a *reactive system*, such problems represent mere conflicts between private individuals in which the state does not need to intervene. In an *activist state* that does not rely on law and courts to implement its vision of change, there may be administrative bodies or labour boards dealing with this problem. But in a *transformative legal system* where law is the key instrument to bring about social change, courts come into play. And when they do, they have to deal with a wealth of questions: Is it the government that has not provided workers with a mandatory health insurance scheme or that has possibly obstructed worker unionization which is responsible, or is it the private employer who exploits the demand for labour, or is the worker himself responsible for failing to procure private insurance? If detailed regulation is lacking or appears insufficient, courts have to deal with these multi-faceted, complex questions by themselves. Because they decide individual cases and have to take different facts into account each time, it will often be difficult to develop a consistent set of legal standards. Of course, here too, things may get easier over time, but the more comprehensive our vision of constitutional law is and the less perfect existing institutions are, the more new issues will keep surfacing.[3]

This represents a challenge for any legal system, but even more so for those built on a hierarchical culture of authority. At the core of hierarchical systems is an understanding of law as a science to be dealt with by professionally trained experts at a very *specific* task; while this specific task does not

[1] This applies first and foremost to Indian Public Interest Litigation; see e.g. Upendra Baxi, 'Taking Suffering Seriously: Social Action Litigation in the Supreme Court of India', *Third World Legal Studies*, (1985) 107.

[2] See Daniel M. Brinks and Varun Gauri, 'Human Rights as Demands for Communicative Action', *World Bank Policy Research Working Paper*, 5951 (2012), <http://ssrn.com/abstract=1988039>.

[3] For the importance of newness in constitutional review see James Fowkes, 'Socio-economic Rights and the Newness Hypothesis', Max Planck Lecture, delivered 29 January 2014 and James Fowkes, *Building the Constitution: The Practice of Constitutional Interpretation in South Africa since 1994* (Cambridge: Cambridge University Press, forthcoming 2016).

necessarily have to involve only legal interpretation, there needs to be a sense of doing something narrower than managing and addressing various problems of social injustice in order to justify claims to professional authority. The sheer breadth of transformative constitutionalism and its drive for bringing about real change, which demands close attention to social context, however, make legal adjudication a difficult managerial exercise,[4] involving lawyers in all sorts of societal problems.

Transformative constitutionalism is not, however, only a Global South phenomenon or a feature of developing economies. Rather, it depends on society's desire for social change. In the 1950s in Germany, social change seemed indispensable after the moral catastrophe of the Holocaust and the Second World War. Obviously, something had been rotten in the German state and together with other actors the Constitutional Court set itself the task of fixing it, using the Basic Law as its tool. And though the Basic Law was initially meant to provide only a provisional framework, the Court understood it, at least initially, as a framework for broader social change. As the Court explained in its judgment prohibiting the Communist party, the 'free democratic order of the Basic Law ... assumes that the [existing state and social conditions] can and must be improved. This presents a never ending task that will present itself in ever new forms and with ever new aspects'.[5] Yet the Court lost its position as frontrunner of social progressivism in the 1970s when calls for change had again become a more partisan affair, attached to a particular progressive agenda rather than a shared commitment of all parties.[6] In this environment, the Court could no longer draw as heavily on the need for change as a legitimating paradigm; it now needed to increase its reliance on other sources of authority or run into conflicts with other state institutions. The hierarchical paradigm provided such an alternative source of legitimacy, allowing the German Court to preserve and entrench its early transformative landmark decisions even though it was now lacking the early drive for change and thus an important potential basis of legitimacy. Even today many jurisprudential arguments and doctrines are direct successors of the Court's turn to an activist paradigm of constitutional law. Reconciling a hierarchical legal culture and its transformative understanding of law, German lawyers created their own particular style of jurisprudence, Value Formalism. As a result, Value Formalism reflects the conflicting demands both of transformative constitutionalism and a hierarchical culture of authority.

[4] James Fowkes, 'Civil Procedure in Public Interest Litigation: Tradition, Collaboration and the Managerial Judge', *Cambridge Journal of International & Comparative Law*, 1 (2012), 235.

[5] BVerfGE 5, 85. [6] For details see Chapter 2.

B. The Transformative Paradigm

I. Access to the Court

In order to effectively realize a transformative constitution, access to courts must be easy. It is no accident that we can observe even in the United States an expansion of standing during the high time of US activist constitutionalism in the 1970s.[7] Courts can facilitate access in two ways: either by liberalizing the procedural requirements or by expanding the scope of substantive constitutional law.

The German Court has mostly chosen to expand the scope of rights rather than relax procedural requirements. There are, nevertheless, a number of procedural features—some explicit in the constitutional text, some jurisprudential innovations—that support an activist approach. The most important of these is abstract review, which allows certain non-affected parties to challenge the constitutionality of laws merely in the objective interest of ensuring their constitutionality. It therefore goes beyond reactive systems and their concern for conflict solution in providing for judicial redress absent any violation of the plaintiff's own rights. But abstract review is not the only feature that points to the Court's willingness to realize constitutional values even where a real case or controversy is lacking. The Court has also repeatedly decided constitutional cases even after the parties had withdrawn the case, in the interest of a public clarification of the legal question at hand.[8] It has moreover granted injunctions without a petition by one of the parties and rejected cases on grounds of substantive law without addressing the question of the admissibility of the complaint first.[9] Going beyond the traditional reactive conception of law as a means of solving conflicts and restoring peace, these decisions exhibit a clearly activist approach: Not only is no actual case or controversy necessary to trigger the Court's apparatus, but once a case has been opened, the managerial imperative of the 'best possible implementation' may also prevail over the interests of the parties or procedural restrictions.

[7] See e.g. Abram Chayes, 'The Role of the Judge in Public Law Litigation', *Harvard Law Review*, 89 (1976), 1281; Antonin Scalia, 'The Doctrine of Standing as an Essential Element of the Separation of Powers', *Suffolk University Law Review*, 17 (1983), 881. For a critique and the later changes, see Abram Chayes, 'The Supreme Court 1981 Term—Foreword: Public Law Litigation and the Burger Court', *Harvard Law Review*, 96 (1982), 4; Cass Sunstein, 'What's Standing After Lujan? Of Citizen Suits, "Injuries," and Article III', *Michigan Law Review*, 91 (1992), 163.

[8] See e.g. BVerfGE 98, 218; see also Christoph Möllers, *Gewaltengliederung* (Tübingen: Mohr Siebeck, 2005), p. 151.

[9] See e.g. BVerfGE 53, 100; BVerfGE 69, 1; BVerfGE 79, 223.

Nevertheless, these procedural innovations seem rather tame compared to developments in other legal systems where access to courts has been significantly expanded under the label of public interest litigation. The Indian Supreme Court, for example, now merely requires that the plaintiff have sufficient interest to start a lawsuit and not be a 'mere busybody or meddlesome interloper'.[10] Under this model, NGOs or publicly spirited individual citizens can raise almost any issue that constitutes some breach of legal rules or constitutional principles in court. Similarly, the South African Constitution provides in its s. 38 (d) for standing in cases of public interest and the South African Constitutional Court has taken a broad approach to standing questions in its jurisprudence so far.[11]

The comparative German restraint in this regard owes itself to two main factors: First of all, German law's activist potential is reduced because the imperative of social change has decreased over time; second and more importantly, the hierarchical paradigm, with its emphasis on the distribution of different tasks to different institutions, inhibits procedural flexibility to some degree because it relies on preserving certain characteristic institutional features of the judiciary that distinguish its workings from those of other branches. One of these features is that judicial processes are individualized: *Individual* plaintiffs seek ex-post redress for encroachments of their *individual* rights in a *concrete* case or controversy.[12] In contrast, politics involves *collective* decision-making aiming to further *common* goods. In public interest litigation, it is, however, not one individual trying to defend himself against a violation of his rights, but rather a publicly spirited citizen presenting a question of public interest. As a result, the line between law and politics gets blurred. Courts that aim to preserve strict dividing lines between political institutions thus have an interest in keeping the judicial process individualized. This does not preclude expansions, but it does tend to restrain them somewhat.

The German Constitutional Court has instead focused on the expansion of individual rights. In order to bring a constitutional complaint, citizens only need to demonstrate that one of their rights may have been violated. By taking both a broad approach to what counts as a fundamental right and to what counts as an infringement, the Court has ensured that this requirement is comparatively easy to fulfil. The Court has, for example, allowed citizens to challenge measures taken in the EU financial crisis based on the right to vote—arguing that the right to vote implies the right to vote for a parliament

[10] *S. P. Gupta vs President of India*, 1981 Supp. (1) SCC 87.

[11] See Justice O'Regan in *Ferreira vs Levin NO and Others*, 1996 (1) SA 984 (CC); *Lawyers for Human Rights vs Department of Home Affairs*, 2004 (4) SA 125 (CC).

[12] Christoph Möllers, *Die drei Gewalten* (Weilerswist: Velbrück, 2008), pp. 100 et seq.

that still has something important to say and is not unduly constrained by financial obligations it has entered into. More importantly, the Court has interpreted Art. 2 para. 1 of the Basic Law as a general right to individual liberty to do or not to do whatever one pleases, as opposed to a more specialized right protecting only certain core expressions of personality.[13] In doing so, it has significantly expanded the scope of its own jurisdiction. And it has taken a similarly generous approach to infringements: According to the standard formula, any state action that wholly or partly makes it impossible for an individual to make use of her fundamental rights constitutes an infringement of that right, whether or not it is intentional, direct or indirect, has legal or factual effects,[14] or is accompanied by state sanctions.[15] The classic German example is a case in which the plaintiff challenged a sign prohibiting horse-riding on certain hiking paths in a forest—under Art. 2 GG, horse-riding represents a constitutionally protected activity and the traffic signs prohibiting it on certain paths therefore qualify as an infringement of this liberty.[16] And while, of course, infringements may still be justifiable, this broad definition of rights and what constitutes an infringement makes it easy for individuals to bring a constitutional complaint. Moreover, plaintiffs are not only not initially required to hire a lawyer to bring a case, but may also apply to the Court for legal aid to hire one depending on their need and chances of success.[17] This jurisprudence therefore provides a functional equivalent of the extensions of standing in other courts by allowing many more people to bring constitutional complaints. Indeed, this line of jurisprudence has been so successful that the Court receives routinely about six thousand new cases each year in spite of some subsequent attempts to curtail this caseload.[18]

II. Value jurisprudence

That rights have an objective function has long been a cornerstone of transformative German constitutional doctrine. This objective function of rights,

[13] See the discussion of the *Elfes* case in Chapter 2.

[14] The distinction between legal and factual effects indicates whether the act that limits the right in the concrete case is itself a law or is merely factual conduct (irrespective of whether there is a legal basis for this factual conduct), i.e. acoustic surveillance or a prison guard beating up a prisoner.

[15] Bodo Pieroth and Bernhard Schlink, *Grundrechte. Staatsrecht II, 28th ed.* (Heidelberg: C. F. Müller, 2012), pp. 49–51.

[16] BVerfGE 80, 137.

[17] Klaus Schlaich and Stefan Korioth, *Das Bundesverfassungsgericht: Stellung, Verfahren, Entscheidungen*, 9th edn (München: C. H. Beck, 2012), para. 59; see also BVerfGE 1, 109 for the first decision on legal aid.

[18] For details see Schlaich and Korioth, *Das Bundesverfassungsgericht*, pp. 280 et seq.

initially conceptualized as values, has been the subject of much scholarly writing.[19] For our purposes, the most important characteristic of values is their teleological character.[20] To better understand what this means, we can draw on the German theorist Robert Alexy, who has described constitutional norms as 'optimization principles' and pointed out that this understanding is roughly equivalent to the Court's value conception.[21] Like optimization principles, it is inherent in the idea of a value that it has to be realized to the fullest degree possible. This imperative of realization has—unlike legal principles or rules—no boundaries of its own. The concept of a value suggests that the more of it there is, the better.[22]

As a matter of law, this implies two things: First, if we seek to realize values, this fits well with a teleological approach to judicial interpretation. A narrow formalist or textualist approach hardly matches with the demand for full realization. As I have demonstrated with my co-author in a short recent study of forty landmark decisions, teleological arguments were present in every single one of them. This is not only a result of the conception of rights as values, of course—otherwise we would expect this to have changed in recent years—but it is one factor among others. The constitutional text, by contrast, only ever provides the first step, and never the endpoint, of constitutional analysis.[23] Teleological arguments may include looking to the historical purpose of the text, but more often the Court seeks to determine the objective purpose of a constitutional norm beyond its original purpose. In doing so, the Court refers quite frequently to a specific idea of mankind (often based on a number of constitutional provisions) or ideas about what constitutes a life worth living or a democratic society. As these concepts are rather broad and incorporate ethical ideas, it is fair to characterize German constitutional interpretation in this regard as quite open and flexible.

[19] For many see Jürgen Habermas, *Between, Facts and Norms: Contributions to a Discourse Theory of Law and Democracy*, trans. William Rehg (Cambridge: MIT Press, 1998), pp. 255 et seq.; Bernhard Schlink, *Abwägung im Verfassungsrecht* (Berlin: Duncker & Humblot, 1976); or more recently Benjamin Rusteberg, *Der grundrechtliche Gewährleistungsgehalt* (Tübingen: Mohr Siebeck, 2009).

[20] See Habermas, *Between, Facts and Norms*, p. 255.

[21] Robert Alexy, *A Theory of Constitutional Rights* (Oxford: Oxford University Press, 2002), pp. 47 et seq.

[22] See Habermas, *Between, Facts and Norms*, p. 255.

[23] See Michaela Hailbronner and Stefan Martini, 'German Report', in *Comparative Constitutional Reasoning*, ed. A. Jakab, A. Dyevre, and G. Itzcovich (Cambridge: Cambridge University Press, forthcoming).

But values imply more than teleological methodology. Because they have objective effect, they expand the scope of constitutional law. As objective values, individual rights are no longer merely tools for individuals to preserve their freedom vis-à-vis the government, but rather assume a much broader scope and function. And even though in recent times talk of values has become more rare in Germany, this objective dimension of rights remains key to German constitutional law.

It also has, according to established doctrine, a number of important implications.[24] First, as objective law constitutional rights have a radiating effect into the broader legal order and can be applied in disputes between private persons through so-called general clauses and other broadly formulated legal norms (*Drittwirkung*). Second, in their objective dimension rights assume a protective function (*Schutzpflichtfunktion*) that obliges the state to protect fundamental rights against encroachments by other private persons. They also have certain procedural and organizational dimensions that compel the state to provide for the procedural and organizational mechanisms that enable individuals to make actual use of their rights. And finally, some rights entail so-called institutional guarantees (*Einrichtungsgarantien*). Institutional guarantees grant constitutional protection to certain long-standing institutions connected to the exercise of individual rights, among them property or marriage, but also public institutions such as schools or the right of municipalities to self-government. The doctrinal development of these different functions has been described as the 're-subjectivisation of objective law' insofar as the (previously developed) objective function of rights now serves as a basis for further individual rights.[25] For our purpose here, the most interesting aspects of German rights are their indirect effect and their protective function, to which I will now turn.

*1. The protective function of rights (*Schutzpflichten*)*

The text of the Basic Law sets out few protective duties. Among those few are, most famously, the duty to protect human dignity, the duty to protect families and mothers, and even a duty to protect Sundays (through an incorporation of some articles from the Weimar Constitution). In the Court's jurisprudence and academic writing, it is, however, by now accepted that other (if not all) fundamental rights have a protective dimension, even if the constitutional

[24] For this and the following, see e.g. Pieroth and Schlink, *Grundrechte*, pp. 28 et seq.

[25] Oliver Lepsius, 'Die Maßstabsetzende Gewalt', in *Das entgrenzte Gericht: Eine kritische Bilanz nach sechzig Jahren Bundesverfassungsgericht*, ed. Matthias Jestaedt, Oliver Lepsius, Christoph Möllers, and Christoph Schönberger (Berlin: Suhrkamp, 2011), pp. 157–278, p. 196.

text does not explicitly say so.[26] This protective dimension underpins some of the most expansive judgments in the Court's history. Though the Court routinely argues that the state's duty to protect rights leaves the legislature wide discretion how to fulfil this obligation, it has nevertheless sometimes developed quite far-reaching standards of its own.

The Court's first decision on abortion of 1974 represents an early elaboration of what protective duties can imply; it remains to this day one of the most expansive judgments in the Court's jurisprudence. In it, the Court invalidated a statute that allowed abortions after mandatory counselling within the first term of the pregnancy and thereafter under certain exceptional conditions.[27] The right to life, the Court argued, included unborn life and the objective character of constitutional rights obliged the state to protect it by criminalizing abortion. This obligation outweighed the mother's liberty, which was a priori confined by the public order and other constitutional values (such as the protection of unborn life).

In subordinating a negative right (the mother's liberty) to a duty to protect a right, the first abortion decision is extremely expansive and today perhaps no longer entirely representative. This at least suggests the Court's more recent decision addressing the shooting down of a plane in a 9/11 situation where the Court took the opposite approach, subordinating instead the state's protective duty to protect its citizens on the ground to the innocent passengers' right to life. Nor did the Court ever go as far again in demanding criminal sanctions as the only effective means of protecting a right; indeed, in the second abortion decision in 1992 the Court allowed for first-trimester abortions to go unpunished.[28] Yet, the first abortion decision is important because it demonstrates how protective duties may play an important role in justifying expansive judicial action and how little room may in fact be left to the legislature, which formally enjoys broad discretion in fulfilling its protective obligations. At the time, the decision prompted one of the most stinging dissents in the Court's history, written and (in an unusual move) read aloud from the bench by the Court's only female Justice, Rupp von Brünneck, who, together with her colleague Justice Simon, criticized the majority opinion harshly for its

[26] See for an overview, Eckard Klein, 'Grundrechtliche Schutzpflicht des Staates', *Neue Juristische Wochenzeitschrift (NJW)* (1989), 1633.

[27] For a detailed historical account, with an emphasis on the role of the churches, see Simone Mantei, *Nein und Ja zur Abtreibung: Die evangelische Kirche in der Reformdebatte um [Paragraph] 218 StGB (1970–1976)* (Göttingen: Vandenhoeck & Ruprecht, 2004), pp. 45 et seq. See also Reva B. Siegel, 'Dignity and Sexuality: Claims on Dignity in Transnational Debates Over Abortion and Same-Sex Marriage', *International Journal of Constitutional Law*, 10(2) (2012), 355, pp. 361 et seq.

[28] BVerfGE 88, 203.

lack of judicial self-restraint. In its aftermath, a group of radical feminists attempted to bomb the Court, albeit without causing much damage.[29]

Protective duties nevertheless still play an important role in German constitutional law. The Court has, for example, developed an individual right to participate in the licensing of nuclear plants from the right to life, as well as comprehensive state duties to regularly investigate and minimize the risks associated with nuclear energy.[30] The right to dignity and the social state principle have served to invalidate the calculation of welfare grants,[31] to increase grants for asylum seekers,[32] and even to provide for a right of access to specific medication in life-threatening situations where no alternative remedy exists and there is at least a chance of improvement.[33] The Court has also argued that while the freedom of profession does not oblige the state to create new universities, it does oblige existing universities to exhaust the full potential of their existing capacities[34]—with the result that each year a number of students who do not get a place at a university sue their way into academic programmes.

And to take a more recent run-of-the-mill case, the Court has held that the Berlin legislature had neglected its constitutional duty to protect Sundays in allowing shops to open their business on the four consecutive Sundays before Christmas and on four other Sundays during the year in cases of public interest.[35] While the Court acknowledged that constitutional law did not entail an absolute protection of Sundays because certain exceptions had always been accepted, it struck down the pre-Christmas exception for failing to guarantee an adequate level of protection. Neither the specific function of Berlin as a 'metropolis' nor the economic interests in the pre-Christmas shop openings could change the Court's mind. The second part of the statute, providing for shop openings on four other Sundays in cases of public interest, was then read down to incorporate a number of restrictions. As the Court clarified, only a narrow definition of public interest would be constitutional and opening hours were to be confined to the time between 1 p.m. and 8 p.m.

Decisions such as this one demonstrate how far German constitutional rights have travelled from their initial framing as restraints on state action to much more comprehensive values or principles. In the Sunday trading decision, no individual claimed to be inhibited in her freedom to practise her religion by the fact that other people were selling

[29] For an account of this largely forgotten event, see <http://www1.wdr.de/themen/archiv/stichtag/stichtag1064.html>; for further references, see Justin Collings, *Democracy's Guardians: A History of the German Federal Constitutional Court 1951–2001* (Oxford: Oxford University Press, forthcoming 2015), chapter 3 (F.).

[30] BVerfGE 49, 89. [31] BVerfGE 125, 175. [32] BVerfGE 132, 134.

[33] BVerfGE 115, 25. [34] BVerfGE 33, 303. [35] BVerfGE 125, 39.

or buying things (the plaintiffs were the churches). What the Court protected was therefore no longer really an individual right, but rather an objective, social interest.[36] The meticulous nature of many of the Court's inquiries into protective aspects of rights, such as in the welfare cases or the Sunday trading decision, demonstrates moreover that the Basic Law in the Court's jurisprudence entails not merely a rough guideline, but sometimes rather detailed prescriptions for the regulation of a wide range of policy areas.

2. Drittwirkung

Another important implication of the Court's turn to values is the concept of *Drittwirkung*, the indirect horizontal application of constitutional law. Unlike other activist constitutional regimes such as the South African system, where constitutional rights are explicitly accorded both indirect and direct horizontal effect against private parties,[37] German *Drittwirkung* represents a jurisprudential innovation based on the idea of the Basic Law as an objective order of values. It is indirect insofar as private persons are not bound by constitutional norms per se, but existing statutory law must be interpreted in light of the constitution, especially when broad general clauses open up spaces for interpretation. In the Court's words:

> An order of values that is centered in the social community of freely developing human personalities and their dignity, has to be taken as the basic constitutional decision for all areas of law; legislation, administration and adjudication derive stimuli and guidelines from it; no private law statute can contradict it, each one has to be interpreted in its light.[38]

The doctrine of indirect effect significantly expands the Court's power because it allows individuals to challenge judicial decisions of ordinary courts in the Constitutional Court if a judicial interpretation of statutory law abrogates their constitutional rights. Because many statutory provisions can be understood to give expression to one or other constitutional right such as the residual right to liberty, the Court's discretion to interfere in private law disputes is almost boundless. As a general rule, about 95 per cent or more of all incoming constitutional complaints, which themselves constitute over 95 per cent of all incoming cases,[39] will be directed against judicial decisions and usually a little

[36] Möllers, 'Legalität, Legitimität und Legitimation des Bundesverfassungsgerichts', in *Das entgrenzte Gericht*, p. 398.

[37] See Constitution of the Republic of South Africa, ss. 8 (2), 8 (3), and 39 (2).

[38] BVerfGE 7, 198 (27).

[39] See official statistics for the years 1951–2013, <http://www.bundesverfassungsgericht.de/DE/Verfahren/Jahresstatistiken/2013/gb2013/A-I-4.html>.

less than half of them are private law disputes.[40] Nearly half of all its decisions hence concern conflicts between private persons. The Court has developed doctrinal restrictions to limit the ensuing flood of new cases, but these restrictions have remained vague and leave the Court substantial discretion in choosing which cases to take on.[41]

III. Focus on substantive law

As we would expect in a transformative system, German constitutional law is also heavily focused on rights rather than procedural and organizational questions. This shows not only in the Court's docket, 95 per cent of which consists of rights cases,[42] but it is also reflected in academic writings which have long focused on working out the doctrinal implication of rights and the *Rechtsstaatsprinzip* (the rule of law) while paying considerably less attention to organizational questions and questions of competences.[43] Realizing constitutional rights required first and foremost the transformation of previous German administrative law, where legal means to challenge the state had initially been confined to particular forms of action and therefore been limited. The new awareness of the fundamental rights of citizens, students, soldiers, and others changed this, creating new avenues for judicial challenges to safeguard one's rights.[44] This development has sometimes been described as the 'perfecting'[45] or the 'hypertrophy'[46] of the German *Rechtsstaat*.

German law can also be described as substantive in a deeper sense, following Jacco Bomhoff's analysis.[47] Linking the comprehensive scope of German constitutional law to its basis in value jurisprudence, Bomhoff emphasizes

[40] See official statistics for the years 1991–2013, for the proportion of complaints against decisions of civil law courts, <http://www.bundesverfassungsgericht.de/DE/Verfahren/Jahresstatistiken/2013/gb2013/A-IV-4.html>, and for the proportion of complaints against judicial decisions more generally for the year 2013, <http://www.bundesverfassungsgericht.de/DE/Verfahren/Jahresstatistiken/2013/gb2013/A-IV-8.html>.

[41] I am referring to the doctrine that the Constitutional Court will only control for violations of 'specific constitutional law' rather than any misinterpretation of statutory law. Though the Court has developed a number of sub-categories, their effect in concretizing what 'specific constitutional law' is, is limited: see Schlaich and Korioth, *Das Bundesverfassungsgericht*, p. 284.

[42] Official statistics available at <http://www.bundesverfassungsgericht.de/DE/Verfahren/Jahresstatistiken/2013/gb2013/A-I-1.html>.

[43] Oliver Lepsius, 'Rezension von: Frieder Günther: Denken vom Staat her. Die bundesdeutsche Staatsrechtslehre zwischen Dezision und Integration 1949–1970', *Sehepunkte*, 4 (2004), <http://www.sehepunkte.de/2004/05/5714.html>.

[44] For many and with further references, see Michael Stolleis, *Geschichte des Öffentlichen Rechts in Deutschland: Vierter Band 1945–1990*, pp. 216 et seq.

[45] See Lepsius, 'Rezension Günther'.

[46] Stolleis, *Vierter Band 1945–1990*, p. 216.

[47] Jacco Bomhoff, *Balancing Constitutional Rights. The Origins and Meanings of Postwar Legal Discourse* (Cambridge: Cambridge University Press, 2013), see especially chapter 3 (pp. 93 et seq.) and chapter 5.

that German constitutional law does not understand itself as a set of neutral principles for governance[48]—and this, one may add, has at most changed marginally with the more recent move away from value jurisprudence. While the Court's language may be technical and neutral, German constitutional law is still concerned with a 'scientific' analysis of the moral and political concepts contained in the Basic Law. Insofar as it is formal, this formality does not, as Bomhoff points out, eschew judicial discretion in the construction of a moral universe as in the United States,[49] but rather treats this as the epitome of a comprehensive expert understanding of the Basic Law and its central ideas.

C. The Challenge of Hierarchical Authority

As I have argued, the German Court's most significant achievement over the past decades has been the reconciliation of its new activist paradigm of constitutional law with the established hierarchical German legal culture. A number of different factors and features, some external, others internal, have made this possible.

I. Institutional self-presentation and selection of judges

The Court's decision-making practice reflects the influence of a hierarchical legal culture. The rarity of dissents[50] and the high rate of unanimous decisions have allowed the Court to build up an institutional identity where the personalities of individual office-holders or their party political affiliation do not matter very much. The selection of candidates for the Court further reinforces this emphasis on expertise and political independence. Even though the Court was originally conceived of by many as a 'political institution' in whose deliberations political arguments might have a role to play and which would hence benefit from judges with political experience,[51] the current selection practice strongly emphasizes legal rather than political expertise. As a matter of law (Art. 94 GG), the Bundesrat (the Second Chamber where the German states are represented) and the Bundestag each elect half of the judges. Up until 2015, the Bundestag, however, had delegated this task to a

[48] Ibid. [49] Ibid., pp. 215 et seq.

[50] Only 8 per cent of all cases come with a dissenting opinion: see official statistics, <http://www.bundesverfassungsgericht.de/DE/Verfahren/Jahresstatistiken/2013/gb2013/A-I-7.html>.

[51] See Martin Drath, 'Die Grenzen der Verfassungsgerichtsbarkeit', *Vereinigung der Deutschen Staatsrechtslehrer*, 9 (Berlin: de Gruyter, 1950), 17–111 (for more see Chapter 3).

committee, which was constituted according to the proportional representation of the different parties in the Bundestag. As a matter of tradition and negotiation, the major parties have accorded each other the right to choose a certain number of candidates, depending on their own representation in the Bundestag,[52] which they have jealously guarded even though party political influences on the Court's jurisprudence are overall weak.[53] At the same time, the need for consensual solutions seems to discourage the choice of radical candidates. The lack of any plenary discussion or vote has encouraged backroom negotiation and a general lack of transparency, which have frequently been the subject of criticism.[54] Since 2015, a new statute provides now for the election of the Justices by the entire Bundestag—again, however, without allowing for an open discussion in order to avoid a 'politicization' of the process, as the official explanatory memorandum of that bill states.[55] Moreover, it seems likely that the need for consensual solutions discourages the choice of radical candidates.

Prior political office is more often than not considered a disadvantage if not a clear disqualification for a judgeship, as the failed nomination of former minister of justice Herta Däubler-Gmelin illustrates.[56] The more recent nomination to the Court of former active politician and president of the state of Saarland Peter Müller similarly stirred considerable criticism for his proximity to the political realm, even though it was eventually successful.[57] Compared to the 1950s, the percentage of judges who had at least partly worked in the judiciary before their appointment to the Court increased in the 1960s and 1970s.[58] Today, professors of public law represent the predominant profession in the Court. This trend in many ways reflects the

[52] For a detailed account and discussion, see Christine Landfried, 'Die Wahl der Bundesverfassungsrichter und ihre Folgen für die Legitimität des Bundesverfassungsgerichts', in *Das Bundesverfassungsgericht im politischen System*, ed. Martin Möllers and Rober C. Ooyen, pp. 229–42 (Wiesbaden: Verlag für Sozialwissenschaften, 2006); also see Ernst Benda, Eckart Klein, and Oliver Klein, *Verfassungsprozessrecht: ein Lehr-und Handbuch* (Heidelberg: C. F. Müller, 2012), p. 5 Die Richter.

[53] Landfried, 'Die Wahl der Bundesverfassungsrichter'.

[54] See e.g. recently, Rolf Lamprecht, Klammheimlich: Unsere Richterwahl muss demokratisch warden, *DIE ZEIT N. 49/2014*, 13 December 2014, <http://www.zeit.de/2014/49/bundesverfassungsgericht-bundestag-richter-wahl>.

[55] See <http://dip21.bundestag.de/dip21/btd/18/027/1802737.pdf>. This change came even though the Court itself had recently upheld the selection mechanism as constitutional, see BVerfG, decision of June 19, 2012-2 BvC 2/10, <http://www.bundesverfassungsgericht.de/SharedDocs/Entscheidungen/DE/2012/06/cs20120619_2bvc000210.html>.

[56] Sascha Kneip, 'Bundesverfassungsgericht: Auf Demokratie ausgerichtet', *Tagesspiegel*, 29 July 2012, <http://www.tagesspiegel.de/meinung/bundesverfassungsgericht-das-gericht-hat-schon-immer-schwerwiegende-und-umkaempfte-entscheidungen-gefaellt/6933720-2.html>.

[57] Kneip, 'Bundesverfassungsgericht'.

[58] Based on my own counts, the biographies are available online.

desire for more specialization: As former professors of public law, they are better equipped to address questions of constitutional law than judges or lawyers who cannot usually specialize in constitutional law.[59] Even if academic candidates have focused on fields other than constitutional law before their appointment, they will typically have written at least one book (either their dissertation or their Habilitation) that addresses questions touching on constitutional law. The Justices further specialize within the Court, where they are assigned specific fields of constitutional law. In these fields, they are primarily responsible for screening and pre-selecting the cases the Court will eventually take on. They do so with the help of their staff, which consists mainly of members of the ordinary judiciary (judges and sometimes prosecutors), rather than comparatively inexperienced law school graduates as in the United States.

As one would expect in a hierarchical system, the German Court has to accept cases once they fulfil the statutory requirements. Nevertheless, constitutional complaints, the predominant source of its cases, require the explicit admission of the Court (sitting in chambers of three Justices).[60] As a matter of law, the Court must admit complaints if they raise questions of fundamental constitutional importance or are necessary to realize the plaintiff's constitutional rights in the sense that she would otherwise suffer severe disadvantages. However, these categories are sufficiently vague to grant the Justices de facto wide leeway in their selection of cases.[61]

Together, these features allow the Court to style itself as an institution that can command respect because of its professional expertise in constitutional interpretation rather than the personal dignity of its individual Justices or its contribution to making the world a better place.

II. Value Formalism

The Court's most important instrument in securing its authority, however, is its particular style of reasoning: Value Formalism. Value Formalism denotes the transformation and taming of activist constitutionalism through doctrinal formalization.

1. Rhetoric and style

The moralistic tone of judicial writings, which often comes with value jurisprudence, ill fits the demands for professional detachment and technical

[59] For members of other professions, it is not usually feasible to focus on constitutional law as a matter of professional practice because there are too few cases.

[60] Schlaich and Korioth, *Das Bundesverfassungsgericht*, paras 258 et seq.

[61] Ibid.

rationalization in a hierarchical system. The German Court hence typically avoids using strongly moralistic language or rhetorical flourish. Whether it deals with abortion or tax law, its judgments retain a dispassionate voice and depersonalized style, speaking in the name of 'the Court' rather than that of individual Justices. The contrast to the US[62] or the Canadian Supreme Courts is striking: Even in a dissenting vote, German Justices are unlikely to ever write a sentence like 'I must, however, respond to a few of the more outrageous arguments in today's opinion, which it is beyond human nature to leave unanswered'.[63] And even when they refer to ethical standards, such as when dealing with convictions of former GDR officials responsible for shootings at the Berlin Wall, they will not become lyrical in doing so,[64] unlike the Canadian Supreme Court ('Difficult as the goal of equality may be it is worth the arduous struggle to attain. It is only when equality is a reality that fraternity and harmony will be achieved. It is then that all individuals will truly live in dignity').[65] In contrast, the German Court's strongest expression may amount to a sentence like the following: 'Human dignity as guaranteed in Art. 1 para. 1 GG cannot be modified as a matter of immigration policy'.[66]

As a result, German constitutional jurisprudence is often hard for lay-persons to access and the Court's primary audience remains the expert community of other lawyers. This, too, marks a contrast to other activist constitutional regimes. As Kalyani Ramnath points out, many judgments of the Indian Supreme Court are multi-layered in that the Court goes beyond its plain legal reasoning to respond to the—in strict legal terms—irrelevant social context.[67] In this second layer, judges liberally dispense wisdom with regard to the broader context in which the case is situated and sometimes offer advice directed less at the legal community than at the Court's multiple other audiences. Judgments may thus provide a language for activists or social movements that can help them make their case and in terms of which the Court tries to establish its own authority. Ramnath points in this context

[62] See also Ulrich Haltern, *Europarecht und das Politische* (Tübingen: Mohr Siebeck, 2005), p. 315, who argues that the opinions of the US Supreme Court are one of the major sources of political rhetoric in the United States.

[63] *Planned Parenthood v Casey*, 505 US 833 (1992), Scalia dissent.

[64] BVerfGE 95, 96.

[65] *Cory J., Vriend v Alberta* [1998] 1 SCR 493.

[66] Das Bundesverfassungsgericht, 'Entscheidungen', <http://www.bundesverfassungsgericht.de/entscheidungen/ls20120718_1bvl001010.html>, 121.

[67] Kalyani Ramnath, 'The Runaway Judgment: Law as Literature, Courtcraft and Constitutional Visions', *Journal of Indian Law and Society*, 3 (2012), 1.

to the 'de-professionalization of justice' that enables the Court to build its 'public credibility'—again a rather foreign move to the German Court.

2. *Formalization: the role of doctrine*

The lack of objective standards for dealing with competing value claims sets another, more serious challenge. '*Dogmatik*' (doctrine) provides the Court's main tool of support here. If in the United States, '(m)ost judges would believe it absurd to think that a real case can be resolved by trying to come to terms with, and evaluate, the scholarly literature',[68] this certainly does not apply to Germany. Doctrine holds out the promise of a 'right' interpretation and is understood to contribute significantly to the goal of achieving legal certainty. According to long-standing tradition, doctrine can be ordered into two major categories: the 'ruling opinion' (*herrschende Meinung*, referred to as 'h.M.'[69]) and minority opinions (*Mindermeinungen*, m.M.).[70] While, therefore, 'some scholar is always available to support any position',[71] the categorization of doctrine into majority and minority opinions provides a mechanism in dealing with the problem of arbitrariness. This division between majority and minority opinion requires not only a quantitative but also a qualitative assessment of the available writings on the subject, where different weights are accorded to different writings depending on their institutional origin (court or scholarship) and the form of their publication.[72] In this system, diverging from the 'h.M.' is not impossible, but it requires significant additional argumentative efforts, roughly comparable to the overruling of settled precedents in common law.[73] Doctrine therefore provides a common language that all justices share and in terms of which they have to justify their decisions to the public and each other. It also serves as a tool to confine debates about legal meaning to certain recognized arguments. As

[68] Paul W. Kahn, *The Cultural Study of Law: Reconstructing Legal Scholarship* (Chicago: University of Chicago Press, 2000), pp. 27–8. See also Richard Posner, *How Judges Think* (Cambridge: Harvard University Press, 2008) for the limited relevance of academic writing to judicial practice in the United States.

[69] The '*herrschende Meinung*' consists of the decisions of higher courts and the scholarly writings in the most important commentaries, handbooks, and law journals. See for a discussion, Ingwer Ebsen, *Das Bundesverfassungsgericht als Element gesellschaftlicher Selbstregulierung* (Berlin: Duncker & Humblot, 1985), pp. 22 et seq.

[70] Some further nuances can be found, such as the 'h.L.' standing for *herrschende Lehre*, which refers to the ruling opinion among academics, thus not including judicial decisions.

[71] Kahn, *The Cultural Study of Law*, p. 28.

[72] For more, see Ebsen, *Das Bundesverfassungsgericht als Element gesellschaftlicher Selbstregulierung.*

[73] Thomas Drosdeck, *Die herrschende Meinung—Autorität als Rechtsquelle* (Berlin: Duncker & Humblot 1989), pp. 21 et seq. for a quantitative analysis of the cases where the German Supreme Court (BGH) turns against the *herrschende Meinung.*

such, it closes off legal discourse to arguments from other disciplines such as economics or political science.[74] External arguments first have to be fit into existing doctrinal categories before achieving legal relevance. Because this process narrows down the interpretive space, doctrine enhances legal certainty.

That said, formalization works on two levels: On the one hand, the building up of legal doctrines through judicial precedents and legal scholarship in fact reduces the range of admissible legal arguments and methods, thereby alleviating some of the uncertainty associated with transformative constitutionalism. On the other hand, not all new doctrinal tools actually produce much certainty, especially if they replace vague constitutional text with other, not much more determinate legal tests. A casuistic approach is often unavoidable, yet at the same time it is of little help when new cases come up which do not fit the established categories. Nevertheless, even in those cases formalization works at least on the level of appearances by simulating the existence of clear guidelines and ultimately of legal determinacy. These processes of formalization are often intertwined and together they provide the foundation of the German Court's authority.

III. Decontextualization and judicial maximalism

One of the most important features of German constitutional jurisprudence is its maximalist approach to constitutional interpretation. Judicial reasoning is maximalist if the Court provides arguments that are both deeper and broader than they need to be in order to justify the result in the concrete case.[75] Though maximalism is not a unique feature of activist constitutional regimes in a hierarchical culture, it will be a frequent feature of such systems: In *activist* constitutional regimes it is especially important to realize the *objective* vision set out in the constitution, independently of what the parties want. This drives courts to engage in broader judicial reasoning than necessary to deal with the concrete case in question. And it is particularly in *hierarchical* systems that the Court will feel the need to do so with quite as much doctrinal depth and nuance.

Of course, it is debatable what depth and breadth of engagement are necessary to deal with particular cases. If I describe German jurisprudence as

[74] Gregor Kirchhof, Stefan Magen, and Karsten Schneider (eds), *Was weiß Dogmatik? Was leistet und wie steuert die Dogmatik des Öffentlichen Rechts?* (Tübingen: Mohr Siebeck, 2012), there particularly Lepsius, 'Kritik der Dogmatik', pp. 39–62.

[75] See Cass Sunstein, *One Case At a Time: Judicial Minimalism on the Supreme Court* (Cambridge: Harvard University Press, 2001), pp. 10–12 for the definition.

maximalist, it is primarily because of a particular style of reasoning, dominant in the Court's jurisprudence, which Oliver Lepsius has aptly called '*Maßstabsdenken*' (thinking in standards).[76] Before the German Court addresses the factual circumstances in a given case and debates whether the act in question violates constitutional norms, it elaborates the meaning of the relevant constitutional norm in a rather abstract way. It does so by drawing on both prior decisions and scholarly opinions (doctrine), which together form the '*Maßstab*', the standard or considerations the court will then apply to the case at hand. And while the *Maßstab* is developed with some regard to the concrete case, it also usually contains other, more general and not necessarily directly relevant considerations of what specific constitutional norms require.

This *Maßstab* is abstract insofar as it is heavily decontextualized so as to furnish no more than a more detailed account of the constitutional provision in question without considering the facts and context of previous cases. The process of building a *Maßstab*, and therefore of building doctrine, involves both extraction and abstraction: The point on which the decision turns is identified, detached from the factual context in which it arises, and then added to the existing body of doctrine, a process which may or may not require some adjustments of the pre-existing structure.[77] Decontextualization is further assisted by the Court's method of citing precedents not by the year in which cases were decided, but only by the number of the relevant law report in which they are published (except when the decision is not yet published in the official reports, in which case the Court has to refer to other publications usually including their year of publication). Precedents are therefore even further detached from their original factual, but also historical and political, context.[78] In the Court's jurisprudence, this reads as follows:

> As a major expression of the principle of freedom of action, contractual freedom is generally protected by the fundamental right to free development of personality according to Article 2.1 of the Basic Law (see BVerfGE 72, 155 <170>; 81, 242 <254 et seq.>; 89, 214 <231 et seq.>; 103, 89 <100–101>).[79]

This way of proceeding evokes the impression that the Court merely interprets the constitutional text in a way that happens to be consistent with its prior decisions. Presented as a deduction from the constitutional text and unrelated to the context in which these principles arose, the *Maßstab* is

[76] Lepsius, 'Die Maßstabsetzende Gewalt'. [77] Ibid., pp. 235 et seq.

[78] See on this already, ibid., pp. 241–2, and Ulrich Haltern, *Verfassungsgerichtsbarkeit, Demokratie und Mißtrauen: Das Bundesverfassungsgericht in einer Verfassungstheorie zwischen Populismus und Progressivismus* (Berlin: Duncker & Humblot, 1998), p. 79.

[79] BVerfG, 2 BvR 2661/06 from 6.7.2010 (50).

dehistorized.[80] Even though prior cases are cited, they are no longer treated as prior cases, i.e. as decisions in particular individual conflicts that have arisen in specific historical, political, and cultural settings. Instead, they merely serve as reference points for principles that now appear to have always been part of the law. This confusion does not happen as easily in common-law jurisdictions where the judge's lawmaking role is apparent already from the language used, referring to the prior opinions of individual judges by name and often contrasting their opinions with others. Similarly—as Oliver Lepsius has pointed out—the common-law technique of distinguishing cases shifts the emphasis towards the facts involved in the relevant cases and therefore explicitly historicizes and contextualizes them.[81]

In setting out an abstract account of the law, the Court not only stabilizes its own authority as legal interpreter rather than lawmaker, but also de facto creates future legislative constraints. As a matter of law, s. 31 of the Statute regulating the Court's procedures (*Bundesverfassungsgerichtsgesetz*) provides that a holding binds not only the parties, but also other state bodies such as other courts or the legislature. This is coupled with a broad approach to what constitutes the holding. In its decision on the Basic Treaty for example, the Court declared pragmatically that its entire reasoning was relevant to the decision and thus binding.[82] Though this was only repeated once and has been heavily criticized by the academic community, the Court has tended to squeeze a lot of material into the so-called *Leitsätze* (the holding), which contain the basic legal arguments on which the decision will be based.[83]

80 Lepsius, 'Die Maßstabsetzende Gewalt', pp. 241–2.

81 Ibid., pp. 198 ff.

82 Schlaich and Korioth, *Das Bundesverfassungsgericht*, para. 488; BVerfGE 36, 1 (36).

83 See also the long 'Leitsätze' of the Court's *Hartz IV* decision, BVerfGE 125, 175: '1. The fundamental right to the guarantee of a subsistence minimum that is in line with human dignity from Article 1.1 of the Basic Law (Grundgesetz—GG) in conjunction with the principle of the social welfare state contained in Article 20.1 of the Basic Law ensures to each person in need of assistance the material prerequisites which are indispensable for his or her physical existence and for a minimum of participation in social, cultural and political life. 2. As a guarantee right, this fundamental right from Article 1.1 of the Basic Law takes on autonomous significance, in its conjunction with Article 20.1 of the Basic Law, in addition to the right from Article 1.1 of the Basic Law to respect for the dignity of each individual, which has an absolute effect. Fundamentally, it is not subject to the legislature's disposal and must be honoured; it must however be lent concrete shape, and be regularly updated, by the legislature, which has to orientate the benefits to be paid towards the respective stage of development of the polity and towards the existing conditions of life. It has latitude in bringing about this state of affairs. 3. In order to ascertain the extent of the claim, the legislature has to realistically and comprehensively assess all expenditure that is necessary for one's existence in a transparent, expedient procedure on the basis of reliable figures and plausible methods of calculation. 4. The legislature may cover the typical needs to ensure a subsistence minimum that is in line with human dignity by means of a fixed monthly amount, but must grant an additional benefit for securing a special need beyond this which is irrefutable, recurrent and not merely a single instance.'

But even independently of the holding, the Court's reasoning will have significant practical effects: Lower courts, administrators, and legislators will usually take the Court's reasoning into account in their own practice in order to avoid being overturned in the future. The broader and deeper the Court's reasoning in a given case, the more it will therefore determine what other courts and legislatures can or cannot do. In an expert-driven culture such as the German, this influence is immense. What the Court says or does not say matters in many ways more than whether or not the Court declares a statute unconstitutional. In the latter case, after all, it is only thwarting parliamentary will in one individual case. But when it develops its broad and deep 'standards', it automatically restricts the room for democratic decision-making (and judicial deliberation of other courts) in the future.

IV. Proportionality analysis

Proportionality analysis is one of Germany's most important legal exports, having become popular in a wide range of jurisdictions around the world. Proportionality takes different forms and shapes in different jurisdictions, but it also fulfils a particularly important function in transformative legal systems and hierarchical cultures of authority. Its usefulness in hierarchical systems may be surprising, since proportionality with its balancing test is often accused of being insufficiently legal, especially in the United States, though not only there.[84] Yet, in creating the appearance of consistency across cases and allowing courts to appear neutral and give credit to both sides, proportionality can be reconciled with the demands of hierarchical systems. Moreover, its openness can be constrained by rights-specific doctrine, as we will see.

So how does proportionality work in Germany? To begin with, proportionality analysis represents the last stage of any limitations analysis and is concerned with the question whether the *limitation* (*Beschränkung*) of a right is proportional to its pursued objective. If it is, the limitation can be justified. If it is not, the limitation becomes an unconstitutional *violation* (*Verletzung*) of a right. German proportionality proceeds in four steps. The first question is whether the limitation of a right serves a *legitimate purpose*, a hurdle that is interpreted generously by the Court. Second, the limitation of a right must be *suitable* to achieve this purpose and, third, represent the *least restrictive means* of doing so. Finally, proportionality requires the *balancing* between

[84] Or Bassok, 'The Supreme Court's New Source of Legitimacy', *University of Pennsylvania Journal of Constitutional Law*, 16 (2013), 153.

the limitation of the right in question and the governmental interest in doing so, i.e. the benefits resulting from the limitation of rights.

Unlike, for example, in South Africa,[85] these four steps are understood strictly consecutively—i.e. if the measure fails one hurdle, the analysis ends and the limitation of a right is deemed an unconstitutional violation of this right. German proportionality analysis is in this regard more structured and may appear more typically legal than elsewhere. Yet, if we compare which steps different courts emphasize, we will see that it is not. Perhaps surprisingly, it is the last two steps and in particular the balancing analysis that lead to the most invalidations in German constitutional jurisprudence.[86] In contrast, in Canada[87] for example, the balancing test represents proportionality's most contested component because it appears most political and least legal. Yet as we have previously observed the German Court has never eschewed broad or vague concepts, and balancing is no different. And here, too, appearances help: With its neat structure that remains consistent across a wide range of cases, proportionality is both flexible and legal enough for German lawyers.

The basis for this multi-functionality lies in its historical development out of two rather different strands of German law: one more liberal and formalist, the other anti-formalist and activist.[88] Prussian courts had initially developed a general principle of proportionality as a means of regulating police action[89] They emphasized the least restrictive means test and applied proportionality altogether in a comparatively rigid and formalist manner. The second important component of proportionality, the balancing between different values or rights, was developed in the school of Interest Jurisprudence, a successor of the German Free Law school which had at its core the idea of balancing different interests and was now infused with a dose of Smend's more value-based understanding.[90]

[85] Kevin Iles, 'A Fresh Look at Limitations: Unpacking Section 36', *South African Journal on Human Rights*, 23 (2007), 68.

[86] Dieter Grimm, 'Proportionality in Canadian and German Constitutional Jurisprudence', *University of Toronto Law Journal*, 57 (2007), 383 and 389.

[87] Grimm, 'Proportionality'.

[88] For the details of this paragraph, see Moshe Cohen-Eliya and Iddo Porat, 'American Balancing and German Proportionality: The Historical Origins', *International Journal of Constitutional Law*, 8 (2010), 276.

[89] Ibid.

[90] See also Bomhoff, *Balancing Constitutional Rights*, pp. 102 et seq. (see also Chapter 2 for an account of Interest Jurisprudence); for another detailed historical overview, see Moshe Cohen-Eliya and Iddo Porat, *Proportionality and Constitutional Culture* (Cambridge: Cambridge University Press, 2013).

The adoption of proportionality by the German Constitutional Court did not originate from any deep theoretical point about the nature of rights in the first place, but came initially without any explanation of its origin,[91] with many of the early decisions confining themselves in somewhat laconic style to stating that the measure in question was also proportional.[92] With its turn to values in *Lüth*, the Court introduced balancing. This was not accidental. The concept of rights as values meant ultimately that their application would be subject only to the concern for other values or public interests; to weigh these different interests or values therefore appeared a natural solution in determining their application in concrete cases. Only in its 1961 *Pharmacies* judgment, the Court finally developed proportionality in more detail, including a least-restrictive means test as well as a balancing requirement.[93]

Proportionality analysis would ultimately be applied routinely across a wide range of topics and cases. This is a valuable property in every legal system—hence its universal popularity—but is especially valuable in transformative systems where new legal questions arise constantly. Because it is sufficiently flexible and does not determine results, it offers an ideal framework to structure legal analysis even in dealing with new issues. Moreover, in spite of this flexibility, it can also be reconciled with a hierarchical legal culture because it provides an appearance of legal consistency: As Stone-Sweet has pointed out, it suggests that 'it is not the law that varies from case to case, but the facts or decision-making context'.[94]

Nor is proportionality just a legal facade for making political choices. In providing a structure that necessarily honours the positions of both parties and considers the arguments for and against their positions, it does not only 'bestow a sheen of politico-ideological neutrality on the Court', but also has real value.[95] Once again, this makes proportionality attractive in many jurisdictions, but especially those that value and trust in legal autonomy and the apolitical nature of courts. With its consideration for both sides, proportionality fits particularly well with an important traditional strand of German constitutional theory, the idea of integration through constitutional law, most famously expressed in the work of Rudolf Smend.[96] This

[91] Grimm, 'Proportionality', pp. 383 et seq.

[92] In these early decisions, the principle had little structure at all and its meaning shifted between something akin to a least-restrictive means test and a balancing of interests.

[93] BVerfGE 7, 377.

[94] Alec Stone-Sweet, 'All Things in Proportion? American Rights Doctrine and the Problem of Balancing', *Emory Law Journal*, 60 (2011), 797, 807 for the quotation.

[95] Ibid., p. 807.

[96] Rudolf Smend, *Verfassung und Verfassungsrecht* (1928); see also for a good secondary account, Bomhoff, *Balancing Constitutional Rights*, pp. 93 et seq.

intellectual tradition was later continued in the work of Konrad Hesse,[97] who argued that balancing should strive for what he called 'practical concordance' by optimally realizing both values at stake. More recent US research on cultural cognition provides some empirical support for this, as well as for Stone-Sweet's neutrality thesis of proportionality. In particular, Dan Kahan has argued that a way to solve the US Supreme Court's enduring neutrality crisis,[98] where citizens perceive the Court as political and non-neutral, is for justices to display 'a plurality of cultural meanings'. By this he means that the Justices should avoid strong statements of absolute security of their position and instead engage seriously with the opponents' ideas.[99] This suggestion is not radically new or surprising, but Kahan bases his conclusions on psychological studies of motivated reasoning, which demonstrate that individuals tend to observe facts differently depending on their worldview and prevailing cultural perceptions of their group. His research shows that they are likely to mistrust declarations of neutrality or objectivity from groups or individuals of generally antagonistic worldviews. As citizens often perceive the Supreme Court as a politicized institution, he argues that the Court may best overcome this cognitive bias if it manages to engage seriously with a plurality of cultural positions, therefore making it harder to identify its reasoning with any one position. While Kahan's research is set in a highly divisive political context, his argument has validity beyond that context. In light of this research, the necessary discussion and weighing of the different positions within the framework of proportionality analysis appears as an ideal instrument to stabilize the Court's authority.

Moreover, critics who accuse proportionality of being too political and indeterminate tend to exaggerate this, and conversely to underestimate the flexibility and openness of US-style constitutional tests.[100] The shifting jurisprudence on the first amendment,[101] the unclear divisions between strict and intermediate scrutiny and rational-basis review,[102] as well as numerous other examples[103] illustrate the de facto flexibility of US constitutional doctrine

[97] Konrad Hesse, *Grundzüge des Verfassungsrechts der Bundesrepublik Deutschland*, 20th edn (Heidelberg: C. F. Müller, 1999), p. 72. Konrad Hesse was one of the most famous constitutional theorists at his time and Justice of the Constitutional Court in the late 1970s and 1980s.

[98] BVerfGE 34, 269; see more on this case in Chapter 5.

[99] Dan M. Kahan, 'The Supreme Court 2010 Term—Foreword: Neutral Principles, Motivated Cognition, and Some Problems for Constitutional Law', *Harvard Law Review*, 125 (2011), 1.

[100] Stone-Sweet, 'All Things in Proportion?'.

[101] See e.g. Robert C. Post, 'Racist Speech, Democracy, and the First Amendment', *William and Mary Law Review*, 32 (1990), 267.

[102] See e.g. Richard H. Fallon, Jr., 'Strict Judicial Scrutiny', *UCLA Law Review*, 54 (2006), 1267.

[103] See Kristin M. Engstrom, 'Establishment Clause Jurisprudence: The Souring of Lemon and the Search for a New Test', *Pacific Law Journal*, 27 (1995), 121.

which moreover often strongly resembles proportionality arguments.[104] German proportionality analysis also leaves ample room for right-specific doctrines to fill in the details. Judicial precedents and scholarship often provide guidance that structure proportionality's subtests in more detail, for example by providing arguments that are particularly relevant when balancing rights, e.g. the value of free speech for democracy. As a result, proportionality analysis becomes more determinate than its bare structure would suggest and than its critics sometimes assume. Take as an example the Court's analysis in a case where the government had infringed the right to privacy in order to allow for the collection of data, which did not comply with the principle of proportionality. The Court recounted a number of factors it had established in its prior jurisprudence that increase the weight of the specific infringement of the right to privacy in this kind of case. Among those were the specific method of data collection 'from complex information technology systems (see re such cases for instance BVerfGE 113, 29; 115, 166; 117, 244)', the fact that individuals may be affected by the surveillance who may be merely 'communication partners of the target person ... (see on telecommunication surveillance BVerfGE 113, 348 (382–383); furthermore BVerfGE 34, 238 (247); 107, 299 (321))', and finally, the 'secrecy of state encroachment measures' which are 'the exception in a state based on the rule of law, and (...) require(s) special justification (see Federal Constitutional Court, Order of 13 June 2007–1 BvR 1550/03 et al. –, Neue Juristische Wochenschrift 2007, p. 2464 (2469–2470))'. Of course, the existence of such a pre-structure does not rule out the consideration of new factors, but then again, law is never entirely determinate. With its openness towards broad ethical and political considerations and its consistent structure across cases and concern for both sides, proportionality is therefore in many ways the doctrinal heart of Value Formalism.

V. Appearances and reality

Much of this suggests that hierarchical features in German constitutional law are mainly serving to convey certain appearances: The rarity of dissents and the deductive style of reasoning suggest that law is determinate. Some political scientists such as Alec Stone-Sweet have therefore treated important features of European constitutional review as a trick on the part of European judges to conceal the 'crisis of legitimacy' resulting from the divergence between the reality of constitutional review and the Kelsenian idea of judges

[104] See Stone-Sweet, 'All Things in Proportion?', pp. 844–5.

as only negative lawmakers. In the characteristic spirit of a political scientist, Stone-Sweet is impatient with the European insistence on a long-outdated idea of judging and calls for a more realistic theory that acknowledges that 'constitutional law is developed within interpretative communities, comprised not only of constitutional judges, but also of legislators, administrators, ordinary judges, scholars, and the interested public'.[105] While I find this picture appealing and accept the value of theories that engage with these issues, it is important to recognize that in cultivating its particular image, the Court participates in a deeper hierarchical legal culture with a specific approach to legal education, the selection of judges, and reliance on legal scholarship for judicial reasoning—features that go beyond the mere presentation of a certain picture to the public.

Moreover, there is at least a plausible argument to be made that maintaining certain appearances drives reality to develop in certain ways. This argument is related to a widespread claim in the literature that US Legal Realism and attitudinal studies may have become self-fulfilling prophecies in the United States.[106] There are good reasons to treat these claims as at least partly correct and to assume that the German insistence on legal certainty may indeed make legal interpretation more certain and predictable. To begin with, the German emphasis on legal certainty has been shown to influence procedural mechanisms and thereby in fact to influence the degree of predictability of German judicial decision-making.[107] But the effects of a strong emphasis on legal certainty cannot be confined to changes in procedural provisions. Drawing on psychological studies of self-fulfilling prophecies, Scott Altman argues, for example, that introspection of judges into their hidden, non-positivist motivations for deciding cases might well incline them to cynicism, creating the impression that 'anything goes', which would be detrimental to the idea of rational jurisprudence and legal certainty.[108] Conversely, we may assume that belief in the possibility of legal certainty and constant effort to make the legal system more determinate can contribute to an actual increase in its determinacy. If judges believe that there exists a right or at least a best answer to every legal question, they may be more willing to make an effort to determine this answer and to discard personal ideological

[105] Alec Stone-Sweet, *Governing with Judges: Constitutional Politics in Europe* (Oxford: Oxford University Press, 2000), p. 132.

[106] See e.g. Möllers, *Die drei Gewalten*, p. 103; James R. Maxeiner, 'Legal Certainty: A European Alternative to American Legal Indeterminacy?', *Tulane Journal of International and Comparative Law*, 15 (2007), 541–607.

[107] Maxeiner, 'Legal Certainty', pp. 553 et seq.

[108] See Scott Altman, 'Beyond Candor', *Michigan Law Review*, 89 (1990), 296; differently Posner, *How Judges Think*, pp. 120–1.

preferences for the sake of another solution that better fits existing legal doctrine and the legal system as a whole.

D. Conclusion

Value Formalism represents the successful synthesis of two different intellectual paradigms: an idea of transformative law and a hierarchical culture of authority. In reconciling these different strands of legal thought, it creates its own particular style of jurisprudence. Rooted in a transformative, comprehensive understanding of the Basic Law, German constitutional reasoning tends to be both broad and deep with a strong teleological bias, often more focused on setting out the 'objective' constitutional meaning than solving individual conflicts. At the same time, this breadth is contained by the dry deductive style and the abstract decontextualized categories of a hierarchical culture, which highly value legal autonomy. Legalistic and expansive, Value Formalism underwrites the power of the German Constitutional Court.

5

Judicial Self-reflection and Institutional Awareness

If we want to understand the German Constitutional Court's authority in contemporary political culture, we must look at the way the Court presents itself in its jurisprudence. In the previous chapters, we have seen how German constitutional law is conceptualized as a science to be dealt with by professionals, thus feeding into a broader German culture of hierarchical authority. It is now time to explore the hierarchical aspect of the Court's self-understanding in more detail. In other words: How does the Court view and describe its own role vis-à-vis other institutions in its jurisprudence? And does this affect how expansive its judgments are?

These questions are connected to the way in which the Court divides legal from political questions. In Chapter 3, we have seen that German lawyers' standard answer is that legal questions are different from political ones only as a matter of methodology, but not as a matter of subject field. A legal question can be answered in terms of law, by drawing on legal arguments. And this, we might say, is in keeping with recent trends that have seen a number of jurisdictions rejecting an explicit political question doctrine; or perhaps more precisely: that many jurisdictions increasingly pick out only one of the components of the political question doctrine in its formulation in *Baker*[1] (the lack of legal standards to decide a question) as relevant. Even in its home country, the United States, the political question doctrine no longer plays the important role it used to play.[2] All this represents a growing global consensus that there should be no realms of power unchecked by law.[3] We have become used to what Etienne Mureinik once famously called 'a culture of

[1] *Baker v Carr*, 369 US 186 (1962).

[2] Marc Tushnet, 'Law and Prudence in the Law of Justiciability: the Transformation and Disappearance of the Political Question Doctrine', *North Carolina Law Review*, 80 (2001), 1203.

[3] Rachel E. Barkow, 'More Supreme than Court? The Fall of the Political Question Doctrine and the Rise of Judicial Supremacy', *Columbia Law Review*, 102 (2002), 237.

justification';[4] we expect that governments are accountable not only through elections, but also through law. Partly, it also represents the trend towards more transformative understandings of constitutionalism. The idea of comprehensive legal accountability—be it when governments restrain the rights of individuals or when they do not do enough to guarantee these rights—is part and parcel of transformative law.

Nevertheless, the slow demise of the political question doctrine has prompted new questions, which are scarcely addressed in current scholarship and which I can only touch upon here. In countries like the United States that follow a more coordinate model of authority, courts naturally share their powers with other institutions and thus are in constant need of finding an equilibrium. In this context, courts tend to be institutionally aware and to justify more explicitly in their jurisprudence why *they* are getting involved as opposed to other institutions. This tends to be different, however, in more hierarchical cultures where courts inhabit a firmer position within a particular hierarchy of institutions; here, their place is clear and so there is less to say about their role. This does not mean that courts in hierarchical systems may not have some doctrine that tells judges when and where to exercise self-restraint as a means of dividing law from politics. But if—for whatever reasons—there is no such doctrinally entrenched way of conceptualizing self-restraint, then hierarchical courts will typically not feel the need to discuss their own role; only strong political pressure in high-profile cases may then force them to engage more with questions of self-restraint and institutional legitimacy.

This at least, I argue, is what has happened in the German case. The security of the Court's position comes at a price. This price is not usually that the Court will be overly expansive when the political stakes are high and it operates under political pressure. Rather, the risk is that it will do so in the run-of-the-mill type of cases where there is no such strong political pressure. Moreover, even when the Court does defer to other institutions, it is often not able to adequately engage with the institutional questions arising and explain in a more detailed way why it defers. Attracting international attention for its potentially disastrous consequences for the European fiscal policy, the German Court's recent jurisprudence in this field illustrates this lack of a consistent concept of judicial self-restraint that can explain in any principled way why the Court defers when it does and when it won't. But this is only the end of a development that goes back to the Court's first years.

[4] Etienne Mureinik, 'A Bridge to Where? Introducing the Interim Bill of Rights', *South African Journal on Human Rights*, 10 (1994), 31, 32.

A. A Political Question Doctrine?

When the German Court saw itself confronted with the divisive question of German rearmament in the 1950s (see Chapter 2), the Justices debated whether they might draw on a political question doctrine to decline jurisdiction. Internal memos provide evidence that a number of judges including Zweigert and Leibholz advocated the adoption of such a doctrine that would exempt certain questions entirely from the Court's jurisdiction.[5] When the Treaty on the French–German Defence Union was eventually rejected by the French parliament, however, the issue became moot. The Court could therefore avoid deciding whether it should adopt a political question doctrine. As it tackled a number of highly political questions in the following years and never made recourse to a political question doctrine, it finally became established doctrine that the Basic Law left no room for such a concept.

So at least many of the Court's Justices in the early 1960s seemed to think. At the annual public law professors' meeting in 1961, a young constitutional scholar, Horst Ehmke, who had spent considerable time in the United States, urged the Court to consider in its interpretation of rights what he called 'functional–legal' (*funktionell–rechtliche*) aspects. Functional–legal considerations were meant to address the function of judicial review and the role of the Constitutional Court and other state organs in the interpretation of constitutional law. Drawing on US constitutional law, Ehmke emphasized the value of a political question doctrine and a doctrine of preferred freedoms. He criticized the Court's broad interpretation of liberty in the *Elfes* as well as the *Pharmacies* case for overreaching and a lack of deference.[6] His suggestions, however, did not fare well with the majority of the participants or with the three Justices of the Constitutional Court, Ernst Friesenhahn, Gerhard Leibholz, and Martin Drath, who were present at the meeting. In particular, Leibholz had now made up his mind against a political question doctrine. He criticized the lack of justiciable criteria to determine whether a question was political or legal and suggested that every issue falling within the scope of legal norms be treated as legal.[7] The two other Justices, Friesenhahn and

[5] Justin Collings, *Democracy's Guardians: A History of the German Federal Constitutional Court 1951–2001* (Oxford: Oxford University Press, forthcoming 2015), chapter 1 (II. A.) for more details. This concept of a political question doctrine also seemed to hold a certain attraction for the Court's then president Höpker-Aschoff, ibid.

[6] Horst Ehmke, 'Prinzipien der Verfassungsinterpretation', *Vereinigung der deutschen Staatsrechtslehrer*, 20 (1963), 74 et seq.

[7] Ibid., discussion Gerhard Leibholz, 117 et seq.

Drath, argued that the Basic Law unlike the US Constitution did not lend itself to a political question doctrine.[8]

Their approach eventually became accepted. In an interview in 1999, the Court's former president Ernst Benda argued again that a political question doctrine was to be rejected 'because it would politicize the Court' by forcing it to make a decision 'which was itself not legal, but political'.[9] It also foreshadowed later arguments against a functional–legal approach that would take a more institutional perspective on legal interpretation. Ingrained in this position is the transformative idea of the constitution as a comprehensive roadmap for state action that leaves no realms of power untainted by law. It is not accidental that the South African Constitutional Court has similarly never explicitly referred to a political question doctrine and that South African judges have rejected its adoption with the argument that '[i]n a substantive constitutional state such as ours, there can be no so-called "political question" doctrine leading to a conclusion different to that dictated by the Constitution'.[10]

B. Institutional Awareness

Scholars have, however, pointed out that the German Court has in the past referred to arguments in its decisions that are in the United States part of the political question doctrine as formulated in Baker.[11] If this is true, then maybe the issue is terminological and whether courts adopt an explicit political question doctrine matters little?

It is certainly not important how we label arguments about self-restraint or political discretion. Nor, for that matter, are the exact doctrinal categories, according to which a court will exercise restraint, particularly important. Whether the German Court hence grants legislative or executive discretion in the exact *same* terms as a political question doctrine would, reflects to some degree political and historical contingencies. What we should care

[8] Ibid., discussion Ernst Friesenhahn and Martin Drath, 121, 127 ff.

[9] Interview with Ernst Benda by the Bavarian Broadcasting Agency (*Bayrischer Rundfunk*), 27 April 1999.

[10] Lourens W. H. Ackermann, 'Opening Remarks on the Conference Theme', in Jonathan Klaaren (ed.), *A Delicate Balance: The Place of the Judiciary in a Constitutional Democracy* (Cape Town: SiberInk, 2006), quoted according to Theunis Roux, 'Principle and Pragmatism on the Constitutional Court of South Africa', *International Journal of Constitutional Law*, 7(1) (2009), 106–38, fn. 160.

[11] Christian Rau, *Selbst entwickelte Grenzen in der Rechtsprechung des United States Supreme Court und des Bundesverfassungsgerichts* (Berlin: Duncker & Humblot, 1996).

about, however, is whether there is *some* doctrinally entrenched way of asking and addressing the Court's own role and, alongside it, the questions of self-restraint and legislative discretion. This, I contend, is not the case in the German Court's jurisprudence. Though there are some recurring arguments for legislative and executive discretion in the Court's jurisprudence, they do not amount to a fully fledged legal doctrine that is consistently applied and structures the legal inquiry to come. Of course, a legal-realist sceptic might point out that courts are never entirely consistent and doctrine does not decide cases anyway. There are two replies to this challenge: For once, the more deeply entrenched a doctrine is, the more consistently courts will usually apply it. In the German case, proportionality, for example, represents a strongly entrenched doctrine that is constantly applied in the Court's jurisprudence—so much so, that it is now unthinkable that the Court might suddenly decide to forego it. Second, while doctrine may not decide cases, it still structures legal argument and provides a particular way of thinking about certain questions. It draws attention to certain facts, but not to others, and this is important.

Courts in coordinate legal cultures may have less need for a particular doctrine on self-restraint because they share their authority with other institutions and therefore constantly need to justify what they are doing and why. In hierarchical systems, however, courts are more isolated from other institutions and their legitimacy rests on their professional expertise and independence, which renders their authority more stable. They are therefore not in the same way confronted with the expectation to address questions of legitimacy. Absent any entrenched doctrine that routinely forces the issue of self-restraint onto the judicial agenda therefore, hierarchical courts will often shy away from considering, let alone openly addressing, this question. It is therefore not surprising if the German Court only rarely and inconsistently engages with its own role vis-à-vis other institutions in any explicit way. As a result, its judgments read very differently to the US Supreme Court's, which often engage in detail with the institutional questions at stake, even when not drawing on a political question doctrine.

This is particularly true when the German Court engages with the interpretation of *rights*. This is because rights cases deal typically with the *product* of institutional action: the law or the administrative act that violates rights. As a result, the institutional questions themselves do not naturally arise in the legal analysis, except for the rare cases where there are explicit procedural or organizational flaws in the law or act in question. The legal questions that arise are therefore substantive questions, whether rights may justifiably be limited or not. But before we turn to analysing the Court's rights' jurisprudence, how does it approach its own role in organizational conflicts?

I. Organizational and institutional conflicts

Organizational and institutional conflicts address by nature primarily questions of institutional boundaries and competences. As a result, the German Court cannot avoid addressing institutional questions in the same way as in rights cases. And at least implicitly, such cases often raise questions about the Court's own relationship to other institutions. The Court can address its own role mainly through two different avenues: The obvious way is to develop standards for legislative discretion and vice versa judicial self-restraint; the second, less common route is to draw on existing state practice in the interpretation of constitutional norms. The German Court uses both of these methods in its organizational cases, albeit only to a limited degree.

1. Considering state practice

The German Court will sometimes invoke state practice as a supporting argument for a particular understanding of a constitutional norm. However, it is hard to say how much state practice actually matters given that it is typically used in support of other arguments. The Court's language suggests that state practice will not be able to overcome what the Court otherwise considers a better understanding of the Basic Law. For state practice is the

> object not the review standard of its constitutional evaluation. Certainly, tradition and practice as they have been developed over time must be considered in interpreting (an institution's) rules of procedure. This, however, only implies that a state practice that keeps within the constitutional framework may not be replaced by a judicial interpretation, even if it thinks it preferable. Moreover, when doubts arise over the meaning of a norm state practice must be taken into account. State practice cannot, however, replace clear constitutional standards or those gained by interpreting a constitutional norm.[12]

Given this, it is hard to determine how much influence state practice actually has on the results. At least in some cases, however, the reference to state practice seems to have cashed out in a more lenient degree of judicial scrutiny, such as when the Court was dealing with the dissolution of the German Bundestag, which it upheld in spite of the largely strategic nature of this move by both Helmut Kohl and later, Gerhard Schröder.[13]

[12] BVerfGE 91, 148.

[13] BVerfGE 61, 1 and 114, 121. These and some other cases have led to the claim that the Court decreases its scrutiny when dealing with a certain core of executive competences (Rau, *Selbst entwickelte Grenzen*, pp. 190 et seq.), but this claim is hard to sustain considering that there is little in the reasoning of these cases to suggest such a more comprehensive approach.

2. *Foreign policy discretion*

Foreign policy decisions form an important part of the Court's institutional and organizational conflicts. As elsewhere, foreign policy has long been considered in German doctrine a field where the government enjoys particularly large discretion.[14] This is especially apparent in some of its early judgments, such as the decision on the Saar-Statut where the Court stated that a political treaty that replaced occupational regimes with another temporary political regime was only justiciable insofar as *central principles* of the Basic Law (Art. 79 or Art. 19) would otherwise be clearly violated.[15] However, the Saar decision would not turn out to be representative for the Court's later jurisprudence. For even in the field of foreign policy, the German Court has often shown remarkably little institutional awareness, though it has ultimately been strategic and restrained itself where necessary.

The reason for this is that the Court has never developed a fully fledged doctrine on legislative discretion. There is hence no routine requirement for the Court to engage with this question seriously on a regular basis and its jurisprudence therefore remains highly inconsistent. Not only is it hard to say in advance when and where the Court may discuss legislative discretion, but even when it does, such passages are often mere rhetorical gestures. Its expansive understanding of the Basic Law means that the Court will find broad criteria and categories to subject foreign policy to judicial scrutiny even in the absence of constitutional standards. Strategic considerations and, sometimes, political pressure, however, ultimately force the Court to backpedal, leaving it to dodge questions entirely or take refuge in gestures of deference not backed up by any more coherent doctrine. Take as a first example the Court's perhaps most famous foreign policy decisions in its history, the decision on the Basic Treaty, which also contains one of the rare explicit statements on the Court's own role.

a) The Basic Treaty decision

The Basic Treaty sought to reform West Germany's relationship with the GDR and was part of the global attempt at a detente between East and West in the aftermath of the Cuban missile crisis. In it, the West German government acknowledged for the first time a limited sovereignty of the GDR

[14] See e.g. BVerfGE 4, 157 (on the Saar-Statut); BVerfGE 36, 1 (about the *Grundlagenvertrag*) and BVerfG, 2 BvE 4/11 vom 19.6.2012 (on the measures taken with regard to the European financial crisis). See also for a discussion Rau, *Selbst entwickelte Grenzen*, pp. 171 et seq.

[15] BVerfGE 4, 157.

in exchange for the lifting of certain travel restrictions and the facilitation of family reunions, among other things.[16] This incensed the Christian Democrats because it suggested a break with long-established West German foreign policy doctrine (the so-called Hallstein doctrine, named after an undersecretary of the German Foreign Office). According to this doctrine, Germany would not recognize East Germany as a separate state, nor would it recognize other states which recognized the East German government. The idea behind this doctrine was to avoid that Germany's separation would over time become a both politically and legally accepted state of affairs. Christian Democrats now feared that with the Basic Treaty, Chancellor Brandt was giving away too much. Some of them argued that this violated the Basic Law's preamble that included reunification as a 'directive principle'. And even though Brandt had just won the federal elections with a clear majority for his coalition government and an electoral campaign that had centred on his foreign policy reforms, the Bavarian government challenged the treaty, which was still being negotiated, before the Court.[17] Brandt's administration showed little patience for the judicial proceedings. Feeling justified to push on with the ongoing treaty negotiations, it indicated it was not giving the Constitutional Court much time to decide on the matter. Around the same time, a disrespectful statement of a member of Brandt's inner circle ('I won't let the eight assholes in Karlsruhe destroy my Ostpolitik') was circulated in the press.[18]

The Court ultimately upheld the treaty. It did so, however, only after an expansive reading of the Basic Law's preamble, whose justiciability was strongly contested. From the preamble, it deduced a number of conditions concerning the interpretation of the treaty and the future conduct of East–West relations. It emphasized that

> no constitutional organ of the Federal Republic of Germany may abandon restoration of national unity as a political goal, that all constitutional organs are obliged in their policy to work towards attaining this goal—which includes the requirement to maintain the claim to reunification alive domestically and vigorously defend it externally—and refrain from anything that might prevent reunification.[19]

[16] Heinrich A. Winkler, *Der lange Weg nach Westen. Deutsche Geschichte vom 'Dritten Reich' bis zur Wiedervereinigung* (München: C. H. Beck, 2000), pp. 307 et seq.

[17] Ibid., pp. 308–9.

[18] Rolf Lamprecht, *Ich gehe bis nach Karlsruhe: Eine Geschichte des Bundesverfassungsgerichts* (München: DVA, 2001), p. 148.

[19] BVerfGE 36, 1 (headnotes), translation by University of Texas Law School, Institute for Transnational Law, available at: <http://www.utexas.edu/law/academics/centers/transnational/work_new/german/case.php?id=589>.

At the same time, it acknowledged that the government was free to decide how best to fulfil its obligation to seek re-unification, announcing that it would only control the outer limits of the government's discretion.[20] Outlining its own role in rare detail, the Justices pointed out that,

> (a)mong the interpretive principles important particularly in connection with the constitutional review of treaties is also that in interpreting constitutional provisions relating to the Federal Republic's relationships with other States, their demarcatory character, that is the room for manoeuvre they allow in policy making, ought not to be left out of account. In this demarcation the Basic Law sets legal limits to every political power, in the area of foreign policy too; this is the essence of the rule of law constituted by the Basic Law. The implementation of this constitutional order is incumbent ultimately on the Federal Constitutional Court.[21] The principle of judicial self-restraint that the Federal Constitutional Court imposes on itself does not mean a curtailment or weakening of its powers as just set out, but refraining from 'playing politics,' that is, intervening in the area of free policy making set up and demarcated by the Constitution. It accordingly aims at keeping the leeway for free policy making guaranteed by the Constitution for the other constitutional organs open.[22]

Note that the Court's emphasis on the Basic Law's demarcatory character and the notion of judicial self-restraint suggested a low standard of scrutiny and concern for its own role and the boundaries of its power. The following lines revealed this, however, to be an empty rhetorical gesture. The Court's decision is—at least with some temporal distance[23]—taken by many scholars and politicians to be one of its most expansive judgements based on a broadly formulated preamble as the sole doctrinal basis from which the Court drew very concrete prescriptions for the conduct of foreign policy.[24] Nor did the Court provide any indication what the 'demarcatory character' of constitutional norms implied, except the idea that the Court must not play politics, which remains again an empty formula.

[20] Among those outer limits, however, it counted the prohibition to yield any legal titles that served the aim of reunification or create new titles that could be invoked against it in the future, BVerfGE 36, 1.

[21] BVerfGE 36, 1 (74); translation by University of Texas Law School, Institute for Transnational Law, available at: <http://www.utexas.edu/law/academics/centers/transnational/work_new/german/case.php?id=589>.

[22] Ibid.

[23] The initial reactions were more mixed insofar as all sides declared victory to save face, see Richard Häußler, *Der Konflikt zwischen Bundesverfassungsgericht und politischer Führung* (Berlin: Duncker & Humblot, 1994), p. 64.

[24] Klaus J. Grigoleit, *Bundesverfassungsgericht und deutsche Frage. Eine dogmatische und historische Untersuchung zum judikativen Anteil an der Staatsleitung* (Tübingen: Mohr Siebeck, 2004), p. 284 with further references.

b) Dealing with the European financial crisis

Ever since European markets collapsed in the wake of the 2008–9 financial crisis, economic debates about how to respond to the crisis have been dividing Europeans. Like no other court else, the German Constitutional Court has participated in this debate and frequently threatened to invalidate the financial measures taken to rescue in particular the Greek economy, even though it has ultimately never (yet) done so. And here, too, its jurisprudence exhibits the by now familiar tendency towards an expansive interpretation of the Basic Law coupled with pragmatic deference. As a matter of law, its judgments in this field are based on the right to vote, but functionally they concern institutional and organizational questions since they discuss the limits of European integration and parliamentary powers. The Court has read the right to vote as a right to vote for a parliament that can still make meaningful political decisions and is not entirely sidelined by European institutions. It has argued that this also implies that the German Bundestag may not relinquish its budgetary autonomy by binding itself in a way that leaves it no room for political decision-making in the future.[25] This fits into a broader pattern of jurisprudence aimed at strengthening the powers of the Bundestag, both in the realm of foreign policy[26] and in internal matters (see Chapter 3). This emphasis on the Bundestag often operates to the detriment of other, especially supranational institutions such as the European parliament[27] or, more recently, the European Central Bank (ECB).[28] Yet, when it comes to determining its own relationship with the legislature, the Court's jurisprudence varies strongly.

In its most recent decision on the European financial stabilization mechanism, the Court deferred very explicitly to the legislature.[29] It stressed that it would only interfere if the parliament had taken over legal obligations that would *legally* oblige it to take over unspecified financial obligations for the future and it subjected *factual* risks merely to an evidence control, i.e. whether they evidently bound the Bundestag in its financial autonomy for the future. Yet, it adopted a different tone in evaluating the ECB's decision to consider purchasing government bonds of selected Member States under certain conditions (OMT-decision) in order to stabilize their economies. For one thing, the Court now applied a different,

[25] See more later in the chapter.

[26] See e.g. the decisions on out-of-area missions of the German military, BVerfGE 90, 286 or in the realm of European integration, BVerfGE 89, 155.

[27] BVerfGE 123, 267.

[28] BVerfG, 2 BvR 1390/12, decision of 18 March 2014.

[29] Ibid.

very high standard of review towards the ECB (para. 58), thereby interfering in a highly contested economic debate and displaying a lack of sensitivity in assessing the powers of other institutions besides parliament.[30] In particular, the Court's argument for adopting a high standard of scrutiny appears somewhat ironic in this regard: Emphasizing that independent bodies such as the Central Bank constitute an exception to the democratic principle and their mandate must therefore be interpreted narrowly, one wonders why this should not equally apply to the Constitutional Court itself. Second, the Court's analysis must be read in light of the fact that the plaintiffs had essentially asked the government to 'do something' against another institution's transgression of its mandate. As one of the two dissenters in the case, Justice Lübbe-Wolff, argued, the complaint should therefore have been declared inadmissible. For '(h)ow Bundestag and Federal Government are to react to a violation, martial or non-martial, of German sovereign rights is a question that cannot reasonably by answered by rules making certain predetermined positive actions mandatory' (Lübbe-Wolff).[31] Then again, the Court ultimately decided to involve the European Court of Justice (ECJ), not touching on the question of remedies and thus keeping a way open to avoid future conflict if necessary.[32] Other decisions on the financial crisis have proceeded among similarly inconsistent lines—some with explicit consideration for the government's and the Bundestag's discretion, others nearly completely silent on this and dodging some of the most important questions.[33]

Even in the realm of foreign policy, therefore, the German Court has not managed to develop any more consistent, explicit doctrine of judicial deference. Though it will in practice not put large obstacles in the way of foreign policy initiatives, its reasoning often starts from an expansive conception of constitutional rights that contributes to the development of sometimes quite detailed standards of conduct for foreign policy.

[30] Ibid. For a more detailed English analysis, see Matthias Goldmann, 'Adjudicating Economics? Central Bank Independence and the Appropriate Standard of Judicial Review', *German Law Journal*, 15 (2014), 265.

[31] BVerfG, 2 BvR 1390/12, decision of 18 March 2014, dissenting vote Justice Lübbe-Wolff, para. 12.

[32] The ECJ has recently upheld the OMT decision, European Court of Justice, C-62/14, 16 June 2015. It will have to be seen how the German Court now reacts to this ruling.

[33] See especially BVerfG, 7 September 2011, NVwZ 2011, 1515; BVerfG, 16 June 2012, NVwZ 2012, 954; BVerfG, 12 September 2012, NJW 2012, 3145 ff. See for a discussion of the 2011 case the interview with Christoph Möllers on the Verfassungsblog (7 September 2011), <http://www.verfassungsblog.de/de/die-vorlage-ware-die-saubere-losung-gewesen/#.UhyyCWT09cQ>.

II. Rights' review

If the Court's jurisprudence on foreign policy—a traditional area of low-level review or even non-justiciability in most jurisdictions—varies in its attention to institutional roles, its rights' decisions are even less open to this kind of argument. This applies both with regard to its style of reasoning and its development of standards for legislative discretion.

To begin with, references to constitutional or state practice hardly play any role in the Court's reasoning in rights cases. Between 1998 and 2014 only a handful of decisions mention state practice in the context of fundamental rights at all. Moreover, all of these decisions mentioned state practice in a very particular context (reunification) that raised specific questions of trust in state practice.[34] Since 1998 at least, the Court has in its fundamental rights decisions not once explicitly drawn on state practice to support a particular interpretation of fundamental rights.[35] Nor does German rights doctrine incorporate any comprehensive legal doctrine that sets out when and where the Court should exercise self-restraint or when and where it should accord discretion to the government.

This has much to do with the fact that German constitutional law focuses like many transformative systems on substance that is ultimately on (substantive) rights, rather than procedures and institutions. German lawyers think about the question what the constitution means, but not about the question what the Court should do. This marks a crucial difference in constitutional methodology compared to other countries such as the United States, which have not restricted judicial argumentation in the same way. I will say more about the United States later, but take Adrian Vermeule's theory of judging under uncertainty as a poignant counter-example to the German approach:

> The methodological thesis is that institutional analysis is indispensable to any account of legal interpretation. The question in law is never 'How should this text be interpreted?' The question is always 'What decision-procedures should particular institutions, with their particular capacities, use to interpret this text?'[36]

In Germany, it is precisely the other way around. Functional considerations play hardly any role in rights review.

[34] BVerfG 2 BvR 2356/9 vom 25 February 2000, 2 BvR 2352/99 vom 24 February 2000, 2 BvR 2353/99 vom 24 February 2000, 2 BvR 2371/99 vom 24 February 2000, 2 BvR 61/96 vom 12 May 1998, 2 BvR 2560/95 vom 7 April 1998.

[35] See for details, Michaela Hailbronner, 'We the Experts. Die geschlossene Gesellschaft der Verfassungsinterpreten', *DER STAAT*, 53 (2014), 425.

[36] Adrian Vermeule, *Judging Under Uncertainty: An Institutional Theory of Legal Interpretation* (Cambridge: Harvard University Press, 2006), p. 1.

Instead, the question is what a particular right entails in a given case. Even on a higher level of abstraction, German constitutional scholarship is primarily concerned with the question of how to approach a given legal text (methodology of interpretation) and what functions this particular text may fulfil (theories about the nature and function of rights). The traditional canon of legal interpretation forms the core of the Court's interpretative repertoire; it consists of five methods: grammatical, logical, systemic (holistic), historic, and (more recently) teleological interpretation. In addition to those, or under the label of teleological interpretation, the Court may also draw on arguments about the nature and function of constitutional norms such as the idea of the constitution as an order of values or of the constitution as a mere framework order (*Rahmenordnung*).[37] Most of these theories are about the nature and function of individual rights. Among them is, for example, the idea that an important function of individual rights is to protect individual freedom against governmental intervention or against third parties, or to protect valuable institutions (press, civil service, etc.).[38] This canon does not, however, contain a theory of judicial review and therefore does not provide an institutional perspective. Take free speech cases as an example: The Court will be able to refer to the importance of the freedom of political speech for the constitutional order with its protections of freedom and democracy.[39] Or it might be referring to the constitutional idea of man as an autonomous being to justify the state's duty to religious neutrality.[40] It will, however, not address this question in terms of why it, the *Constitutional Court*, is legitimately deciding this question as opposed to the legislature. If a substantive legal argument is found to apply, it is (implicitly) seen as settling any institutional questions.

There were and occasionally still are, of course, some exceptions where scholars or even the Court itself take(s) a more institution-centred perspective on constitutional interpretation. However, they have not become sufficiently doctrinally entrenched in the sense that they provide a consistently applied and structured way of thinking about the Court's role in particular cases. And in those rare cases where the Court does take a more institutional perspective and considers functional-legal considerations, this is

[37] Ernst-Wolfgang Böckenförde, 'Grundrechtstheorie und Grundrechtsinterpretation', in *Staat, Verfassung, Demokratie: Studien zur Verfassungstheorie und zum Verfassungsrecht*, ed. Ernst-Wolfgang Böckenförde (Frankfurt am Main: Suhrkamp, 1992).

[38] For an overview of the different functions of fundamental rights, see e.g. Hufen, *Staatsrecht II Grundrechte*, 3rd edn (München: Beck, 2011), pp. 53 et seq.; Bodo Pieroth and Bernhard Schlink, *Grundrechte Staatsrecht II* (Heidelberg: C. F. Müller, 2012), pp. 21 et seq.

[39] BVerfGE 93, 266.

[40] BVerfGE 108, 282.

often considered an intrusion into the established doctrine driven by the substantive-law question and indeed an impermissible non-legal consideration. A widely cited textbook on the Court's procedural law formulates this point as follows: 'For this reason questions such as the following should not be asked: In the concrete case, the question is therefore whether it is primarily the Court's or the legislature's task to solve multidimensional rights conflicts'.[41] If the Court does, in a rare case, take a more institutional perspective, it is typically as a result of judicial strategy and personal feelings of responsibility of individual judges. This in turn reinforces the mainstream opinion that so-called functional-legal considerations do not yield sufficiently consistent legal standards.

Now it is sometimes argued that courts simply cannot step outside of their role to take an external perspective, which would be necessary to engage with their own legitimacy.[42] From a Luhmannian perspective, Moritz Renner points out that law cannot critically reflect itself ,[43] and neither can courts for that matter. However, not only do some courts cross this line more or less frequently, but this restriction also does not apply to legal scholarship. Especially in the last two decades, comparatively few German scholars have engaged with questions of legitimacy. There is probably no academic universe in the world that equals the richness of US discourse in this regard, but the poverty of institutional thought in Germany is nevertheless striking considering the nuance and complexity of German legal thought on other subjects. The US universe of constitutional theorizing ranges from originalist methods (in German terminology subjective historical) to ethical (Dworkin[44]) over structural ones (Black[45]) to institution-centred approaches such as minimalism (Sunstein[46]), passive virtues (Bickel[47]), or representation

[41] Klaus Schlaich and Stefan Korioth, *Das Bundesverfassungsgericht: Stellung, Verfahren, Entscheidungen*, 9th edn (München: C. H. Beck, 2012), who cite for this proposition Gunnar Folke, *Funktionell-rechtliche Grenzen der Verfassungs-interpretation* (Königstein im Taunus: Athenäum, 1980), p. 43.

[42] Christoph Möllers, 'Legalität, Legitimität und Legitimation des Bundesverfassungsgerichts', in *Das entgrenzte Gericht: Eine kritische Bilanz nach sechzig Jahren Bundesverfassungsgericht*, ed. Matthias Jestaedt, Oliver Lepsius, Christoph Möllers, and Christoph Schönberger (Berlin: Suhrkamp, 2011), pp. 279–419, p. 281.

[43] Moritz Renner, 'Kontingenz, Redundanz, Transzendenz? Zum Gerechtigkeitsbegriff Niklas Luhmanns', *Ancilla Iuris*, 62 (2008), 70–1.

[44] Ronald M. Dworkin, *Law's Empire* (Cambridge: Harvard University Press, 1986).

[45] Charles Lund Black, *Structure and Relationship in Constitutional Law* (Woodbridge: OxBow Press, 1985).

[46] Cass R. Sunstein, *One Case At a Time: Judicial Minimalism on the Supreme Court* (Cambridge: Harvard University Press, 2001).

[47] Alexander M. Bickel, *The Least Dangerous Branch: The Supreme Court at the Bar of Politics* (New Haven: Yale University Press, 1962).

reinforcing review (Ely[48]). While some of these methods understand themselves as strictly legal (i.e. originalism, structural interpretation) and are similarly employed by Germans, others instead provide guidelines for judicial behaviour (Bickel) by drawing on considerations of legitimacy that are not strictly legal[49] and are therefore inacceptable to German lawyers. And sometimes, the bridge from legitimacy to legality is explicitly crossed and the two are connected: This is, for example, the case for Ackerman's theory of constitutional law.[50] Ackerman takes a classical legitimacy argument—the heightened and repeated expression of popular sovereignty during certain constitutional moments—to draw the legal conclusion that the Constitution has been amended by the (repeated) expression of popular sovereignty.

Nor is this language of judicial legitimacy confined to the domain of legal scholarship; in numerous decisions the US Supreme Court has explicitly addressed questions of legitimacy. Take as an example the following excerpt of the Supreme Court's decision in *Planned Parenthood v Casey*:

> The root of American governmental power is revealed most clearly in the instance of the power conferred by the Constitution upon the Judiciary of the United States and specifically upon this Court. As Americans of each succeeding generation are rightly told, the Court cannot buy support for its decisions by spending money and, except to a minor degree, it cannot independently coerce obedience to its decrees. The Court's power lies, rather, in its legitimacy, a product of substance and perception that shows itself in the people's acceptance of the Judiciary as fit to determine what the Nation's law means and to declare what it demands. (...) Where, in the performance of its judicial duties, the Court decides a case in such a way as to resolve the sort of intensely divisive controversy reflected in Roe and those rare, comparable cases, its decision has a dimension that the resolution of the normal case does not carry. It is the dimension present whenever the Court's interpretation of the Constitution calls the contending sides of a national controversy to end their national division by accepting a common mandate rooted in the Constitution...[51]

Like the American Supreme Court Justices, their Indian colleagues do not shy away from self-consciously addressing their own role and the limitations attached to their knowledge and expertise:

> It is inevitable that the social philosophy and the scale of values of the judges participating in the decision should play an important part, and the limit to

[48] John Hart Ely, *Democracy and Distrust: A Theory of Judicial Review* (Cambridge: Harvard University Press, 1980).

[49] I have benefitted here from reading James Fowkes, *Building the Constitution: The Practice of Constitutional Interpretation in South Africa since 1994* (Cambridge: Cambridge University Press, forthcoming 2016).

[50] Bruce Ackerman, *We the People. Foundations* (Cambridge: Harvard University Press, 1991).

[51] *Planned Parenthood v Casey*, 505 US 833 (1992).

their interference with legislative judgment in such cases can only be dictated by their sense of responsibility and self-restraint and the sobering reflection that the Constitution is meant not only for the people of their way of thinking, but for all, and that the majority of elected representatives of the people have, in authorizing the imposition of the restrictions, considered them reasonable (Indian Supreme Court).[52]

Of course, none of these courts is always open towards this kind of argument—sometimes a legalistic approach prevails and a court stresses its independence from extra-legal considerations (and in those cases even assumes the more technical depersonalized language, speaking of 'the Court' instead of 'we', for example).[53] This is similarly reflected in the changes and shifts in its jurisprudence on the Fourteenth Amendment, which wavers between acknowledging Congress's independent right of constitutional interpretation and a conception that emphasizes legal autonomy from constitutional culture.[54] But it nevertheless seems remarkable that this language is ultimately available to many courts and in some jurisdictions quite regularly drawn upon.

Compare this to the only case in the German Court's history that confronted the Court directly and explicitly with the question of the judicial role vis-à-vis that of other branches, the *Soraya* case in 1973: The case dealt with the question if the German Supreme Court had overstepped its competences as a court in granting financial compensation for a violation of privacy that was not provided for in the text, but based on an analogy with violations of other rights that triggered this sanction.[55] The Constitutional Court thus saw itself confronted with the unusual challenge to define the limits of the judicial

[52] Justice Shastri in State of *Madras v V. G. Row*, AIR 1952 SC 192, 608; I am referred to this by Ramnath, 'The Runaway Judgment', 16.

[53] See e.g. *Bush v Gore*, 531 US 98 (2000).

[54] See *Katzenbach v Morgan*, 384 US 641 (1966), but later *City of Boerne v Flores*, 521 US 507 (1997). See also Robert C. Post and Reva B. Siegel, 'Protecting the Constitution from the People: Juricentric Restrictions on Section Five Power', *Indiana Law Journal*, 78 (2003), 1.

[55] BVerfGE 34, 259. The facts of the case were quite interesting: The ex-wife of the Iranian Shah, Soraya, sued a German, magazine for compensation because it had published an entirely invented interview with Soraya ('the Shah no longer wrote to me'). As the journal became aware that the interview was invented, it retracted the story publicly; it refused, however, to pay compensation as Soraya had requested it. According to the German Civil Code, the press's position seemed reasonable. German law provided for compensation only when specific rights such as bodily integrity were violated, not, however, the right to privacy which had been violated in this case. Whether this law should be changed to include violations of privacy rights had previously been the subject of a lengthy debate, recommendations had been formulated, and the Bundestag had adopted a draft to amend the bill, but there was also considerable resistance to the idea and the bill was never passed. The Supreme Court now took the opportunity to remedy this, in its eyes, dismal situation; it accorded Soraya financial compensation based on an analogy with the existing rules.

role more clearly in order to determine if the Supreme Court had overreached by creating new law. It tackled this challenge in its typical style, by combining a broad approach to the judicial role with a nearly complete lack of any broader institutional framework. It emphasized in particular that courts had to reveal and realize ethical standards immanent in the constitutional order, but not necessarily always explicit in the statutes themselves (para. 39). In doing so, courts might even go beyond the wording of individual statutes to draw on broader ideas of justice rooted in society. This broad understanding of the judicial role was not, however, then embedded in any broader institutional argument. In addressing the institutional questions the case posed, the Court failed dismally, given that a draft bill had already been proposed and debated in the parliament, but had not ultimately been passed. This, however, features only marginally in the Court's reasoning when it explains that the Supreme Court did not need to wait for the legislature to decide the question:

> For while the government attempted twice to find a statutory solution for the problem of the protection of the right to privacy with regard to third parties, its draft bills from 1959 and 1967 were abandoned in the early stages of the drafting process—without this suggesting that the legislature had actually wanted to leave matters as they were (para. 45).

This absence of any serious engagement with the two-fold abandoning of the draft bills by the legislature strikes one as unthinkable in a US court. It is all the more puzzling as the decision discusses in depth what the scholarly debates were at the time and how the legal community more broadly had approached the interpretive question.

1. Historical development

There are, however, some instances where the Court and scholars have taken a more institutional perspective and it is worth taking a closer look at these. In response to the Court's conflict with the government during the 1970s, suggestions to approach constitutional interpretation from a more functional-legal perspective were quite popular.[56] And even the Court itself has occasionally taken a more institutional perspective.

a) Judicial scrutiny for predictions of future factual developments

At the height of the conflicts over its role in the 1970s, the Court had to address the constitutionality of one of the Social Democrats' great reform projects and certainly one closest to its traditional base, the introduction of

[56] See Chapter 2.

labour co-determination, i.e. of labour representation in the highest company boards. Company owners claimed that the law violated their right to property and ran counter to the Basic Law's supposed choice in favour of a free market economy. The decision, written by Konrad Hesse, represents a masterpiece of judicial reasoning, with its thorough analysis both of the facts and the legal questions involved and its nuanced consideration of the meaning of legislative discretion and judicial self-restraint.[57] In particular, the Court argued that the appropriate degree of judicial scrutiny depended on a number of factors, among them 'the characteristics of the policy field in question, the possibilities to form a sufficiently certain opinion and the importance of the legal values at stake'. Depending on the interplay of these factors, it would adopt different standards of review, ranging from controlling merely for evident misuse of legislative discretion, to the reasonableness of the measure,[58] to a more intensified substantive examination.[59] The law in question involved regulation in a politically and scientifically complex policy field where factual predictions were hard to make, and on the other hand, neither life nor personal liberty was at stake. The appropriate standard of scrutiny was consequently determined to be low rather than high. In any case, the government's assessment of the facts withstood a reasonableness test since it had thoroughly evaluated all the facts at hands, had debated all sides of the argument intensively, had conducted several stakeholder hearings, and had even adapted its regulation in response to the hearings.

The co-determination case built on an earlier case where the Court had emphasized legislative discretion in delegating powers to the administration with regard to the licensing of risky nuclear technologies (*Kalkar I*).[60] In both cases, the Court stressed that it was primarily the legislature's task to take decisions in situations of future factual uncertainties. However, the attempt in the co-determination case to formulate a more comprehensive theory of judicial scrutiny and restraint would ultimately not be successful. In the end, it was mainly the substantive law part of the test (the importance of the legal values in question) that survived; its more institutional components (the possibility to form a judgment and the characteristics of the policy field in question) would over time play a much lesser role. For this position, too, the Court could rely on judicial precedents. Already a year before the

[57] BVerfGE 50, 290.

[58] Reasonableness here seeks to translate the German term *Vertretbarkeit*, and hence it does not refer to reasonableness standards in Common Law.

[59] For a comparative overview of the development of the Court's jurisprudence on legislative discretion, see Rau, *Selbst entwickelte Grenzen*, pp. 158 et seq., who gives the Court, however, too much credit for what it claims to do.

[60] BVerfGE 49, 89.

co-determination decision, it had in the life-long imprisonment case suggested that in cases where grave infringements of constitutional rights were at stake, factual uncertainties should not necessarily provide an argument in favour of legislative discretion and then engaged in its own detailed analysis of the facts at hand.[61] The difference between this case and the *Kalkar* case has been attributed mainly to the fact that in *Kalkar*, the plaintiffs desired legislative action, whereas in the life-long imprisonment case, individual rights were involved in their traditional liberal, freedom-securing function.[62] Another, but slightly un-German argument to make sense of the difference would, of course, be an Ely-like argument: The life-long imprisonment case is clearly one dealing with discreet, insular minorities who had little chance to advance their agenda in the usual democratic channels and were thus more in need of judicial protection. In contrast, the general decision about dealing with nuclear energy could be said to be best left to the democratic process, where its risks and chances could be appropriately assessed. The German Court itself chose neither of these approaches and cited the *Kalkar* case in the life-long imprisonment decision, ironically even in support of its argument.[63]

And while frequently reiterating the co-determination formula in later cases, the Court nevertheless declared not long afterwards that 'external factors or those which the legislator can influence such as urgency or insufficient consultation' had to be disregarded.[64] This unqualified exclusion of external factors seemed hardly consistent with the co-determination formula itself that had acknowledged the difficulty of assessing future developments as a relevant factor in assessing legislative discretion. It fit, of course, with the idea of a science of constitutional law that was pure and untainted by social facts. In 1993 the Court distanced itself even further from the co-determination formula in the second abortion decision: While reiterating that the legislature's discretion depended on a number of different factors, 'whether one could derive from this three different degrees of constitutional scrutiny', the judgment explained 'need not be debated': In any case, it would examine 'if the legislature had considered the mentioned factors sufficiently and exercised its discretion reasonably'.[65] The Court thus reversed the sides: It was now not the Court itself but the legislature that would now have to consider these factors, with the Court then checking the analysis. This turn towards controlling the legislature's reasoning marked the beginnings of a new trend. The Court's then new president Papier had earlier criticized the co-determination

[61] BVerfGE 45, 187. [62] Rau, *Selbst entwickelte Grenzen*, pp. 205 et seq.
[63] BVerfGE 49, 89, 133.
[64] BVerfGE 106, 62 (152). See also Schlaich and Korioth, *Das Bundesverfassungsgericht*, p. 532.
[65] BVerfGE 88, 203.

decision on the basis that legislative discretion could apply only with regard to specific fundamental rights and their limitation, rather than providing an independent consideration of its own that would take social and political context into account.[66] Perhaps under his influence, the Court increasingly referred to the co-determination arguments only within the first three steps of proportionality analysis, which never had much bite, thereby reducing its relevance.[67]

b) The turn to procedure

The Court's turn to more procedural forms of scrutiny suggests at first glance a more institutionally aware approach, based on recognition of the epistemic limits of constitutional interpretation. Procedural scrutiny is in many ways better equipped to take institutional capabilities and limits into account; it can enable courts to take over functions of other institutions when they are failing because the emphasis on process makes it less likely that courts merely substitute their own preferences for those of other institutions. Yet, the German Court's turn to procedures is at least so far incomplete and institutionally deficient. Rather than a turn to institutional awareness, it represents the final consequence of its transformative conception of the Basic Law.

The new emphasis on procedure builds on a more expansive reading of the right to equality. For about thirty years, the German Court had interpreted the Basic Law's equality clause as a mere barrier to arbitrary state action; this changed only in a number of decisions in the 1980s in which the Court adopted a new formula: Within one group of cases, the old arbitrariness standard would still apply, but in another, where different groups of citizens were treated unequally, the Court would now require a 'reason of a kind and weight that could justify the unequal treatment',[68] a formulation that introduced a standard very similar to proportionality analysis. This line of jurisprudence led to a new, quiet kind of judicial expansionism particularly in the field of tax policy and welfare law, the main areas of the Court's contemporary activity.[69]

The *Hartz IV* case, named after a social reformer under the Schröder administration, makes perhaps for the best example in this line of jurisprudence.

[66] Hans-Jürgen Papier, 'Das Mitbestimmungsurteil des Bundesverfassungsgerichts–Eine kritische Würdigung aus verfassungsrechtlicher Sicht–', *Zeitschrift für Unternehmens-und Gesellschaftsrecht*, 8(4) (1979), 455.

[67] See e.g. BVerfGE 88, 203; BVerfGE 90, 155; BVerfGE 116, 69; BVerfGE 120, 224.

[68] BVerfGE 55, 72.

[69] Tax law and social welfare have the highest invalidation rates among policy fields, see Sascha Kneip, *Verfassungsgerichte als demokratische Akteure: Der Beitrag des Bundesverfassungsgerichts zur Qualität der bundesdeutschen Demokratie* (Baden-Baden: Nomos, 2009), p. 302.

It also shows how easily the Court could overcome one of the remaining institutional arguments, namely that the government enjoys particular discretion in fulfilling its protective duties under the Basic Law, which had been a recurring argument in a number of its previous cases.[70]

A lower court had brought the *Hartz IV* case, arguing that the federal law setting out social welfare grants failed to meet constitutional requirements. The Constitutional Court agreed and declared the respective legal provisions to be incompatible with the Basic Law, giving the legislature some months to fix them.[71] Its reasoning is worth taking a closer look at. First, the Court derived a right to a subsistence minimum from the constitutional duty to protect human dignity in Art. 1, which it read in conjunction with the social state principle (Art. 20). It then acknowledged that it could not deduce the exact scope of the right to subsistence from the constitution, because it depended on prevailing social views of what constituted a dignified existence as well as political and fiscal circumstances.[72] Instead, the Court set out to examine merely if the benefits provided were evidently insufficient and, if that was not case, if the procedure leading to the calculation of the grant was unsuitable.

The Justices ultimately concluded that the amount of welfare allocated to both adults and children was not evidently insufficient, since it covered at least the requirements for physical existence, but they objected to the method of calculation insofar as it had not been consistently applied: For the drafters had chosen a statistical model to assess the needs of the poorest quintile of the population and then deducted in a second step from the expenditure of these households certain percentages, depending on the type of expenditure in question. These deductions were thought to exclude expenses considered unnecessary to secure the subsistence minimum. While this was generally acceptable, the Court objected to the lack of any thorough empirical analysis as a basis for the deductions as opposed to the mere 'at random' estimates made by the legislature. For example, deductions had been made to except goods such as furs and tailor-made clothes or camping gear without any empirical basis as to the question if the lowest quintile of income owners did actually invest in such items. If no empirical data was available to assess the necessary deductions, the Court concluded, the government had to avoid these deductions altogether. Examining the positions accounted for in the government's calculation in meticulous detail, it found that many of the deductions lacked any solid empirical basis.

[70] See e.g. BVerfGE 55, 349; BVerfGE 77, 170; BVerfGE 79, 174.

[71] BVerfGE 125, 175. [72] Ibid., para. 138.

The same criticism applied to the calculation of child grants that had—again—been done by deducting a certain percentage, depending on the age group, from the amount allocated to adults without any sound empirical analysis of the actual needs of children. The Court also observed that the government had tied the rise of welfare grants to the increase of pensions, which provided an unsuitable yardstick because pension payments depended on factors that were irrelevant for assessing the subsistence minimum. Finally, the Court objected to the absence of any provision allocating higher welfare grants in cases where needs arose which were 'irrefutable, recurrent and not merely a single instance if this is necessary in individual cases for a subsistence minimum that is in line with human dignity'[73] and which were not covered by the provisions regulating exceptional payments in specific individual instances.

The decision is particularly interesting for its unusual combination of a broad transformative approach with a very meticulous standard of procedural control, which breaks to some degree with the traditional focus on substantive law. As Oliver Lepsius points out:

> All of the flaws associated with constructing standards ('Massstäbe,' see Chapter 4) culminate in this case: individual rights are derived from objective law, objective standards are derived from individual rights, the textual basis is unclear, previous precedents are not considered with regard to their particular context in building on them to further develop standards, institutional context is ignored, legal questions that depend on competence and organizational requirements are treated as questions of substantive law.[74]

If the case reminds us of the South African Constitutional Court's similarly procedural approach at first glance, this is only partly accurate. On closer examination, there are significant differences in the way the two courts review legislative procedures. Whereas the South African approach in *Doctors for Life* and the follow-up cases is explicitly geared towards promoting democracy,[75] the German approach is primarily about ensuring rationality. Christoph Möllers has rightly remarked that the German Court's standard of review is similar to the review standards for administrative decisions, and has argued that this ignores the need for compromise and bargaining that characterizes political

[73] Ibid., para. 206.

[74] Oliver Lepsius, 'Die Maßstabsetzende Gewalt', in *Das entgrenzte Gericht*, pp. 157–278, p. 230 (my own translation).

[75] Susan Rose-Ackerman, Stefanie Egidy, and James Fowkes,*'Due Process of Lawmaking': United States, South Africa, Germany and the European Union* (Cambridge: Cambridge University Press, 2015, South African chapter); see also *Doctors for Life International v Speaker of the National Assembly*, 2006 (6) SA 416 (CC).

processes.[76] Though some have argued that Germany as a parliamentary system with strong political parties is less dependent on political bargaining and compromise in order to get bills passed than other political systems such as the United States,[77] even here the necessity and existence of coalitions between different parties cannot do without many compromises and trade-offs between parties. The kind of logic the Court imposes on political actors is moreover very similar to its own (legal) standards of reasoning with their demand for principle and consistency, as opposed to more genuinely political standards of scrutiny that would seek to improve the democratic process as such. The German Court thereby ultimately forces politics into a professional paradigm similar to its own. In doing so, it ensures that governing is at least in Germany indeed a lot like judging (Stone-Sweet[78]).

In the end, it remains to note that the Court's decision did not bring the fundamental rise in welfare grants the plaintiffs had hoped for. A recalculation of the benefits yielded a mere net increase of 5 euros of the general welfare grant and the amounts allocated to children were in the course of their recalculation revealed to be higher than necessary.[79] This, however, would change in the Court's 2012 follow-up decision dealing with the constitutionality of welfare grants to asylum seekers that were substantially lower than *Hartz IV* assistance.[80] Now, the Court went a step further. Not only did it declare the current grants retroactively unconstitutional,[81] but it also made the necessary financial adjustment by itself, providing a precise amount of welfare until the legislature did its own re-calculations. The Court based its conclusions on the fact that the grants for asylum seekers had not been increased since 1993 while general prices had risen by around 30 per cent during this time period. They were therefore, the Court concluded, evidently insufficient and thus unconstitutional. In a second step, it turned again to examining the government's method of calculation, which it found similarly wanting. Reacting

[76] Möllers, 'Legalität, Legitimität und Legitimation', in *Das entgrenzte Gericht*, p. 383; see also Lepsius, 'Die maßstabsetzende Gewalt', in *Das entgrenzte Gericht*, pp. 229–30 and Mehrdad Payandeh, 'Das Gebot der Folgerichtigkeit: Rationalitätsgewinn oder Irrweg der Grundrechtsdogmatik?', *Archiv des öffentlichen Rechts*, 136 (2011), 578, who argues that the principle of consistency is hard to operationalize and hence not very useful as a doctrinal tool.

[77] In this direction Rose-Ackerman, Egidy, and Fowkes, *Due Process of Lawmaking*.

[78] Alec Stone-Sweet, *Governing with Judges: Constitutional Politics in Europe* (Oxford: Oxford University Press, 2000), p. 204.

[79] Stefanie Egidy, 'Fundamental Right to the Guarantee of a Subsistence Minimum in the Hartz IV Decision of the German Federal Constitutional Court', *German Law Journal*, 12 (2011), 1962, 1982.

[80] BVerfG, 1 BvL 10/10 vom 18 July 2012.

[81] The Court argued that the government could have known of the unconstitutionality of the law in question ever since the Court's *Hartz IV* decision in 2010.

to its critics of the *Hartz IV* decision, the Court now explicitly sought to clarify that the Basic Law (and its own standard of scrutiny) 'leave room for negotiations and for political compromise. Decisive is that the constitutional requirements to provide for a dignified existence are met with regard to the *final result*' (author's highlighting).[82] Though hardly convincing, this protest signalled that the Court's proceduralism was instrumental, remaining firmly tied to the substantive claim. It did not suggest a new sensitivity to institutional questions.

III. The Court's nature as a court

The only institutional consideration standardly accepted by contemporary scholarship is the Court's role *as a court*. This means that the Court is procedurally bound to act only on appeal of a plaintiff, to follow the right procedure, and to exercise its control ex-post and in a concrete case or controversy.[83] In contrast, other functional considerations such as the different capacities of different institutions, etc. suggest an inappropriately competitive relationship between court and legislature.[84] *Inappropriately* competitive, because Court and legislature or executive work in different ways and therefore must be distinguished: 'With the exception of a few constitutional duties the legislature can do what it wants, but the Court only decides on what it has been asked to decide'.[85] Beyond that, the principles of separation of powers or democracy are widely believed not to provide any guidelines beyond restricting the Court's function to its role as a court. It is instead the substantive law in question that determines what degree of judicial scrutiny is appropriate: 'Not the Court, but the constitution as the Court's standard of scrutiny is either restrained or clearly intensive'.[86]

C. Conclusion

When it is appropriate for the Court to act and when it should defer to the legislature is hence a question that has become situated outside of the *legal* discourse in the realm of *legitimacy* in Germany. It is therefore not a proper subject for the Constitutional Court to discuss. Nevertheless, the German

[82] BVerfG, 1 BvL 10/10 vom 18 July 2012, para. 96.
[83] Schlaich and Korioth, *Das Bundesverfassungsgericht*, p. 510. See also Chapter 4 and Christoph Möllers, *Gewaltengliederung* (Tübingen: Mohr Siebeck, 2005), p. 151 for some examples of how the Court has sometimes overstepped its role as a court in this sense.
[84] Schlaich and Korioth, *Das Bundesverfassungsgericht*, p. 510.
[85] Ibid.
[86] Ibid., 527.

Court, too, occasionally seeks to signal to the other branches in a more explicit way that it is not overstepping its boundaries. For this reason, the necessity for legislative discretion is an acknowledged topos in the Court's jurisprudence. However, this topos is mostly empty. It is not backed up, as one might expect in German law, by an acknowledged and detailed body of doctrine elaborating when legislative discretion is adequate and when it is not. Judicial self-restraint is more often than not understood as a question of the Justices' *personal understanding* of their role, but not as a question of law, as Justice Baer in a public lecture in 2011 pointed out.[87] As a matter of *law*, judicial self-restraint is obsolete because judges merely interpret the law and thus do not feel the need to restrain themselves in fulfilling this task. As a matter of personal attitudes, the judges are, of course, clearly aware of the political context of their decisions, as numerous interviews with individual judges confirm.[88] But understood as a question of personal attitudes, it receives neither the doctrinal attention other constitutional concepts attract, nor is it usually backed up by any deeper point of constitutional theory. It is therefore not surprising that some of the most detailed discussions of the Court's own role can be found in the Court's few dissenting votes.[89] This is important. But those dissenting votes have not entrenched self-restraint as a standard legal question in ordinary constitutional doctrine. As a result, judicial self-restraint remains under-theorized and often a mere strategic gesture towards the legislature.

This is especially problematic in a legal system with a broad transformative understanding of constitutionalism. For rather than just safeguarding certain individual rights, courts in transformative systems prompt new state action and steer and correct existing measures. They do, in other words, much more than courts used to do only a hundred years ago. Whether or not this is a good thing will often depend on the political context. Courts can do much good, but they can also stifle democratic deliberation and thwart majoritarian decision-making in problematic ways. It is therefore important for them to critically reflect on their own role and position within the system. Transformative law drives change and thus it often drives ideas of expansive judicial action. In a hierarchical system where the judges feel

[87] Final discussion, Speaker Susanne Baer, International Conference: Advocates or Notaries of Democracy? A Comparative Socio-legal Analysis of the Role of Constitutional Courts in Political Transformation Processes, Berlin, 24 September 2011.

[88] See Uwe Kranenpohl, *Hinter dem Schleier des Beratungsgeheimnisses: Der Willensbildungs- und Entscheidungsprozess des Bundesverfassungsgerichts* (Wiesbaden: Verlag für Sozialwissenschaften, 2010), pp. 367 et seq.

[89] See e.g. the dissenting votes to BVerfGE 39, 1, BVerfGE 114, 121 or BVerfG, 2 BvR 1390/12, decision of 18 March 2014.

no institutionalized expectation to ensure and justify that their decision is accepted and implemented by other actors, it is risky to leave judicial self-reflection to the Justices' personal tastes and their sense of strategy. It is too contingent on personalities and political pressure, which may or may not be present. To leave the question of self-restraint to the interpretation of *substantive* law is similarly unsatisfying. For if we are seeking to preserve political capacities and institutional balances, the question is often not *what* the Court should do, but *when* it should act.[90] Substantive law provides no answers to this question. This raises the risk of unsubstantiated legal expansionism in cases where strong political pressure is absent and of skewing the institutional balance in favour of the Court.

[90] Fowkes, *Building the Constitution*, especially chapter 2.

6

We the Lawyers—Dialogue and Constitutional Patriotism

Courts depend on outside support. If they want to make a real impact and change things, they need the help of other branches and the people. What others say and think about the Court therefore matters. How, then, do German institutional actors and the public perceive the Constitutional Court? Have they accepted its hierarchical position as the uncontested expert interpreter of the German Basic Law?

A. Strategy and Popular Support

Public support plays an important role in explaining the German Court's current authority. Opinion polls routinely show that the German Constitutional Court enjoys high levels of public approval, with ratings considerably higher than those of the German Bundestag. According to a 2012 poll, 40 per cent of the participants expressed very high or high trust in the Constitutional Court, whereas only 14 per cent showed comparable trust in the Bundestag.[1] Another 2012 poll demonstrated that most citizens approve of the Court's political influence; only 5 per cent of the poll's participants thought that the Court had too much influence.[2] Citizens also tend to believe that the Court is more responsive to them than parliament[3] and that it is more oriented

[1] Oliver W. Lembcke, *Über das Ansehen des Bundesverfassungsgerichts. Ansichten und Meinungen in der Öffentlichkeit 1951–2001* (Berlin: Berliner Wissenschafts-Verlag, 2006), p. 20; for a more recent poll, see Michael Schlieben, 'Großes Vertrauen in Karlsruhe, wenig in die Regierung', *ZEIT*, 7 September 2012, <http://www.zeit.de/politik/deutschland/2012-07/umfrage-institutionen-karlsruhe>.

[2] See Renate Köcher, 'Das Bollwerk', *Frankfurter Allgemeine*, 21 August 2012, <http://www.faz.net/aktuell/politik/inland/bundesverfassungsgericht-das-bollwerk-11863396.html>.

[3] Werner Patzelt, 'Warum verachten die Deutschen ihr Parlament und lieben ihr Verfassungsgericht?—Ergebnisse einer vergleichenden demoskopischen Studie', *Zeitschrift für Parlamentsfragen*, 36 (2005), 517, 521.

towards the common good, whereas parties are accused of pursuing narrow factional interests.[4]

This is not surprising. Most constitutional courts enjoy high public support, especially compared to legislatures: For example, 34 per cent of respondents in a recent Gallup poll trusted the US Supreme Court quite a lot or even a great deal compared to only 10 per cent who showed comparable trust in Congress.[5] In line with this broader pattern, German researchers have suggested that the comparatively high levels of trust in the Court may stem from the fact that parliament is evaluated in the light of everyday politics and the performance of the respective government at the time; in contrast, the Court is perceived in the light of its general function within the political systems and the constitutional principles it interprets.[6] Moreover, the press usually focuses on cases where the Court strikes down statutes, whereas most constitutional complaints that are immediately dismissed by the Court will not make the news. Press reports will therefore typically convey a skewed account of the Court's work by suggesting that the Court is taking the citizens' side against the political establishment more often than is actually the case.[7] The Court in turn contributes to this impression with its own public relations policy. This includes, for example, a visitors' day where the Court invites the public to audit oral arguments in specific cases whose success rate is considerably higher than the statistical average.[8]

These findings and the similarly high trust in courts in other countries leave us wondering if public trust can tell us much about the German Court's *specific* kind of authority. For if citizens everywhere trust their courts and this has to do with the way press reporting works, this offers little help in explaining why—unlike in the United States—hardly anyone in Germany today seeks to challenge the Constitutional Court's power. It also raises a second question, namely how much public support actually matters as a driver for expansive judicial action.

[4] Patzelt, 'Warum verachten die Deutschen ihr Parlament und lieben ihr Verfassungsgericht?', 526–7.

[5] Elisabeth Mendes and Joy Wilke, 'Americans' Confidence on Congress Falls to Lowest on Record', *Gallup*, 13 June 2013, <http://www.gallup.com/poll/163052/americans-confidence-congress-falls-lowest-record.aspx>.

[6] Patzelt, 'Warum verachten die Deutschen ihr Parlament und lieben ihr Verfassungsgericht?', 521.

[7] This is not at odds with the observation that increases in press coverage often entail increases in negative comments on the courts because most of the coverage may still be positive, especially during times when there is less reporting.

[8] Andre Brodocz and Steven Schäller, 'Hinter der Blende der Richterbank—Über den Tag der offenen Tür am Bundesverfassungsgericht', in *Die Deutungsmacht der Verfassungsgerichtsbarkeit*, ed. Hans Vorländer (Wiesbaden: Verlag für Sozialwissenschaften, 2006), pp. 235–58.

Even though this book owes much to their historical and analytical work, political scientists and historians have generally little to offer as an explanation for the German Court's *specific* kind of authority, as it is rarely the focus of their research.[9] This applies especially to one of the major approaches of German political science which seeks to capture the Court's authority with the concept of '*Deutungsmacht*' (the power of exegesis/interpretation).[10] Because '*Macht*' (power) usually implies that an actor can enforce its decisions, but the Constitutional Court has no such enforcement power in the narrow sense, political scientists have offered '*Deutungsmacht*' (interpretive power) as a better description of the Court's authority. *Deutungsmacht*, then, depends on whether the Court can offer a convincing interpretation of the Basic Law. When it comes to determining the conditions for *Deutungsmacht*, we are, however, confronted with a large, non-exhaustive list of factors (a 'complex interplay of symbolic-communicative conditions, instrumental framework requirements and practical effects'[11]). Alas, if everything matters, this tells us little we do not already know. Most importantly, it does not tell us much about the foundations of the German Court's *particular* authority and comparative strength.

Justin Collings offers another, both more specific and more useful reply to the German Court's specific appeal and authority.[12] Partly, his account, too, emphasizes the continuities between German nineteenth-century legal traditions (see the discussion in Chapter 2 on this), but it also goes beyond this in pointing out that Germans came to view the Court as an integral part of German democracy, recognizing the Court's contribution to the successful transformation of Western Germany in the 1950s and 1960s. As Collings rightly remarks, in particular the German press has during the last decades repeatedly emphasized the importance of the Court's contribution to the foundation of a democratic and liberal German state after the war. This is an important observation and it certainly plays a role in explaining the Court's

[9] See in particular the magisterial work by Michael Stolleis, *Geschichte des öffentlichen Rechts in Deutschland: Vierter Band 1945–1990* (München: C. H. Beck, 2012), as well as Richard Häußler, *Der Konflikt zwischen Bundesverfassungsgericht und politischer Führung* (Berlin: Duncker & Humblot, 1994) and Oliver Lembcke, *Hüter der Verfassung Eine institutionentheoretische Studie zur Autorität des Bundesverfassungsgerichts* (Tübingen: Mohr Siebeck, 2007), all of which have provided very important material and inspirations for this book.

[10] Hans Vorländer (ed.), *Die Deutungsmacht der Verfassungsgerichtsbarkeit.*

[11] Hans Vorländer, 'Die Deutungsmacht des Bundesverfassungsgerichts', in *Das Bundesverfassungsgericht im politischen System*, ed. Ooyen and Martin H. W. Möllers (Wiesbaden: Verlag für Sozialwissenschaften, 2006), pp. 189–200, p. 194.

[12] Justin Collings, *Democracy's Guardians: A History of the German Federal Constitutional Court 1951–2001* (Oxford: Oxford University Press, forthcoming 2015), in particular the introduction and conclusion.

public acceptance today, but it also raises the question why the German Court can now, in a mature German state, continue its expansive jurisprudence.[13] The answer to that question, I contend, has much to do with the fact that the Court understands and presents itself as an expert institution that occupies a certain place within the institutional hierarchy and that this understanding has largely come to be accepted by political elites and the public.

A statistical analysis of the German Court's jurisprudence by Georg Vanberg provides further insights. Vanberg argues that the German Court takes more expansive decisions when it does not have to worry about implementation.[14] This, he suggests, is the case when transparency (i.e. when citizens are likely to notice if political actors disregard the Court's judgment)[15] and popular support are both high. However, because popular support cannot adequately be measured, since there are no sufficiently comprehensive studies that survey popular opinion in reaction to specific decisions and the Court generally enjoys high diffuse popular support, Vanberg eventually focuses entirely on *transparency*.[16] To assess transparency, he takes four factors into account: 1) public awareness of an issue; 2) external popular support by social movements; 3) the complexity of the policy in question; and 4) the governmental interest in sustaining the law.[17] Within this framework, public awareness is statistically measured in relation to a) the Court holding oral hearings, and b) the number of amicus briefs that outside groups have filed.[18] Outside popular support is measured by the content of amicus briefs both from outside groups and governments, i.e. whether they argue for the law's unconstitutionality.[19] Finally, complexity is accounted for by dividing the Court's jurisprudence into more and less complex fields of policy and governmental interest by assessing whether the government has filed a brief arguing against the statute's constitutionality.[20] Vanberg's study shows that public awareness, outside support, and complexity seem to influence the probability that the Court will invalidate the law in question, whereas governmental interest does not seem to matter in the statistical analysis.

These are interesting insights, in particular with regard to the influence of social movements on the Court's jurisprudence. The influence of social movements on the creation of a rights culture is a rich field of study in the United States and elsewhere,[21] but is deeply under-researched for Germany.

[13] Collings himself also raises this question in his conclusion as a challenge to the Court's current, still expansionist jurisprudence, ibid.

[14] See e.g. Georg Vanberg, *The Politics of Constitutional Review in Germany* (Cambridge: Cambridge University Press, 2005), pp. 13 et seq.

[15] Ibid., pp. 23 et seq., pp. 45 et seq. [16] Ibid., pp. 100–1. [17] Ibid.

[18] Ibid., p. 103. [19] Ibid. [20] Ibid., p. 104.

[21] See especially, but not only, Charles R. Epp, *The Rights Revolution: Lawyers, Activists, and Supreme Courts in Comparative Perspective* (Chicago: University of Chicago Press, 1998).

In specific fields such as asylum law, experts note that many of the asylum law cases brought to the Constitutional Court in the early 1990s were financed and pushed by charitable organizations or churches,[22] but no study yet offers any conclusive quantitative evidence that would permit one to draw or reject an Epp-type conclusion for Germany. Other scholars claim—without offering any supporting evidence, however—that '[i]nterest groups rarely play a significant role in preparing or assisting constitutional complaints or other forms of constitutional litigation' and conclude that '[g]enerally, the Court is not seen as a platform for advancing causes pursued by social movements'.[23] Vanberg's analysis suggests that social movements may at least have a certain influence, though it remains hard to say how exactly things work. His study also runs, however, into a number of problems. For one thing, it is somewhat surprising that a study that seeks to assess public awareness of constitutional cases does not take the Court's media coverage into account. German studies have suggested that the high degree of media attention paid to the Court often came with more negative reporting and conversely, that the decrease in coverage of the Court during the 1960s and from 2000 onwards coincided with more positive evaluations.[24] If we assume that negative newspaper reporting will influence public opinion and make it more likely that the public will take sides against the Court, this suggests that the link between the public awareness of the Court and its ability or willingness to strike down statutes may be more complicated than Vanberg's analysis suggests. Nor is his division of fields into complex and less complex policy fields entirely plausible given that complexity will often depend on the facts in a particular case. Vanberg's main thesis, however, that German Justices take the implementation of their judgments into account in their decision-making, is nevertheless convincing and backed up by interviews, which routinely confirm that the Justices pay attention to the effects of their judgments and the political context.[25]

This is perhaps not particularly surprising, but it is still an important point to make, particularly in the law- and court-centred universe of German

[22] Professor Kay Hailbronner, University of Constance, May 2012. See also Doreen Müller, *Flucht und Asyl in europäischen Migrationsregimen: Metamorphosen einer umkämpften Kategorie am Beispiel der EU, Deutschlands und Polens* (Universitätsverlag Göttingen, 2010), pp. 148–9.

[23] Thomas Gawron and Ralph Rogowski (eds), 'Introduction. Constitutional Litigation as Dispute Processing: Comparing the U.S. Supreme Court and the German Federal Constitutional Court', in *Constitutional Courts in Comparison* (New York: Berghahn Books, 2002), p. 9.

[24] Lembcke, *Über das Ansehen*, pp. 36 et seq.

[25] See also Uwe Kranenpohl, *Hinter dem Schleier des Beratungsgeheimnisses: Der Willensbildungs- und Entscheidungsprozess des Bundesverfassungsgerichts* (Wiesbaden: Verlag für Sozialwissenschaften, 2010), pp. 367–72.

scholarship. It is also in line with some of our observations in the cases we have encountered in the previous chapters. The famous *Lüth* decision, for example, strongly reflected the changing attitudes of German elites in dealing with the German past. The *Elfes* and *Pharmacies* judgments must be read in the context of the Cold War and West German attempts to distinguish its government clearly from the GDR.[26] And when the Court for the first time struck down a major governmental project, Adenauer's public TV channel, in 1961, it is important to note that this measure had in fact never been very popular, not even within Adenauer's own party.[27] The Court's decision to uphold the Basic Treaty reordering West Germany's relationship with East Germany (in spite of severe concerns) not only represented increased deference in foreign affairs; it was also an implicit acknowledgement of the fact that the government had just won a federal election based on a campaign heavily focused on this question.[28] In more recent times, the Court's judgments with regard to the European Union and the ECJ can similarly be understood as strategic insofar as the Court has so far avoided any actual conflict with the ECJ or, for that matter, interfering too much in European financial policy.

But neither Vanberg's study nor these individual cases tell us much about what kind of support matters, and when and in what way it influences the Court. For courts do not always act strategically, but sometimes defy public opinion. In the 1990s, the German Court provoked strong public protests when it declared that mandatory crosses in primary school classrooms violated the religious freedom of children and parents of other ideological denominations.[29] Considering that many of the Court's most expansive rulings are taken against a background of major political disagreement or in the absence of public support for the government's measure, we can, however, provide at least a tentative answer to the question under what conditions judges may overrule public opinion: The Court usually avoids making decisions that run simultaneously against the interest of unified political institutions *and* popular opinion, if it is aware of these factors. Comparative lessons from other countries suggest that courts will be able to resist public opinion, particularly if they are defending sufficiently socially entrenched ideas or enjoy elite support.[30] While popular support for specific constitutional

[26] See Chapter 2 for details. [27] See Häußler, *Der Konflikt*, p. 51.

[28] Manfred Görtemaker, *Geschichte der Bundesrepublik Deutschland. Von der Gründung bis zur Gegenwart* (München: Beck, 1999), p. 563.

[29] BVerfGE 93, 1.

[30] See James Fowkes and Michaela Hailbronner, 'Courts as the Nation's Conscience: Empirically Testing the Intuitions Behind Ethicalization', in *Ethik und Recht—Die Ethisierung des Rechts/ Ethics and Law—The Ethicalization of Law*, ed. Silja Vöneky, Britta Beylage-Haarmann, Anja Höfelmeier, and Anna-Katharina Hübler (Heidelberg: Springer, 2013), pp. 395 et seq.

propositions, or rather the lack of it, thus plays a role, the political elite has a key role in implementing and enforcing judicial decisions. We can therefore sometimes see courts that enjoy little popular support—both generally and with regard to a particular issue—nonetheless take unpopular decisions if they enjoy the support of the political leadership, such as the South African Constitutional Court when it declared the death penalty unconstitutional against prevailing popular opinion.[31] Public opinion is therefore not decisive on its own and neither is elite support.

This also means, however, that the Court's room for manoeuvre is often considerable, as not every governmental project matters to the general public. The Basic Treaty decision provides one example of a case where popular opinion and pressure by political actors were aligned, with the result that the Court deferred. In contrast, in the *Kruzifix* case, where popular sentiment and political actors were largely in agreement, but the Justices did not realize this and failed to take it into account in their decision,[32] the judgment's implementation was threatened: According to newspaper reports a year after the decision, the number of crosses in Bavarian schools had hardly decreased.[33] Yet, even then, political resistance did not amount to a more fundamental attack on the Court's last word in the matter, as we will see in the next section. And in the standard, run-of-the-mill cases where the Court is not confronted with such unanimous opposition, the threat of political backlash will not usually be decisive in determining the Court's behaviour.

B. Institutional Support and Political Elites

All this raises the question how other important political institutions perceive the Court? A comprehensive answer to this question would require a book of its own, but I can offer at least a partial answer for the most important German institution in this context: the German Bundestag (the federal parliament). In the parliamentarian German system, the Bundestag elects and controls the government and is also key when it comes to evaluating the Court's institutional support. After all, it is *its* laws the Court regularly invalidates and *it* is the institution that has to react to judicial action by changing and amending its

[31] *S v Makwanyane* 1995 (2) SACR 1 (6 June 1995), for details see James Fowkes, *Building the Constitution: The Practice of Constitutional Interpretation in South Africa Since 1994* (Cambridge: Cambridge University Press, forthcoming 2016), chapter 1.

[32] See Kranenpohl, *Hinter dem Schleier*, p. 427.

[33] See Vanberg, *The Politics*, pp. 3–4.

laws. I have therefore examined the protocols of the German Bundestag's plenary sessions in 2012 to see what exactly parliamentarians are saying about the Court and how they are reacting to its judgments.

This survey provides two insights: The first is that parliamentarians only rarely criticize the Court, and if they do, they do so very carefully. Of course, not all criticism of the Court takes place in the Bundestag, but criticism here to some degree has a more important political function because of its institutional origin. The second point goes more to the core of my thesis—validating (once again) Alec Stone-Sweet's claim that governing has become increasingly like judging:[34] Parliamentarians frequently emphasize the necessity of expertise in constitutional law and quite often use specifically legal terminology when discussing constitutional issues.

Overall, there are sixty-five protocols of the Bundestag's plenary sessions from 2012, forty-seven of which mention the term 'constitutional court' either as a noun or an adjective ('*verfassungsgericht*' was my German search term). Not all, but most of these mentions refer to concrete judicial decisions of the Federal Constitutional Court. On average, each protocol mentions the search term nineteen times, though this number includes a very small number of references to state constitutional courts.[35] This shows that the Court and its jurisprudence are important reference points in parliamentary debates.

To begin with, only about ten statements about the Court out of roughly 902 overall mentions are explicitly critical. Even considering that some statements mention the search term more than once, this represents a low number. Moreover, even those statements that are critical are usually very carefully phrased, shying away from overt polemical attacks on the Court. This is quite unusual considering the Bundestag's frequently quite rough style of debating. Five out of ten critical statements refer to the Court's revisions of electoral law, with the speakers belonging to very different political parties. This diverse authorship and high degree of criticism has its roots most probably in the multi-partisan authorship of electoral laws: Since they are products of combined efforts of Christian and Social Democrats, the Court's invalidation has hurt both of these parties equally. Court criticism, which draws attention to one's defeat in the Constitutional Court, is thus less likely to have immediate political costs. Yet, note the formulation of what are perhaps the two most critical statements overall:

[34] Alec Stone-Sweet, *Governing with Judges. Constitutional Politics in Europe* (Oxford: Oxford University Press, 2000), p. 197.

[35] The protocols also include some written statements by parliamentarians that they wish to attach to their vote to explain their decision in particular cases to their constituents.

The [Court's] latest decision pushing us to this electoral law was in its reasoning in some respects quite astonishing. (...) The Senate is aware that [the Court's pronouncement] as an act of judicial concretization cannot be fully explained. I do hope that I can say in the name of the entire house: Such an abandonment of reasoning should not become standard in the Constitutional Court. As legislators we are increasingly confronted by Karlsruhe with higher standards of rationality with respect to lawmaking. (...) I would appreciate if the Court itself followed this rule in the future, as it has in the past.[36]

My colleague Oppermann and I am both well-educated and thus don't criticize the Court in strong terms. I will therefore adopt the criticism of the dissenting vote by Mrs. [Justice] Lübbe-Wolff: 'Should those engaged in lawmaking'—that's us!—'have thought that they might at least be able rely safely on the Court's established case law if nothing suggested it had ever been contested within the Court itself, the following decision will surprise them.' It did surprise. Without any warning an electoral law established since the postwar era has now been declared unconstitutional and we were confronted with a problem.[37]

Particularly the second statement is interesting in its reference to standards of conduct for criticizing the Court. It suggests that etiquette prohibits open critique of the Court's judgments, taking refuge in quoting the dissenting vote. The same careful approach appears in the statement of the colleague mentioned (Oppermann) declaring his intention 'not to criticize the Court from this place', though 'finding it hard to understand its decision'.[38] If we look around further, we repeatedly find statements emphasizing parliamentary self-restraint towards the court, combined with a clarification that the Court and the Court alone is charged with the task of constitutional interpretation:

Dear Colleague Veit, if we're talking about decisions of the Federal Administrative Court or the Constitutional Court, I will as a member of legislature be restrained and not claim that these are wrong decisions, that they should be decided otherwise.[39]

...I may point out that it is not the parliamentary factions who are charged with declaring the unconstitutionality of statutes, not even the Bundestag itself, but the Federal Constitutional Court. In my opinion, we owe our colleagues and the constitutional order of competences that minimum degree of respect not to claim any special competences in this regard.[40]

[36] Krings, in Protocol of the German Bundestag No. 17/215, 14 December 2012 <http://dipbt.bundestag.de/dip21/btp/17/17215.pdf>, pp. 26519–20. The translation here and for the following Bundestag quotes are my own.

[37] Wieland, in Protocol of the German Bundestag No. 17/215, pp. 26523–4.

[38] Protocol of the German Bundestag No. 17/215, p. 26510.

[39] Wieland, in Protocol of the German Bundestag No. 17/182, 25 May 2012 <http://dipbt.bundestag.de/dip21/btp/17/17182.pdf>, p. 21771.

[40] Lammert, in Protocol of the German Bundestag No. 17/188, 19 June 2012 <http://dipbt.bundestag.de/dip21/btp/17/17188.pdf>, p. 22735.

Constitutionality or unconstitutionality is something to be determined by the Constitutional Court and is not a matter of parliamentary consideration...[41]

Other statements ridicule suggestions by parliamentarians whose constitutionality seems doubtful according to the Court's jurisprudence:

I can see that you are apparently more qualified to interpret the Basic Law than the Federal Constitutional Court.[42]

Talking about the Rechtsstaat: We have to provide you with the opportunity for a discussion here, ladies and gentlemen, but certainly with not the competence to discuss decisions of the Federal Constitutional Court.[43]

What should we make of this overwhelming restraint with regard to the Court's jurisprudence? To some degree, the Court's high rates of public support make any open opposition against it a politically costly affair.[44] Nevertheless, considering that both government and the opposition suffered a number of important defeats in the Constitutional Court in the course of 2012, we would probably expect more criticism. Even if we take some of the less explicitly critical and more ambiguous statements into account, for example when parliamentarians point out the rise of applications for asylum from certain 'safe' countries as a result of the Court's rise of welfare payments to asylum seekers, there are hardly more than about another nine critical statements. Contrary decisions (as determined with respect to one's own political standpoint) of the Court are often acknowledged without comment as technical constraints to be taken into account in the future and treated as 'homework'[45] the Bundestag has to get done. If several parties have participated in the drafting of an unconstitutional law, one's own responsibility is sometimes shamefully acknowledged ('no reason for pride'), but also measured against the (greater) responsibility of the other party involved.[46] And not infrequently, the Court receives considerable praise. Its 'excellent decisions' are declared to have improved the quality of parliamentary debate and the Court is said to be 'further than all of us'. Given that, the explicit call upon the Court to engage in lawmaking (*'rechtsschöpferisch' tätig zu werden*)[47]

[41] Binding, Protocol of the German Bundestag No. 17/188, p. 22757, in attached written statement.

[42] Wieland, in Protocol of the German Bundestag No. 17/182, p. 21771.

[43] Schuster, in Protocol of the German Bundestag No. 17/182, p. 21772.

[44] Kranenpohl, *Hinter dem Schleier*, pp. 367–8.

[45] Kampeter, in Protocol of the German Bundestag No. 17/194, 26 September 2012 <http://dipbt.bundestag.de/dip21/btp/17/17194.pdf>, p. 23266.

[46] Schwanitz, in Protocol of the German Bundestag No. 17/176, 27 April 2012 <http://dipbt.bundestag.de/dip21/btp/17/17176.pdf>, 20927.

[47] Uhl, in Protocol of the German Bundestag No. 17/204, 8 November 2012 <http://dipbt.bundestag.de/dip21/btp/17/17204.pdf>, 24738.

is hardly surprising. Nor is the regret of two parliamentarians to have to debate and vote on the question whether male circumcision should be explicitly permitted by law before the Constitutional Court had dealt with the issue, accompanied by applause from the Social Democrats: 'I wish that after this decision of the district court there had been a high/constitutional court decision, for it is an issue involving the balancing of fundamental rights'.[48]

Parliamentarians also emphasize the importance of legal expertise among themselves. Take as an example the following brief exchange:

> My ladies and gentlemen of the 'Left,' dear Mrs. Krellmann, if you had done your legal homework, you would know the decision of the Constitutional Court of 1967—(Jutta Krellmann, member of the 'Left Party': I am not a lawyer like you.')—At the time, time work was prohibited. The Constitutional Court then declared this prohibition to be unconstitutional (...) You have pragmatically ignored this decision. I just heard your interjection you weren't a lawyer.—(Jutta Krellmann: I'm an economist and union secretary.)—Now, that really is a complete confession of failure. Fact is that the legislator must respect the law and especially the Basic Law—that applies even to you, Mrs. Krellmann.[49]

Moreover, parliamentary debates routinely involve a number of parliamentarians engaging in explicit law-talk. Some of the best illustrations for this can be found in the debate on male circumcision.[50] Frequently, parliamentarians frame the question—legally correctly—as one of finding the correct 'balance' between different constitutional values, the child's well-being, and the parents' right to educate their children as well as their religious freedom. They also do not shy away from discussing the legal details and the explicit merits of their respective legislative drafts to guarantee the necessary legal certainty.

This emphasis on legal expertise may stem in part from the high percentage of lawyers both in government and the Bundestag itself. In the federal government, the average percentage of legal professionals since 1990 has been 38.75 per cent, with only one governmental term below 20 per cent and three terms with rates higher than 40 per cent. In parliament, the average rate of

[48] Lamprecht, in Protocol of the German Bundestag No. 17/189, 19 July 2012 <http://dipbt.bundestag.de/dip21/btp/17/17189.pdf>, p. 22831; see also Ruppert, in Protocol of the German Bundestag No. 17/192, 13 September 2012 <http://dipbt.bundestag.de/dip21/btp/17/17192.pdf>, p. 23169. This question had come up in a verdict by a local district court (*Amtsgericht*) which had held the circumcision of a little Jewish boy to be a criminal offence, albeit in a case where the boy later had to be admitted to hospital, as the procedure had been unprofessionally executed.

[49] Connemann, Plenarprotokoll des Bundestages 17/166, 8 March 2012 <http://dipbt.bundestag.de/dip21/btp/17/17166.pdf>, p. 19789.

[50] Protocol of the German Bundestag No. 17/189, 19 July 2012 <http://dipbt.bundestag.de/dip21/btp/17/17189.pdf>.

lawyers since 1990 has been 21.45 per cent, and since the last election in 2013, 138 out of 634 parliamentarians have previously worked with the law (*Rechts- und Vollstreckungswesen*), even though not all of them will have completed the full legal training at university.[51] With so many lawyers present, it makes sense that debates are more likely to focus on the legal points. Legally uninformed arguments in turn are, as we have seen, quickly discredited.

C. Court Criticism and Legislative Re-enactments

These observations feed into a broader picture of a hierarchical legal and political culture. Though individual scholars have in the past invoked a more dialogic understanding of constitutional interpretation, these ideas have had little influence on the ideological mainstream. This was true, for example, for Peter Häberle's concept of an 'open society of constitutional interpreters', which stressed the role of other institutions as well as citizens in interpreting the Basic Law.[52] Even though Häberle did not draw any radical conclusions from this, but merely argued for a more institutional perspective on judicial interpretation, his suggestions encountered broad resistance from the legal mainstream and accusations of blurring the boundaries between law and politics.[53]

The plenary protocols demonstrate how strongly entrenched the German Constitutional Court's position is among parliamentarians. Even when parliamentarians take part in the professional law-talk and criticize the Court from a professional legal perspective, they are easily ridiculed along the lines of 'you really think you know better what the constitution means than the court'. An unwritten code of conduct seems to rule out strong court criticism as inappropriate. Moreover, those who are lawyers in the German parliament will themselves be socialized in the German legal mindset with its belief in legal autonomy and judicial determinacy. Since constitutional law is not an actual area of practice for lawyers (except academics),[54] their understanding

[51] Deutscher Bundestag, 'Datenhandbuch', <http://www.bundestag.de/blob/273350/eaf72e426cc17a9e14916ad235e36e9a/kapitel_03_11_berufsstruktur-pdf-data.pdf>.

[52] Peter Häberle, 'Die offene Gesellschaft der Verfassungsinterpreten', *Juristenzeitung* (1975), 297.

[53] See remarks by Joseph Kaiser and Roman Herzog, in 'Grundrechte im Leistungsstaat', *Vereinigung der Deutschen Staatsrechtslehrer*, 30 (Berlin: de Gruyter, 1972), 148 and 157; see also Frieder Günther, *Denken vom Staat her: Die bundesdeutsche Staatsrechtslehre zwischen Dezision und Integration 1949–1970* (München: Oldenbourg, 2004), p. 311.

[54] There are not sufficient cases for constitutional law to be a field of practice, and moreover the cases that do arise usually develop in the lower courts and are then taken by the same lawyers dealing with the normal statutory question to the Constitutional Court. Insofar as constitutional

of constitutional review will usually be strongly shaped by the training and education they have received during law school. German legal education has, however, in the more recent decades provided few incentives for a critical engagement with the power of constitutional review. In standard German constitutional law textbooks, judicial self-restraint features either extremely marginally or not at all.[55] Parliamentarians who are trained as lawyers are therefore unlikely to have developed a critical stance towards the Court's jurisprudence. At the same time, as lawyers they will claim special expertise when it comes to discussing the Court's jurisprudence or its role; they are therefore likely to dominate the discourse about the meaning of the Basic Law within the parliament and contribute to the general acquiescence in the Court's expansion of its competences.

This acceptance of the Constitutional Court as the final constitutional interpreter is not a recent phenomenon either. Unlike in the United States, political actors in Germany have—with one exception—never claimed an independent competence for constitutional interpretation. The one exception is Thomas Dehler, then Head of the Justice Department, and his fate suggests why his example did not last. In the controversies over German rearmament, Dehler not only declared the Court's decision to be not in accordance with the law, but also called himself a 'guardian' of the Court.[56] His stance provoked a strong public defence of the Court by all major media outlets. Furthermore, his repeated public outbursts eventually led Adenauer to distance himself from Dehler and not to reappoint him after the next elections. Moreover, the institutional foundations for the guardian role Dehler had claimed for himself broke down soon afterwards when the Court managed to achieve budgetary and institutional autonomy from the Department of Justice with the *Statusdenkschrift*.[57] In later years, no politician would ever claim to be the Court's guardian again. There would certainly be protests against the Court and attempts to cut down its powers—from both Christian and Social Democrats. But even when tensions were running high, as in the 1970s, Court critics such as then Chancellor Helmut Schmidt would do no more than remind the Court of the necessity of 'self-restraint'

law experts do get involved, they will usually be law professors who often act as advocates before the Court.

[55] One of the most widely read textbooks (Bodo Pieroth and Bernhard Schlink, *Grundrechte. Staatsrecht II*, 28th edn (Heidelberg: C. F. Müller, 2012)) never explicitly discusses the Court's role and mentions legislative discretion only a couple of times with respect to specific doctrines (such as proportionality) or rights. The same applies to Hufen, *Staatsrecht II. Grundrechte* (München: Beck, 2007).

[56] Häußler, *Der Konflikt*, p. 34; see also Collings, *Democracy's Guardians*, chapter 1 (I.B.).

[57] See Chapter 3, and for more details Collings, *Democracy's Guardians*, chapter 1 (I.B.).

(*Selbstbeschränkung*).[58] Protest against its decisions would not fundamentally challenge its interpretive monopoly. Indeed, even the Bavarian prime minister Edmund Stoiber's comparatively strong show of resistance against the decision banning mandatory crucifixes in Bavarian classrooms was framed differently: Aiming to contravene the decision's spirit and preserve Bavarian crosses in classroom, the Bavarian government adopted what it described as a narrow interpretation of the Court decision. It did not, however, explicitly and formally disregard the Court's judgment, as Stoiber publicly emphasized.[59]

Legal doctrine supports such caution by setting limits for court criticism and the re-enactment of laws previously declared unconstitutional. Court criticism is not per se prohibited, of course.[60] Scholars routinely invoke the need to maintain an open discourse in a democracy and prevent abuses of power. In a 1996 paper, Andreas Vosskuhle, today the Court's youngest Chief Justice, even put forward Peter Häberle's concept of the 'open society of constitutional interpreters' as a general argument as to why court criticism was admissible. At the same time, however, he like most other scholars agreed that there must be legal limits to such a critique, though German law does not contain a general contempt of court doctrine. Legal limits to Court criticism are instead based on the constitutional argument that different branches owe each other respect and must not threaten judicial independence. Perhaps unsurprisingly, the historical roots of this argument can be found in the Court's early fights with the government when the Court had issued a statement outlining the limits of permissible criticism.[61] Today, the broad rule with regard to criticism is that it may not be abusive and/or damage the Court's authority.[62] Though the details are contested, scholars tend to distinguish between criticism directed at the Court as such (its 'procedure and the competence of its members') from ex post critiques of individual decisions—the former being generally more problematic than

[58] Häußler, *Der Konflikt*, p. 73.

[59] Die Welt, 16 September 1995, 'Stoiber erzürnt der Vorwurf des Verfassungsbruchs', <http://www.welt.de/print-welt/article662152/Stoiber-erzuernt-Vorwurf-des-Verfassungsbruchs.html>.

[60] See Häußler, *Der Konflikt*, pp. 224 et seq.; Alexander Lorz, *Interorganrespekt im Verfassungsrecht: Funktionenzuordnung, Rücksichtnahmegebote und Kooperationsverpflichtungen: eine rechtsvergleichende Analyse anhand der Verfassungssysteme der Bundesrepublik Deutschland, der Europäischen Union und der Vereinigten Staaten* (Tübingen: Mohr Siebeck, 2001), pp. 476 et seq.; Robin Mishra, *Zulässigkeit und Grenzen der Urteilsschelte* (Berlin: Duncker & Humblot, 1997), pp. 236 et seq.; Andreas Voßkuhle, 'Der Grundsatz der Verfassungsorgantreue und die Kritik am BVerfG', *Neue Juristische Wochenschrift (NJW)* (1997), 2216.

[61] Rolf Lamprecht, *Ich gehe bis nach Karlsruhe. Eine Geschichte des Bundesverfassungsgerichts* (München: Deutsche Verlags-Anstalt, 2011), p. 81.

[62] Herbert Bethge, s. 31, in *Bundesverfassungsgerichtsgesetz, Kommentar*, ed. Theodor Maunz, Bruno Schmidt-Bleibtreu, Franz Klein, and Herbert Bethge, 38, EL (2012), para. 199.

the latter. According to Vosskuhle's 1996 paper, statements such as 'If the Court violates the political prerogative of the legislature, this would imply the end of German constitutional review' or statements pointing to the 'anti-parliamentarian effect of eight judges overriding parliament's will' are examples of unacceptable criticism.

Similar restraints apply to legislative re-enactment of laws previously declared unconstitutional by the Court.[63] While the two Senates of the Court have previously disagreed about the question of legislative re-enactments and scholars are similarly divided on the question, many nevertheless seem to converge on the position that the legislature may generally re-enact unconstitutional laws, but only within the boundaries of the respect they owe the other branches. As a result, direct re-enactments without temporal distance and/or changing circumstances are usually considered to hurt the Court's authority and thus to be unconstitutional.[64]

D. Constitutional Change and the People

But, a sceptic may point out, perhaps German constitutional interpretation is only hierarchical because constitutional change is much easier than in the United States. After all, the German Basic Law has been amended fifty-nine times between 1949 and 2013, with many of these amendments including multiple changes to the Basic Law.[65] In other words: Doesn't the realistic possibility of amending the Basic Law more than make up for the diminished role of the people and other institutions in constitutional interpretation? The answer is No.

First, in a hierarchical culture of authority such as the German, the Court's decisions are conceived of less as political decisions than as technical constraints—this is why parliamentarians sometimes refer to the implementation of constitutional decisions as 'homework'. There are, of course, some exceptions to this rule such as the first heavily criticized abortion decision or the *Kruzifix* judgment, but they remain exceptions. Second,

[63] See for an overview of the different positions, Friederike Lange, *Grundrechtsbindung des Gesetzgebers: Eine rechtsvergleichende Studie zu Deutschland, Frankreich und den USA* (Tübingen: Mohr Siebeck, 2010), pp. 167 et seq.

[64] Uwe Kischel, 'Darf der Gesetzgeber das Bundesverfassungsgericht igonorieren?—Zum erneuten Erlaß für nichtig erklärter Gesetze', *Archiv des öffentlichen Rechts (AöR)*, 131 (2006), 219; Voßkuhle, 'Der Grundsatz der Verfassungsorgantreue'.

[65] Deutscher Bundestag (ed.), *Datenhandbuch*, Kapitel 13.2, <https://www.bundestag.de/blob/272508/07819bdd2849c45eaf1442581aeb72ee/kapitel_13_02_grundgesetz-__nderungsgesetze-pdf-data.pdf>.

constitutional amendments may be easier to pass than in the United States, but they still require a two-thirds majority in both houses. Therefore, the two big parties, the Christian Democrats and the Social Democrats, generally have to agree about the necessity of an amendment. In practice, this has meant two things: First, most amendments have not involved the kind of heavily ideological themes that are core to one of the party's particular focus points, but deal with issues that are (at least in Germany) not tied to any particular party agenda such as federalism and finances;[66] second, those amendments that are closer to a particular party's agenda are typically presented as reactions to external constraints that require the respective changes, in order to minimize political resistance.[67] This was, for example, the case with the constitutional amendment to the right to asylum in 1993, which partly constituted a reaction to the Court's previous generous reading of this right.[68] This, however, played hardly any role in the debate and for good reason, because the proposed narrowing down of this right had been heavily contested between Christian Democrats and Social Democrats. When the proposed amendment finally attracted the support of a two-thirds majority in the Bundestag, it was only in response to major changes in the European asylum regime and a significant rise in the number of persons seeking asylum in Germany in the preceding year.[69] These events provided the (supposed) external factors many German politicians felt they needed to act upon. As a result, however, constitutional change even with regard to politicized issues does not appear as a result of the German people's coordinate effort in shaping the Basic Law. Instead, such amendments represent reactions to what is considered necessary in light of technical and often external constraints. As such, they do not convey the impression that the Bundestag takes an active role in determining what kinds of constitutional commitments Germans will take upon themselves.

[66] Astrid Lorenz, 'Substanzbezogenes und alternatives Nutzenmaximierungsverhalten von Akteuren und die Auswirkungen auf das Grundgesetz', in *Verfassungswandel im Mehrebenensystem*, ed. Christoph Hönnige, Sascha Kneip, and Astrid Lorenz (Wiesbaden: Springer, 2011), pp. 94–7. See also Florian Grotz, 'Verfassungsreformen in der Bundesrepublik: 1969–1994–2006', in *Verfassungswandel im Mehrebenensystem*, pp. 108–29.

[67] Lorenz, 'Substanzbezogenes und alternatives Nutzenmaximierungsverhalten von Akteuren', pp. 88–91.

[68] See Dorothee Lauter, Arne Niemann, and Sabine Heister, 'Zwei-Ebenen-Spiele und die Asylrechtsreform von 1993', in *Verfassungswandel im Mehrebenensystem*, pp. 158–78; more broadly Ursula Münch, 'Vorgeschichte, Probleme und Auswirkungen der Asylrechtsänderung 1993', in *Deutschland und das Weltflüchtlingsproblem*, ed. Carsten Tessmer (Opladen: Leske und Budrich, 1994), pp. 103–36.

[69] Lauter, Niemann, and Heister, 'Zwei-Ebenen-Spiele und die Asylrechtsreform von 1993', pp. 158–78.

Compare this to the United States. There is, for one thing, the American tradition of departmentalism: the idea that other branches besides the Court have an independent right to interpret the constitutional meaning.[70] Though true departmentalist episodes have been rare in US constitutional history, the concept is nevertheless an integral part of US constitutional culture. Even within more mainstream constitutional territory, there is considerable literature that emphasizes the role of the people and the political branches in shaping the constitutional meaning. Sanford Levinson, for example, describes American constitutional faith as Protestant because it places with the constitution a written document in its centre that is to be read and interpreted by the people at large rather than merely a privileged caste of judges or scholars.[71]

To be fair, some of this literature may overemphasize the role of Congress or the people: Studies of constitutional deliberation in the US Congress paint a more mixed picture.[72] There are famous examples of strong and independent discussions of constitutional issues,[73] but more recent studies have also drawn attention to congressional disinterest in constitutional matters. They have emphasized that legislators often merely draw on constitutional arguments as elaborated by the Court in support of their own positions—much as German parliamentarians do, in other words.[74] Yet, even if more intensive and independent constitutional deliberation has become rarer, it still exists—perhaps most clearly in those 'constitutional moments' to which Bruce Ackerman's influential account draws attention.[75] And however much constitutional dialogue is practised in particular US institutions such as Congress, it is certainly alive and well in the political rhetoric and to some degree even in the Supreme Court's reasoning. Compare for example Justice Powell's arguments in *Frontiero*, Justice Powell stated, to the German Court's Soraya decision with its disinterest in legislative action (see Chapter 5):

There is another, and I find compelling, reason for deferring a general categorizing of sex classifications as invoking the strictest test of judicial scrutiny. The Equal Rights Amendment, which if adopted will resolve the substance of this precise question, has been approved by the Congress and submitted for ratification by the States. If this Amendment is duly adopted, it will represent the will of the people

[70] Keith E. Whittington, *Political Foundations of Judicial Supremacy: The Presidency, the Supreme Court, and Constitutional Leadership in U.S. History* (Princeton: Princeton University Press, 2007).

[71] Sanford Levinson, *Constitutional Faith* (Princeton: Princeton University Press, 2011).

[72] J. Mitchell Pickerill, *Constitutional Deliberation in Congress. The Impact of Judicial Review in a Separated System* (Durham: Duke, 2004).

[73] Keith E. Whittington, 'James Madison Has Left the Building', *University of Chicago Law Review*, 72(3) (2005), 1137, 1156–8.

[74] Pickerill, *Constitutional Deliberation*, Introduction, see more p. 136.

[75] Bruce Ackerman, *We the People. Foundations* (Cambridge: Harvard University Press, 1991).

accomplished in the manner prescribed by the Constitution. By acting prematurely and unnecessarily, as I view it, the Court has assumed a decisional responsibility at the very time when state legislatures, functioning within the traditional democratic process, are debating the proposed Amendment. It seems to me that this reaching out to pre-empt by judicial action a major political decision which is currently in process of resolution does not reflect appropriate respect for duly prescribed legislative processes.[76]

A similar, much more coordinate approach is also reflected in the judicial doctrine of contempt of court and legislative re-enactments. US contempt of court doctrine is narrower than the German limits on court criticism and usually refers to insulting behaviour, pressure, or interference in specific cases[77] rather than targeting general court criticism, however damaging to the court's overall authority it might be. And it is uncontested that the legislature may re-enact laws previously declared unconstitutional and thus prompt the Court to reconsider its previous judgments—as it has indeed done a number of times.[78] In the words of Senator John Pastore on the question of how to frame the new Civil Rights Act of 1964 with regard to the Supreme Court's 1883 Civil Rights Cases:

'I am a little disturbed about the carefulness we are exercising on both sides here with relation to the inviolability of an opinion of the Supreme Court of 1883. I submit that until it is changed by another opinion of the Supreme Court, or by constitutional amendment, that it is the binding law of the land and we must preserve it. But is there any constitutional prohibition about Congress taking a second bite at the cherry?' The answer by the assistant attorney general, Civil Rights Division, Marshall was: 'No, there isn't, Senator.'[79]

But it is ultimately not these doctrinal differences that matter, but rather the underlying differences in the legal and political culture. Since the mid-1990s the authority of the German Court has not really been challenged in any sustained and fundamental way. Legislative disregard for Court decisions seems mostly to have been confined to the fields of party financing and the crosses in Bavarian classrooms. And though it is not impossible that there are other cases, it is telling that we do not really know about them and hence they do not play a role in shaping the Court's public image.

[76] *Frontiero v Richardson*, 411 US 677 (1973), see Concurring Opinion of Justice Powell. See also for more examples of this kind of reasoning, Bruce Ackerman, *We the People. The Civil Rights Revolution* (Cambridge: Harvard University Press, 2014).

[77] Dan D. Dobbs, 'Contempt of Court: A Survey', *Cornell Law Review*, 56 (1971), 185.

[78] John Agresto, *The Supreme Court and Constitutional Democracy* (Ithaca: Cornell University Press, 1984), pp. 125 et seq.; for a detailed comparison of German and US doctrines with regard to re-enactment, see Lange, *Grundrechtsbindung*, pp. 170–1.

[79] Quoted according to Agresto, *The Supreme Court*, p. 127.

E. Constitutional Patriotism Revisited

Framing the Court's authority as exclusive and expertise-based has consequences for our understanding of German constitutional patriotism—at least insofar as we are employing it as a descriptive rather than a normative concept. Originally developed by conservative scholar Sternberger as an affirmative description, the concept of constitutional patriotism was soon taken up in the political arena and by other academics.[80] In particular, Jürgen Habermas gave the idea a decidedly new and more critical spin. Sternberger himself had developed his idea of the patria as a republic that promoted individual freedom as early as 1959.[81] Drawing on Aristotelian ideas and US experiences, he elaborated the concept in his later writings. There, he coined the term '*Verfassungspatriotismus*' (constitutional patriotism) describing the attachment of German citizens towards the state and its institutions. The citizen was supposed to develop a 'friendship' with the state (*Staatsfreundschaft*[82]) that, so Sternberger thought, distinguished the Federal Republic from Weimar's 'democracy without democrats'. The resulting new patriotism was connected to the newly gained German pride in having finally established a liberal constitutional state that included democratic competition between parties, guarantees for individual freedom, an independent judiciary, and so forth. At the same time, however, the concept did not entail a notion of true 'civic empowerment' and the principal object of its attachment was not the written constitution, but the political order more generally.[83]

In its later Habermasian framing, the concept changed. Against the background of Germany's Nazi past, Habermas argued, Germans could not simply return to any normal, uncomplicated feeling of belonging.[84] Affirming post-war German constitutional democracy, he pointed out, always entailed

[80] See e.g. Paul Kirchhof, 'Der demokratische Rechtsstaat—die Staatsform der Zugehörigen', in *Handbuch Des Staatsrechts IX*, ed. Paul Kirchhof and Josef Isensee (Heidelberg: C. F. Müller, 1997), para. 6.

[81] See Volker Kronenberg, *Patriotismus in Deutschland: Perspektiven für eine weltoffene Nation* (Wiesbaden: Verlag für Sozialwissenschaften, 2006), pp. 189 et seq.

[82] Dolf Sternberger, 'Verfassungpatriotismus: Rede bei der 25-Jahr Feier der "Akademie für politische Bildung" ', in *Verfassungspatriotismus, Schriften 10*, ed. Dolf Sternberger (Frankfurt am Main: Insel, 1990), pp. 17–31.

[83] Sternberger, 'Verfassungspatriotismus', pp. 17–31; see also Jan-Werner Müller, *Constitutional Patriotism* (Princeton: Princeton University Press, 2007), pp. 22 et seq.

[84] See Jürgen Habermas (ed.), 'Apologetische Tendenzen', in *Eine Art Schadensabwicklung* (Frankfurt: Suhrkamp, 1987), pp. 120 et seq.; Jürgen Habermas (ed.), 'Verfassungspatriotismus', in *Die nachholende Revolution* (Frankfurt: Suhrkamp, 1990). See also Müller, *Constitutional Patriotism*, pp. 26 et seq.

and required that one would critically reflect on past history. Building attachment to the post-war German polity could and should therefore only be done in a process of mutual exchange and collective learning. Only then could citizens affirm and give concrete content to Germany's adoption of Western constitutional principles. While Habermas' understanding of constitutional patriotism may provide an attractive normative concept, it is important to note that it was always something to be realized rather than an already present reality (though Habermas' concept is blurry in this respect and has at least some descriptive elements, too).

Whether Germans today are actually constitutional patriots seems unclear. Nor can we really say whether the Court has indeed integrated German society.[85] Much will depend here on what precisely we consider is required for constitutional patriotism to exist. Drawing on the relevance of the Basic Law in public discussions, von Bogdandy argues, for example, that the Basic Law contributes to the forming and shaping of national identity.[86] Moreover, polls show that economic achievements, originally the major subject of pride for Germans, as well as the state's capacity to provide citizens with goods and services, have over time lost some of their importance in building national pride. In contrast, the political achievement of living in a 'free' and rule of law-based state has become more important as a factor for citizens' identification with the German state, which provides some evidence for the existence of a, if perhaps weak, presence of constitutional patriotism.[87]

But even though Sternberger drew on US experiences in developing the idea of constitutional patriotism, a closer look at the United States and Germany points to considerable differences. Sanford Levinson describes American constitutional faith as protestant because it focuses 1) on the written document that 2) is open to interpretation by every citizen rather than just the Supreme Court. Constitutional faith is 'Catholic' in contrast if it

[85] Ulrich Herbert, 'Integration der jungen Republik durch Verfassungsrecht?', in *Das Bonner Grundgesetz: Altes Recht und neue Verfassung in den ersten Jahrzehnten der Bundesrepublik Deutschland (1949–1969)*, ed. Michael Stolleis (Berlin: BWV, 2006); similarly sceptical is Gary S. Schaal, *Integration durch Verfassung und Verfassungsrechtsprechung?: Über den Zusammenhang von Demokratie, Verfassung und Integration* (Berlin: BWV, 2000).

[86] Armin van Bogdandy, 'Europäische und nationale Identität', *Vereinigung der deutschen Staatsrechtslehrer*, 62 (2003), 156.

[87] See generally Jürgen Gebhardt, 'Verfassungspatriotismus als Identitätskonzept der Nation', *Aus Politik und Zeitgeschichte*, 43 (1993), 29; more specifically for an (if older) empirical account of German attitudes towards the state, see Heinz Rausch, 'Politisches Bewußtsein und politische Einstellungen im Wandel', in *Die Identität der Deutschen*, ed. Werner Weidenfeld (Berlin: BPB, 1983), pp. 119 et seq. Affirming the importance of the Basic Law for political identification see also Dieter Grimm, 'Integration by Constitution', *International Journal of Constitutional Law*, 3 (2005), 193.

refers to established traditions and doctrines, and if constitutional meaning is determined by a closed group of office-holders, such as the pope or a caste of priests. Unsurprisingly, Levinson's analysis of the US case is strongly linked to US experiences with departmentalism as well as current US literature on popular constitutionalism.

German constitutional patriotism is different from US constitutional faith in multiple ways. It is not by accident that the German expression is 'patriotism' rather than the religious notion of 'faith'. For unlike in the United States, where religion has largely preserved its charismatic function in public discourse, in Europe the state has taken over most of the churches' social functions, and religious appeals have therefore become rarer.[88] Moreover, in the United States the imagination of the sacred is, to some degree at least, still rooted in the social imagery of the state and the Constitution, which is why Kahn argues that the Schmittian concept of political theology offers a useful way of understanding the United States.[89] In Germany, the downfall of the Third Reich discredited an understanding of the German state as a special and sacred category of constitutional and political discourse.[90] The idea of citizens' sacrifice for the state (or the nation) is no longer an important part of the German cultural imagery. The Court's ability to quickly discard the argument in the Aviation Security Act cases that passengers in a plane abducted by terrorists should sacrifice themselves for the greater good was telling in this regard.[91] Similarly, there is little public attention or ceremony if German soldiers are killed in combat—very much unlike in the United States.

But it is less these differences between faith and patriotism than the Catholic rather than Protestant character of German constitutional patriotism I want to stress here. Jürgen Gebhardt suggests that unlike the US Constitution that draws its strength from a civil religious paradigm of republicanism, the symbolic force of the German Constitution is bound to its distinctly *legal* conception of an order of values as interpreted by the German Court.[92] This is an important observation, which points not only to the central role of the German Court for the Basic Law's symbolic force but also, in its emphasis on a 'legal' conception, to the broader differences between

[88] James Q. Whitman, 'Separating Church and State: The Atlantic Divide', *Historical Reflections*, 34 (2008), 86.

[89] Paul W. Kahn, *Political Theology: Four New Chapters on the Concept of Sovereignty* (New York: Columbia University Press, 2011).

[90] In this direction, see Ulrich Haltern, *Was bedeutet Souveränität* (Tübingen: Mohr Siebeck, 2007), pp. 55 et seq. Haltern's use of the Protestant/Catholic matrix does, however, not correspond with my own usage of these terms here.

[91] BVerfGE 115, 118.

[92] Gebhardt, 'Verfassungspatriotismus', p. 35.

the German and the US approach. As we have previously seen, expertise as expressed in the mastery of '*Dogmatik*' (doctrine) is in Germany seen as a prerequisite for engaging in constitutional interpretation. And if a recent study of US constitutional reasoning points out that the Supreme Court often takes a 'legalistic' approach with a heavy emphasis on the constitutional text,[93] the text is in German constitutional law only ever the starting point for a broader teleological inquiry[94] that is pre-structured by German doctrine (*Dogmatik*). *Dogmatik* thus works as a gatekeeper: It controls not only *what* counts as a legal argument, but also *who* counts as a legitimate interpreter of the Basic Law. In the expertise-based culture *Dogmatik* sustains, only the judges themselves, lower courts and scholars are part of this interpretive community. Other 'non-legal' institutions such as the legislature remain—unlike in the United States—outside of it.[95]

Though German *Dogmatik* is open to their concerns and voices, tying constitutional law to constitutional culture,[96] laymen are therefore only to a very limited degree able to share in the debate over the meaning of our Constitution. The only way in which they can participate in this conversation is as plaintiffs: They may appeal their case to the Constitutional Court, suggesting that a particular act or law violates their fundamental rights. This possibility, most clearly encapsulated in the individual complaint procedure, is no doubt important: The 'ordinary' man or woman is thereby empowered to challenge the once-mighty state par-on-par in the courtroom and the state has to justify its actions before an independent tribunal. This is no small thing. The famous 'walk to Karlsruhe', as the title of a number of books and newspaper headlines runs,[97] has indeed empowered individual citizens to defend their rights. Having opened up its jurisprudence with the help of Art. 2 and the objective order of values, the Court deserves much of the credit for this development. It also forms part of the narrative of the Westernization of German culture—for it is here that Germany has most visibly joined the tradition of liberal Western constitutionalism.

It does not mean, however, that citizens—or indeed legislators—are able to participate in discussing the meaning of the Basic Law without the requisite legal training. As we have seen, the Court does not share its authority

[93] Howard Schweber and Jennifer Williams, 'US Report', in *Comparative Constitutional Reasoning*, ed. A. Jakab, A. Dyevre, and G. Itzcovich (Cambridge University Press, forthcoming).

[94] Michaela Hailbronner and Stefan Martini, 'German Report', in *Comparative Constitutional Reasoning*.

[95] For a more detailed account, see Michaela Hailbronner, 'We the Experts. Die geschlossene Gesellschaft der Verfassungsinterpreten', *DER STAAT*, 53(3) (2014), 425.

[96] Ibid.

[97] See e.g. Uwe Wesel, *Der Gang nach Karlsruhe: Das Bundesverfassungsgericht in der Geschichte der Bundesrepublik* (München: Karl Blessing Verlag, 2004).

in interpreting the German Basic Law with other institutions, even though legal *scholarship* is more important in shaping the Court's jurisprudence than in the United States.[98] This, however, only confirms the emphasis on expertise as a prerequisite for participating in the task of constitutional interpretation. This approach comes with costs.[99] Among these costs are two particular risks: policy distortion and democratic debilitation. According to Marc Tushnet, '(p)olicy distortion occurs when, due to judicial review, legislators choose policies that are less effective but more easily defensible than other constitutionally acceptable alternatives'.[100] Not every adaptation of legislative programmes to ensure that they are in accordance with constitutional law is, however, policy distortion. Rather, distortion happens when legislators unnecessarily seek to preclude invalidation by the Court based on unclear constitutional provisions or previous jurisprudence. In contrast, democratic debilitation supposes that legislators do not sufficiently consider the Constitution because someone else already takes care of it.[101]

Given the high percentage of lawyers in the legislature, and the high political costs of an invalidation by the Court, the German parliament is not generally particularly prone to democratic debilitation. Parliamentary discourse is often conducted in surprisingly technical legal terms, as we have seen. Nevertheless, there is a risk that recognition of the Court's authority may stifle discourse in individual cases, in particular when voting is not dictated by strict party discipline, as it happened in the debate on circumcision when two parliamentarians complained that parliament had to decide the question rather than the Constitutional Court.[102]

The more urgent risk, however, is policy distortion, and the hierarchical German model increases this risk further: Because the Court is publicly conceived as apolitical, invalidations usually bear a stigma of incompetence for the concerned parties and hence a considerable risk of bad press. To avoid this, civil servants and parliamentary committees screen all legislative drafts for compatibility with the Basic Law. When parliamentarians and administrators are unsure about the exact implication and meaning of the Court's jurisprudence, they are likely to err 'on the safe side':

Without any warning an electoral law established since the postwar era has now been declared unconstitutional and we were confronted with a problem. (...) We're

[98] See Chapter 4, also Hailbronner, 'We the Experts'.

[99] Mark Tushnet, 'Policy Distortion and Democratic Debilitation: Comparative Illumination of the Countermajoritarian Difficulty', *Michigan Law Review*, 94 (1995), 245.

[100] Ibid., 250. [101] Ibid., 247.

[102] Lamprecht, in 'Protocol of the German Bundestag', 17/189, 19 July 2012 <http://dipbt.bundestag.de/dip21/btp/17/17189.pdf>, 22831; see also Ruppert, 'Protocol of the German Bundestag', 17/192, 13 September 2012 <http://dipbt.bundestag.de/dip21/btp/17/17192.pdf>, p. 23169.

going to find out if we have solved it. Our solution has been relatively simple: We copy and paste the judgment's text directly into the new statute, according to the motto: They won't declare themselves unconstitutional next time around. (Wieland, Green Party)[103]

If parliamentarians proceed like this, it means that existing spaces for political manoeuvre are not being recognized as such and policy distortion may occur. Rather than thoroughly evaluating their policy choices in the light of the Court's decision, they seek to avoid the risk of defeat in the Court and the bad press that comes with it. German Value Formalism and its maximalist approach to constitutional interpretation further exacerbate the problem because the Court's development of countless objective standards of reasoning (*Maßstäbe*)[104] make it necessary for risk-averse legislators to take enormous masses of judicial material into account, thus further constraining their legislative freedom.

F. Conclusion

If the people think of the Court's judgments as statements of principle, oriented towards the common good rather than narrow group interests, parliamentarians understand them primarily as technical constraints and shy away from explicit court criticism. This cements the Court's hierarchical position as the final interpreter of the German Basic Law, unchallenged by other institutions whose authority to criticize the German Court and re-enact previously invalidated statutes is limited by law. As a result, constitutional patriotism has in Germany a rather Catholic ring to it compared to its Protestant US counterpart: It is experts, not the people at large, that define Germans' most important political commitments.

[103] Plenarprotokoll des Bundestags 17/215, 14 December 2012 <http://dipbt.bundestag.de/dip21/btp/17/17215.pdf>, pp. 26523–4.

[104] Oliver Lepsius, 'Die Maßstabsetzende Gewalt', in *Das entgrenzte Gericht: Eine kritische Bilanz nach sechzig Jahren Bundesverfassungsgericht*, ed. Matthias Jestaedt, Oliver Lepsius, Christoph Möllers, and Christoph Schönberger (Berlin: Suhrkamp, 2011), pp. 157–278.

Conclusion

The German Basic Law and the Federal Constitutional Court have become central elements of the German *Rechtsstaat*. And more than that, they are key to the identity of post-war Germany. In this book, I have offered a way to better understand German constitutionalism with its strong Constitutional Court at the centre. Traditions and transformations play equal parts in this story. A continental legal culture that is based on strict hierarchical divisions between different functions provides the foundations of the house that is German constitutionalism. Yet, its pillars and roof are more modern in origin: Their design reflects the kind of comprehensive constitutional vision that has today become the hallmark of transformative constitutionalism in countries such as South Africa or India.

But not every foundation adequately supports every structure on top. Successfully fitting both past and present together required major efforts by the German legal community. Transformative constitutionalism entails risks for any legal system. Because of the sheer scope of its constitutional vision and the difficulties of realizing such a vision, it is hard to elaborate clear and consistent standards of legal reasoning in advance. In hierarchical cultures of authority, such a priori norms are indispensable. Developing standards that are sufficiently flexible and broad to deal with a broad range of constitutional issues, but that are at the same time sufficiently rigid and legal, was thus a major challenge. Value Formalism represents the successful German answer to this challenge. In framing the Basic Law as an 'order of values', the Court significantly expanded its jurisdiction. Constitutional norms would no longer merely restrain state action encroaching on individual freedom, but, as values, would radiate into the entire legal system; they would affect relationships between private persons and drive state action. But Value Formalism is a means of both realizing and taming values: Based on the Court's jurisprudence and the doctrinal work of generations of German public law scholars, Value Formalism made it possible to keep constitutional interpretation a business for professionals whose authority depends on their specialized expertise.

For the Court's public image this meant that it was not to become a well-reputed third chamber characterized by its pragmatic approach to all matters constitutional (as a purely activist model of constitutional law might have encouraged it to be), but a full-bodied court, rooted firmly in the continental legal tradition. Its rarely questioned authority often appears as the pinnacle of the German *Rechtsstaat*, a state and society governed by law as interpreted by the German Constitutional Court. Yet, this success has come with costs and risks: Institutional thinking that enables the Court to reflect its own role is rare in its jurisprudence, thus increasing the risk of judicial expansionism in cases where strong political pressure is absent. The German emphasis on expert authority also excludes laymen from the task of constitutional interpretation, making German constitutional patriotism a rather Catholic affair and heightening risks of policy distortion.

All of this distinguishes German constitutionalism from its US counterpart. With its traditional emphasis on restraining state action and preserving individual liberties, US constitutionalism has traditionally taken a different, more reactive approach to constitutional law which still shapes—in spite of important changes during the New Deal and the Civil Rights Revolution—US constitutional discourse and jurisprudence today. Recurring departmentalist challenges to the Supreme Court's authority as final constitutional interpreter and widespread support for ideas of (broadly understood) popular constitutionalism mean that the US Supreme Court operates today in a very different universe than the German Court. If the Supreme Court wants to preserve its authority and have its decisions respected, it cannot rely to the same degree on its claim to superior legal knowledge and expertise. To be successful, it also needs to appeal to popular sovereignty.[1]

This raises finally the question of what to make of these different models of constitutionalism. Do we, after all, find the German model normatively attractive? And second, if we do not, is there anything we can do about it? I suspect that my earlier chapters have given away my answer to the first question. In choosing my analytical framework, I have, of course, already decided to focus on certain characteristics of German constitutionalism as opposed to others. Nevertheless, I have attempted to be fair and balanced in my presentation of German constitutionalism, and point not only to what I consider its deficits and problems, but also to its advantages and achievements. It is

[1] Paul Kahn, *Political Theology: Four New Chapters on the Concept of Sovereignty* (New York: Columbia University Press, 2011); for the connection between public opinion and the Supreme Court's authority, see also Or Bassok, 'The Supreme Court's New Source of Legitimacy', *University of Pennsylvania Journal of Constitutional Law*, 16 (2013), 153; and in a somewhat different key, but also emphasizing the importance of popular sovereignty, see Bruce Ackerman, *We the People. Foundations* (Cambridge: Harvard University Press, 1991).

now time to address some of the concerns I have raised previously in a more explicit way.

A. Normative Questions

The previous chapters have touched on a range of questions that all come with their own normative pedigree. Together, they deserve a book-length treatment of their own, entangled as they are in a very rich and deep debate about the legitimacy of constitutional review and the separation of powers. Here, I can only consider some of the most common arguments in the German debate and offer some preliminary reasons we might have for doubting their persuasiveness.

I. Activist constitutionalism

Both activist constitutionalism and coordinate models of authority come with their own particular questions of judicial legitimacy. As we have seen in Chapters 2 and 3, there have always been critics of the Court's turn to *activist* constitutionalism as incorporated in the concept of an objective order of values. Originally propagated by the Schmittians,[2] this critique has since the 1970s increasingly found sympathizers on the political left.[3] Building on Franz Neumann's praise of abstract, general laws as a bulwark against arbitrary state action,[4] Ingeborg Maus[5] and to some degree Jürgen Habermas[6] have taken aim at the indeterminacy of value-based reasoning in German constitutional law from a democratic perspective. Concerned more with the risks to legal determinacy and individual freedom posed by activist constitutionalism, German legal scholars have similarly often voiced criticism.[7] Perhaps the most important

[2] Ernst Forsthoff, 'Die Umbildung des Verfassungsgesetzes', in *Rechtsstaat im Wandel: Verfassungsrechtliche Abhandlungen*, ed. Klaus Frey (München: C. H. Beck, 1976), p. 134, and Carl Schmitt, *Die Tyrannei der Werte*, ed. Christoph Schönberger, 3rd edn (Berlin: Duncker & Humblot, 2011).

[3] See Dieter Grimm, 'Reformalisierung des Rechtsstaats als Demokratiepostulat?', *Juristische Schulung*, 20 (1980), 704.

[4] Franz Neumann (ed.), 'Der Funktionswandel des Gesetzes im Recht der bürgerlichen Gesellschaft', in *Demokratischer und autoritärer Staat* (Frankfurt am Main: Europäische Verlagsanstalt, 1967), pp. 7 et seq.

[5] Ingeborg Maus, 'Liberties and Popular Sovereignty: On Jürgen Habermas' Reconstruction of the System of Rights', *Cardozo Law Review*, 17 (1995), 825.

[6] Jürgen Habermas, *Faktizität und Geltung: Beiträge zur Diskurstheorie des Rechts und des Demokratischen Rechtsstaats* (Frankfurt am Main: Suhrkamp, 1998), pp. 309 et seq.

[7] For a critique of the value-based approach, see e.g. Ernst-Wolfgang Böckenförde, 'Grundrechtstheorie und Grundrechtsinterpretation', in *Staat, Verfassung, Demokratie: Studien zur Verfassungstheorie und zum Verfassungsrecht*, ed. Ernst-Wolfgang Böckenförde (Frankfurt

critique in recent times has been directed against the *objective* dimension of German fundamental rights.[8] Based on the idea that public authority is legitimate if it stems from and enables both individual and collective self-determination, Christoph Möllers in particular argues for a more traditional and narrow conception of the judicial task.[9] If democratic elections and parliamentary legislation express our *collective* self-determination, courts enable individuals to realize their claim to *individual* self-determination, Möllers argues. They do so only upon invocation in an individual case, in individualized procedures, retrospectively, and by means of a particular legal style of reasoning. Under this model, constitutional review and the German objectivization of rights are problematic. Ultimately, Möllers approves of constitutional courts as hybrid institutions between law and politics, but criticizes the concept of objective law for enabling the Court to act in the objective interest of upholding the Basic Law, absent a particular case or controversy where individual rights are at stake.[10]

These critiques raise a number of important points. The indeterminacy that comes with activist constitutionalism is certainly problematic on democratic grounds. It also gives rise to the question how much courts can actually usefully say and contribute to solving pressing issues in our society. The differentiation of modern societies and the development of autonomous social systems that operate according to their own logic mean that a great deal of translation and insight is required for lawyers to usefully engage with problems arising in other social systems.

However, returning to a more narrow, reactive and individual-rights-centred model of constitutionalism is neither the only way to avoid these problems nor perhaps the most promising one. To begin with, the reactive model, with its emphasis on the judicial protection of individual rights in concrete cases or controversies, has long been an abstraction.[11] In no constitutional system have

am Main: Suhrkamp, 1992), pp. 171 et seq.; Helmut Goerlich, *Werordnung und Grundgesetz. Kritik einer Argumentationsfigur des Bundesverfassungsgerichts* (Baden-Baden: Nomos, 1973), pp. 131 et seq.; both a critique of values and a defence present Udo Di Fabio, 'Grundrechte als Werteordnung', *Juristenzeitung* (2004), 1. For a critique of proportionality, see e.g. Schlink, *Abwägung im Verfassungsrecht* (Berlin: Duncker & Humblot, 1976), and more recently Benjamin Rusteberg, *Der grundrechtliche Gewährleistungsgehalt* (Tübingen: Mohr Siebeck, 2009).

[8] Lepsius, 'Die Maßstabsetzende Gewalt', pp. 157–278, p. 196 in *Das entgrenzte Gericht: Eine kritische Bilanz nach sechzig Jahren Bundesverfassungsgericht*, ed. Matthias Jestaedt, Oliver Lepsius, Christoph Möllers, and Christoph Schönberger (Berlin: Suhrkamp, 2011), pp. 157–278; Christoph Möllers, *The Three Branches. A Comparative Model of Separation of Powers* (Oxford: Oxford University Press, 2013).

[9] Christoph Möllers, *Die drei Gewalten* (Weilerswist: Velbrück, 2008).

[10] Ibid.; see also Möllers, 'Legalität, Legitimität und Legitimation des Bundesverfassungsgerichts', in *Das entgrenzte Gericht*, p. 399.

[11] Criminal law, for example, has long not fit this model, even though it has at certain times been perceived largely as a private matter between individuals, such as in Britain before the

the three powers been entirely separated, and today in particular, we are often dealing with hybrid institutions. While this may not fit neatly into existing theories of separation of powers, hybrid institutions are not problematic per se. With the growth of our regulatory states, principal–agent problems have multiplied and courts have frequently become engaged in safeguarding public interests as a result of our collective decision-making. As such, they have become involved in, often prospective, policymaking. On the other hand, collective decision-making is often concerned with ensuring that those whose rights will be affected by a new law or regulation are heard and their concerns taken into account. Many scholars have therefore called for a new model of the separation of powers that replaces the familiar triad of a legislative, executive, and judicative branch with new and different checks and balances.[12] Given these developments, returning to a more reactive conception of constitutional justice risks prizing theoretical purity over the very real challenges of governance in an expansive welfare state.

And there are other good reasons not to abandon the remaining pillars of German transformative constitutionalism: If courts are to protect those important commitments we make to each other as members of a political community, in Germany as in many other states these include a certain measure of social solidarity and equal opportunities as well as a concurrent state duty to realize these promises. What exactly this tradition of the German welfare state implies, is and should be subject to political and legal debate. But the established consensus in post-war and indeed pre-war Germany that holds across the boundaries of the major political parties does certainly entail an activist role for the German state. Germans talk in very different, much more positive terms about the state and its role in society than do Americans—and they do so across the main political parties. And even though it took somewhat longer for constitutional law to reflect this political consensus, it is today an essential part of Germany's constitutional tradition and an adequate reflection of its deep political commitments. Returning to a more reactive understanding of the Basic Law would not only ignore this tradition, but might also provide an obstacle to the state's activist role in the longer term.

eighteenth century. Today, criminal justice is in most states seen as one of the most important public tasks. Though the victim may have certain procedural rights, the trial nevertheless serves mostly the public interest in punishment and at least partly the aim of preventing further crimes. The criminal justice system hence serves to implement our collective agreements rather than an individual's claim to self-determination.

[12] See e.g. Eoin Carolan, *The New Separation of Powers. A Theory for the Modern State* (Oxford: Oxford University Press, 2009); Bruce Ackerman, 'The New Separation of Powers', *Harvard Law Review*, 113(3) (2000), 633–729.

II. Coordinate authority

An alternative reply to the democratic objections against expansive jurisprudence therefore might be to turn towards a more coordinate model of constitutional review. The possibility of inter-branch competition in coordinate systems might provide a certain counterweight to the expansion of judicial powers in activist constitutional regimes. By discarding the concept of one final interpreter, coordinate models can open up the possibility of discourse about constitutional meaning between the different branches. This is, at least from the perspective of procedural and discursive approaches to social justice, a normative advantage.

However, Germans tend to resist typical features of coordinate models. This is expressed first and foremost in their rejection of US-style constitutionalism as 'too politicized and personalized'.[13] The underlying premise of this rejection is that the politicization and personalization of constitutional review are bad things. But are they really? The answer to this question depends on what we mean by politicization and on the characteristics of the political and legal system in question.

To deal with the politicization and personalization argument, it is important to understand it in its context. Some scholars attribute these features of US constitutional review to the loss of faith in law and legal autonomy. This loss of faith in turn is understood to have been propelled by the political science literature on the politicization of courts and sometimes, more broadly, by US Legal Realism and its successor, the Critical Legal Studies movement:[14] If no one believes in legal autonomy any more, the argument runs, this may become a self-fulfilling prophecy and law and courts will become political. However, as yet there is no conclusive empirical evidence to prove the self-fulfilling prophecy. Nevertheless, as I have argued in Chapter 4, there are reasons to treat as at least plausible the proposition that there is a causal link between the importance attributed to judicial determinacy and consistency, and the degree to which these values are actually realized within

[13] See e.g. 'Interview mit Angelika Nußberger', *Legal Tribune*, 14 December 2010, <http://www.lto.de/recht/feuilleton/f/prof-dr-angelika-nussberger-im-interview-die-entscheidungspraxis-sollte-nicht-politisiert-werden/>. See also the explanatory memorandum on the draft bill changing the selection procedure for the Justices of the Court in the Bundestag (Deutscher Bundestag, Drucksache 18/2737, Entwurf eines Neunten Gesetzes zur Änderung des Bundesverfassungsgerichtsgesetzes, <http://dip21.bundestag.de/dip21/btd/18/027/1802737.pdf>).

[14] See e.g. Möllers, *Die drei Gewalten*, 103; James R. Maxeiner, 'Legal Certainty: A European Alternative to American Legal Indeterminacy?', *Tulane Journal of International and Comparative Law*, 15 (2007), 541, 543; Suzanna Sherry, 'Putting the Law Back in Constitutional Law', *Constitutional Commentaries*, 25 (2008), 461.

a given legal system: *Because* legal determinacy and consistency matter less in a coordinate system, we will expect its jurisprudence to be indeed less consistent and legal interpretation to be less determinate. And *because* it is more important for coordinate courts not to be out of sync with public opinion, they are likely to take public opinion more seriously.

If we accept this claim, we must take the politicization charge seriously. But it is then only a *specific kind* of politicization and personalization we are talking about. In particular, politicization and personalization do *not* imply that judges decide based on their personal ideological preferences—that is, that they take decisions without any reference to recognized theories or topoi of constitutional review, or if they do refer to such theories, that their decisions are not really based on these theoretical considerations. (If they act like that, constitutional jurisprudence is likely to become arbitrary with deleterious consequences for judicial authority at large. Even if it may in individual cases produce more just results, this does not seem to compensate for its downsides—at least if judges are persistently applying their personal preferences.) But this understanding of politicization is *not* a likely consequence of coordinate conceptions of judicial authority. While coordinate systems may place less emphasis on the idea of law as a determinate science, this is not equivalent to giving free reign to the judges' personal preferences. Authority in coordinate systems depends on the institution's connection to the public and the ruling elite—something that is hardly guaranteed if judges merely pursue their own personal political preferences.

Rather, politicization in a coordinate system implies that judges are more inclined to take seriously what those in power want or what public opinion suggests. And they might be more prone to a specific style of argument that is less formalist and more open to political and strategic considerations and/or more emotional and rhetorical. Yet, to determine whether this is a bad thing in a democracy is not an easy task—and I can only outline here a preliminary reply to some of the arguments typically associated with a politicization of the judiciary.

As previously, in addressing these questions it is crucial to be aware of the characteristics and stability of the political system in question. My concern here is with Germany and I am looking mainly at the United States for a comparison—both are now stable democratic systems with a broadly functioning government and administration, and strong and independent judiciaries. All this is key to my argument here for a more coordinate conception of constitutional justice. Only a sufficiently robust conception of judicial independence guarantees that courts, whether in hierarchical or coordinate systems, have a basis of authority of their own. Without such independence, the risk is large that courts will have to compete with other political institutions at their own game in order to attract support and establish their authority. Particularly in transformative systems, this is a competition courts are not well-suited to win—achieving real change in society is a difficult task, which courts are not always well equipped to discharge, making them vulnerable to political attack and increasing the risk that they end up merely rubber stamping what happens elsewhere. Where judicial independence is permanently threatened, therefore, where political order is unstable and governments engage in large-scale violation of minority rights, the case for coordinate justice will look very different than in Germany today.

1. Consistency and predictability

From a contemporary German perspective, perhaps the most important objection to a more coordinate conception of authority is that it is likely to produce less consistent and less predictable judicial decision-making. Consistency and predictability are not mere fetishes of some legal scholars in hierarchical systems. If it is not clear who has the last word, state action more easily becomes arbitrary. The equal application of law may be at risk if different actors make different decisions; in particular, politicians may pay less attention to the long-term viability of the system and thus to the values of consistency and equality. As a result, citizens may be impaired in their ability to lead autonomous lives within an established framework of rules and norms.

Yet in a country like Germany where constitutional review is centralized in one institution, these concerns weigh less heavily. Here, constitutional cases are still comparatively rare. Moreover, constitutional terms are generally vague. Constitutional interpretation already has a much lower degree of consistency and determinacy than ordinary statutory law. While there is therefore a risk that consistency and certainty may suffer in constitutional cases, this cost can be borne here more easily than elsewhere.

However, the critic may argue, does my model not suggest that constitutional courts form part of the general legal culture and thus that we cannot have one without the other? This is, of course, true, but only to a degree. In real life, most systems are to some degree hybrids. Because constitutional courts are situated on the boundaries of law and politics, they are more independent from the legal culture at large than other courts. It does not seem inconceivable, therefore, that they may develop a different image more compatible with the dialogic realm of politics than expert-based law. Whether this is a likely prospect, of course, is a different question, which I address in the next section. Nevertheless, a move towards a more coordinate conception will presumably lead to more inconsistent decisions as a result of more dialogic structures of decision-making in the longer term.

2. Minority protection

Related to this problem is another premise frequently underlying the politicization critique, namely that courts should be apolitical in order to better protect minorities and guard against politics going wrong. But even though this idea is popular as a justification for constitutional review in Germany, there is no evidence that the German Court has been comparatively more protective of minorities than other constitutional courts. On the contrary, insights from constitutional doctrine and theory suggest that the German Court's conception of rights might even be less oriented towards protecting minorities than that of other courts such as the US Supreme Court.[15] Nor, to my knowledge, have court advocates ever tried to make the case for a more general quantitative argument that courts protect minorities more often than political institutions. Indeed, even their qualitative argument is not particularly convincing: Though justices enjoy judicial independence and thus are not subject to re-election pressures in coordinate and hierarchical systems alike, they are appointed by the established political class and likely to share their political ideas and ideology.[16] Empirical studies of the United States, India, Britain, Canada, and South Africa suggest broadly that judicial protection of minorities is usually closely connected to their ability to organize politically on a large scale and thus make political headway, simultaneously or before they are successful in courts.[17] It thus may well be more important that judges are sensitive and receptive to political changes rather than merely apolitical legal experts, accepted as final arbiters of constitutional law. The role of courts is, in other words, rather different from the one envisaged by

[15] See Oliver Lepsius, 'Die Religionsfreiheit als Minderheitenrecht in Deutschland, Frankreich und den USA', *Leviathan*, 34 (2006), 345; also Michaela Hailbronner, 'Rethinking the Rise of the German Constitutional Court: From Anti-Nazism to Value Formalism', *International Journal of Constitutional Law*, 12(3) (2014), 626.

[16] Robert A. Dahl, 'Decision-Making in a Democracy: The Supreme Court as National Policy-Maker', *Journal of Public Law*, 6 (1957), 279.

[17] See for a general study of the US, India, Britain, and Canada, Charles Epp, *The Rights Revolution: Lawyers, Activists, and Supreme Courts in Comparative Perspective* (Chicago: University of Chicago Press, 1998); more specifically on the importance of social movements with regard to the success of women's rights in the Supreme Court, Reva B. Siegel, 'Constitutional Culture, Social Movement Conflict and Constitutional Change: The Case of the De Facto Era, 2005–06 Brennan Center Symposium Lecture', *California Law Review*, 94 (2006), 1323; for a detailed analysis of South African jurisprudence, see James Fowkes, *Building the Constitution: The Practice of Constitutional Interpretation in South Africa since 1994* (Cambridge: Cambridge University Press, forthcoming 2016).

those who think that independence and distance to politics make courts bold defenders of minority rights: Courts can entrench political changes or spark them, but they will not usually make the bold anti-majoritarian decisions independent of politics that court advocates imagine them taking.[18] And if they seek to protect minorities or take other unpopular stands, they will be wise to be strategic in order to secure implementation in order to avoid backlash—a role coordinate courts are in many ways better equipped to fulfil than those operating in a hierarchical setting.

3. The stability argument

Another frequent worry is that coordinate conceptions of constitutional review will lead to political instability. However, not every institutional conflict is problematic for political stability. Societies can usually grapple with a significant amount of conflict and this applies especially to more mature democratic societies such as post-war Germany. Indeed, conflict may even be beneficial. For one thing, it reflects the real debate over the meaning of our constitutional commitments. Constitutional provisions often *are* deeply indeterminate and conflicts therefore to be expected. Of course, we can try to build elaborate systems that explain norms in relation to one another. But while structural or systematic arguments certainly are an important part of legal interpretation, they will only get us so far. As Schmitt emphasized, constitutional norms are first and foremost 'formula compromises',[19] or in Sunstein's more contemporary formulation, 'incompletely theorized agreements'[20]—an idea hard to reconcile with a view of law as a determinate system of norms and principles. To provide for the possibility of inter-institutional competition reflects the fundamental indeterminacy of constitutional principles rather than trying to camouflage it.

It also increases the chances of a more open version of constitutional patriotism by enabling a larger group of participants to take part in the enterprise of constitutional interpretation. Ideally, this group should encompass all of us. A constitution represents the commitments we make to each other as a condition for living together in one state and society. To realize these

[18] For a more detailed critique of the idea that constitutional courts can act as a 'national conscience', see James Fowkes and Michaela Hailbronner, 'Courts as the Nation's Conscience: Empirically Testing the Intuitions Behind Ethicalization', in *Ethik und Recht—Die Ethisierung des Rechts/Ethics and Law—The Ethicalization of Law*, ed. Britta Beylage-Haarmann et al. (Heidelberg: Springer, 2013).

[19] Carl Schmitt, *Verfassungslehre* (München: Duncker & Humblot, 1928), pp. 28–32.

[20] Cass R. Sunstein, *Designing Democracy: What Constitutions Do* (New York: Oxford University Press, 2001), pp. 55 et seq.

commitments, it is important that we engage with them—if not constantly (for most of us are private citizens[21]), at least some of the time. A good way to encourage public awareness of constitutional issues is to engage the people and their representatives in a dialogue with the Court over their meaning. If people can challenge judicial interpretation rather than having to merely accept the Court's authority, this is more likely to happen. Conflict over constitutional meaning and backlash against courts can be productive in this regard in reminding us what is at stake and prompting us to rethink and reargue our convictions.[22]

To produce a lively public dialogue, however, it will not suffice to merely provide the institutional mechanisms to challenge an interpretation of the Court. Some Commonwealth countries have done so in a way that ultimately gives the last say to parliament. The British Declaration of Incompatibility or the Canadian Notwithstanding Clause are examples of this approach. But what matters most from a coordinate perspective is not that the Court is formally displaced as the final interpreter by parliament. Instead, it is the possibility of real inter-branch coordination and competition that is important. Famously, the Canadian federal government has never invoked the Notwithstanding Clause and Canadian provinces (most often Quebec) have done so on only a few occasions.[23] This does not mean that this model will not increase the legitimacy of constitutional review even so (I think it does), but if political convention effectively excludes its application, we may not have the kind of lively dialogue about the constitution we might otherwise have. The United States may for this reason make for a better example of a coordinate system: Its constitution's silence on judicial review keeps the question of the ultimate interpreter textually open. Its departmentalist history and long-standing concern with the counter-majoritarian difficulty ensure that opposition to courts is still seen as a viable political option. Of course, here too the stakes have to be sufficiently high. Going against the Supreme Court is politically a high-risk manoeuvre that requires considerable public and institutional support. It may indeed even require the rare constitutional moment.[24] But it is less the frequency of such events that matters and more whether our political and legal culture embraces their possibility.

[21] Ackerman, *Foundations*, pp. 231 et seq.

[22] Robert C. Post and Reva B. Siegel, 'Roe Rage: Democratic Constitutionalism and Backlash', *Harvard Civil Rights—Civil Liberties Law Review*, 42 (2007), 373, 390 et seq.

[23] Rosalind Dixon, 'The Supreme Court of Canada, Charter Dialogue, and Deference', *Osgoode Hall Law Journal*, 47 (2009), 235–86, 248–9.

[24] See Ackerman, *Foundations*.

4. Rationalization

Finally, some may argue that the existence of constitutional dialogue may propel judges to rely on rhetoric and emotional appeals more than rational argument. If courts have to compete with other actors over the final interpretation of constitutional law, they may be at a disadvantage if they confine themselves to dry and technical arguments and be ultimately unable to win the battle for popular opinion. They are therefore likely to use a different style that entails more rhetoric, less technicality, and more emotional appeals.[25] But again, it seems debatable whether this is something to avoid. The technical style of hierarchical courts creates a certain distance to the emotional issues at stake. Emotions, of course, may impact on our ability to think about a case in a fair und unbiased way. We risk being carried away by our feelings rather than trying to see both sides and do justice to them.

But this is not a real problem for coordinate courts, once we distinguish between the oral argument and the judges' deliberations and writing of the judgment. During the former, it seems indeed important to look at things with a certain emotional detachment and to keep consciously in mind the problem of personal bias and ideology. For this reason, it seems important that judges listen not only to the parties, but also to their colleagues with an open mind.[26] With regard to writing decisions, however, a more rhetorical style geared at persuading audiences as well as convincing them appears less troublesome. Indeed, if we want citizens to become constitutional patriots and develop an—if self-reflective and -critical—emotional attachment to the constitution as a common basis for state and society, a somewhat more evocative and emotional style of constitutional jurisprudence may well be useful.

Moreover, rhetoric and appeal to emotions do not themselves diminish the quality of our arguments and discourse. We can passionately argue about something, but do so in a deep and considerate way. Note that this is not inconsistent with my argument for emotional detachment in the process of judicial deliberations. Here, where judges act as decision-makers, they have to be as fair and unbiased as possible. Once they write judgments, however, they act as advocates of their opinions with regard to other political actors

[25] See e.g. Ulrich Haltern, *Europarecht und das Politische* (Tübingen: Mohr Siebeck, 2005), p. 315, who argues that opinions of the US Supreme Court are a major source for political rhetoric in the United States.

[26] The poverty of judicial deliberations in the US Supreme Court, therefore, is not necessarily connected to its nature as a coordinate court, but rather to its internal institutional culture and the Chief Justice's leadership; see e.g. Jeffrey Toobin, *The Nine: Inside the Secret World of the Supreme Court* (New York: Doubleday, 2007).

and the larger public. Yet, even then, an appeal to emotions should not and will not usually stand alone, but will be based on arguments. Legal argument is no different than good political discourse in this regard; it is just that law, with its claim to be generalizable and its structural consistency, can sometimes come close to what is ideal in any public debate. Insofar as reality falls behind, it is important to improve it rather than seek our refuge in the more technical language of law.

5. *Conclusion*

At least in the German context, the arguments against a more coordinate conception of constitutional review are therefore not necessarily compelling. The frequent resistance to American constitutionalism among German legal scholars suffers not only from an inadequate awareness of German blind spots, but also from a shared German opposition to current Republican Party policies and their vocal representatives in the US Supreme Court and academia. They are, however, neither all there is to US constitutionalism nor to coordinate systems of authority more generally. What approach to constitutional justice is more appropriate for Germany is therefore well worth a more open debate. In transformative constitutional systems with their broad vision of constitutional law, coordinate ideas can at least offer a certain counter-weight to the expansion of judicial power by challenging the finality of judicial authority. In the ideal case, they may even encourage public deliberation about our constitutional commitments.

B. Prospects for German Constitutionalism

If there is much to like about coordinate constitutionalism, what are the chances that constitutional review in Germany could become more coordinate, more dialogic? Or is German constitutionalism forever mired in the German hierarchical legal culture?

No less than a traumatic childhood, an existing culture of authority is no straitjacket from which we cannot escape. As I have emphasized in the course of this book, legal culture is but one factor in explaining the rise of German constitutionalism and there are other factors and forces pulling in different directions. Path-dependence is not absolute, and constitutional courts are always to some degree hybrid institutions, working at the boundaries between law and politics. Even if they successfully locate themselves within the realm of law, they are nevertheless more vulnerable to challenges than traditional legal institutions.

Yet, at least in the current political and legal cultural climate, fundamental changes are not likely. While we can perhaps imagine a slight shift to a more political understanding of constitutional justice, it is unlikely that the German Court will turn towards a fully blown coordinate model. This would require more significant transformations in the underlying political and legal culture than we might reasonably expect to happen anytime soon. What changes, then, might we realistically expect? And what might a somewhat more coordinate conception of constitutional justice look like and lastly, which elements of the German hierarchical model of constitutionalism would be likely to stay?

At the core of German legal culture are its scientific approach to law and legal interpretation and, related to that, the importance of expertise for judicial office. Many other characteristics—such as the frequency of dissents and rhetorical style—are only expressions of this core idea. Given that, can we reconcile these core ideas with a more coordinate conception of justice? An example of such an approach can be found in the French system, where 'government' itself assumes the character of a special discipline to be studied. Here, courts may be drawn into this sphere of specialized government as an important part of 'politics'. Staffed with a number of former politicians as well as laypersons, the Conseil Constitutionnel is often described as a political body rather than a court. If it formulates its judgments nevertheless in the traditional judicial style of French courts, this must not trick us into assuming its judicial character. Rather, we must understand it as part of the French culture of government as professional administration.[27] The most notable French example of this kind of institution is the Conseil d'Etat, which is partly legal counsel to the government and partly a court.[28] It fulfils both its roles under the same roof, and its judges and civil servants not only regularly swap sides, but are also in their majority all trained in the same institution, the famous Ecole Nationale d'Administration.

This is, however, not a likely prospect for German constitutionalism. Though Germany has a strong administrative culture, the German parliamentarian and bureaucratic systems differ considerably from the French. The German system accords a much smaller role to the executive and has

[27] I have benefitted from discussions with Hannah Birkenkötter and Quentin Epron about the French case. As is apparent, the French case does not fit neatly into my analytical categories of hierarchical vs coordinate authority; so far, my best understanding suggests that it would be a hybrid.

[28] Bruno Latour, *The Making of Law: An Ethnography of the Conseil d'État*, trans. Marina Brilman and Alain Pottage (Cambridge: Polity Press, 2010). See also Mitchel de S.-O.-l'E. Lasser, *Judicial Deliberations: A Comparative Analysis of Transparency and Legitimacy* (Oxford: Oxford University Press, 2004).

no institution comparable to the Ecole Nationale d'Administration in providing specialized training for the future political-administrative elite. And while the German Bundestag itself is in many ways a working parliament relying on the expertise of its members, this nevertheless makes for a rather different, less bureaucratic political culture than exists in France. It is therefore difficult to imagine the German Court taking a French approach to matters and adopting a political rather than legal character while preserving its expert-centred authority. What we can imagine though, is a more toned-down version. In this scenario, constitutional court judges might be accorded a more statesmen-like role that encompasses *both* legal knowledge and political experience.[29] That way, the Court might still be able to preserve a certain distance from the realm of party politics and establish itself as an independent institution with a certain non-partisan authority. At the same time, the public perception of the Court as a more political institution would make its interpretations more susceptible to public and political criticism and resistance. We would expect the Court to react to this criticism and over time adopt more sensitivity towards political constraints and pressures.

However, to produce even this kind of change in the public perception of the Court would require a considerable degree of sustained court criticism, which seems to come and go in waves. More recently, there is at least among scholars a notable trend towards more critical assessments of the Constitutional Court. A collection of four critical essays by four younger German law professors, called 'The Court without Boundaries' (*Das entgrenzte Gericht*),[30] is the most well-known manifestation of this academic trend. The question of the Court's role as final constitutional interpreter also occupied the younger all-public-lawyers conference in Bern in 2013, demonstrating renewed interest in the question. Nevertheless, most scholars, especially of the younger generation, are firmly supportive of the Court. The organizers of the Bern conference (which included a number of Swiss and Austrian participants who are typically more sceptical towards strong forms of constitutional review) took an interesting poll: After a panel discussion about the relative advantages and disadvantages of weak (Swiss) and strong (German) forms of constitutional review, 151 out of 191 participants voted in favour of the statement 'I reject the idea that constitutional review poses a risk for

[29] The kind of role I have in mind for the judges would resemble the one envisaged by Martin Drath in his seminal presentation at the public lawyers' conference in 1951 (Martin Drath, 'Die Grenzen der Verfassungsgerichtsbarkeit', *Vereinigung der deutschen Staatsrechtslehrer*, Heft 9 (1950), 17–111), albeit in a restricted form since we are now dealing with an established democracy that no longer requires the Court to assume the paternalistic role of educating citizens that Drath initially envisaged.

[30] Matthias Jestaedt et al. (eds), *Das entgrenzte Gericht*.

the primacy of politics', with only forty participants disagreeing—many of them, one suspects, Swiss and Austrian lawyers.

There is, however, a renewed interest in post-war constitutional history and more theoretical and interdisciplinary questions including empirical research, as the recent advisory report of the German Council of Science and Humanities (*Wissenschaftsrat*) 'Perspectives of Jurisprudence' demonstrates.[31] If this trend holds, prompting scholars to assume more often the external perspective of observer rather than the internal one of participant in the legal system, there may be less unquestioning support of the Court in the future. Good historical and empirical research will be useful for developing a more realist picture of the Court and its shortcomings. It is also likely to draw attention to the role of other actors besides the Court that are and have been key to the development of German constitutionalism. Theory in turn can help to stir and sharpen the debate about the legitimacy of constitutional review and to develop a thicker normative account for when the Court should get involved. Nevertheless, scholarly criticism and rethinking is unlikely to have much effect if not backed by political pressure. Whether politicians decide to exercise such pressure depends of course largely on the Court's decisions and the surrounding political factors. Only if the Court's involvement threatens sufficiently important political projects will politicians publicly criticize the Court. Yet, the Court can manage these forces through its judgments to a considerable degree, even if it is not fully in control of them.

Ultimately, however, the development of a more fully coordinate culture of authority seems unlikely. Such a change would imply a shift towards a different, more republican way of thinking about politics in general. True, Germans increasingly demand more direct forms of democratic engagement. This trend has its roots in the political protests in Eastern Germany before German Re-Unification, and on the Western side mainly in the environmentalist and pacifist movements.[32] Today, it expresses itself in major public protests over infrastructural projects, the ascent of the German Pirate Party and their internal-democracy agenda, as well as an increasing opening-up of administrative processes to citizens and the use of referenda in state politics. Direct democracy and chances for civil society engagement are therefore somewhat on the rise. At the same time, it is hard to say how long this trend will persist. Like its East German predecessor, the Round Tables, the Pirate

[31] Wissenschaftsrat, 'Perspektiven der Rechtswissenschaft in Deutschland: Situation, Analysen, Empfehlungen', 9 November 2012, <http://www.wissenschaftsrat.de/download/archiv/2558-12.pdf>.

[32] See e.g. for a discussion, Ingo Bode, Adalbert Evers, and Ansgar Klein, *Bürgergesellschaft als Projekt: Eine Bestandsaufnahme zu Entwicklung und Förderung zivilgesellschaftlicher Potenziale in Deutschland* (Heidelberg: Springer, 2009).

Party has already lost much of its steam again. More importantly, the call for more direct democracy expressed by these movements has so far never even touched on the question of constitutional review or the Court's authority, nor does it seem particularly likely that it will any time soon. As long as the Court is primarily regarded as the only institution able to reign in established political parties, civil society organizations are likely to look to the Court as an ally rather than an institution whose power needs rethinking.

While conflicts over the Court's judgments can therefore always arise, since there are limits to its ability to gauge reactions in advance, little suggests that renewed attacks or criticism would lead to a more sustained change in attitudes towards the Court. The recent amendment of the selection procedure of the judges in the German Bundestag demonstrates this. It has the Bundestag as a whole elect (their half of) the Justices of the Constitutional Court on the recommendation of the selection committee rather than, as it was previously done, letting the committee itself elect the Justices.[33] However, even with these changes, parliamentarians will merely cast their vote without any previous discussion of the candidates in the plenary session. According to the bill's official explanatory memorandum, this is meant to avoid a politicized 'hearing' (English in the original, which demonstrates the US background to the German debate) that might harm candidates and contribute to the politicization of the Court. Moreover, popular support for the Court has remained high over decades, in spite of some temporary bumps in the 1990s, and the feeling that a strong constitutional court is an essential component of post-war German society is widely shared.[34] Even though some adjustments towards a more political conception of the Court can always occur if the Court is causing too much political frustration, it seems unlikely that German constitutionalism will become truly dialogic and coordinate.

C. Postscript

German constitutionalism holds many attractions—not only to Germans, but also to foreign nations and scholars who have taken over famous provisions of the Basic Law and features of the Court's jurisprudence: dignity,

[33] Deutscher Bundestag, Drucksache 18/2737, Entwurf eines Neunten Gesetzes zur Änderung des Bundesverfassungsgerichtsgesetzes, <http://dip21.bundestag.de/dip21/btd/18/027/1802737.pdf>.

[34] Chapter 6, on this aspect in particular, see also Justin Collings, *Democracy's Guardians: A History of the German Federal Constitutional Court 1951–2001* (Oxford: Oxford University Press, forthcoming 2015).

the individual complaint procedure, and proportionality are just some of the examples. Yet, when we look elsewhere, these legal exports often look different from their German originals. German constitutionalism is not easily manufactured abroad, but this may well be a good thing. Admirers of the German model are often insufficiently aware of what this model really entails.

This book has sought to fill this gap. German Value Formalism is much more than the conjoining of a couple of German constitutional doctrines: It is a complex and slightly precarious synthesis of two rather different and often inconsistent ideas of what law and judicial authority are and should be. Only once we understand how it works can we assess the chances that something similar will be successful elsewhere. And only once we see both its problems and advantages can we decide if and when it is something to advocate or admire.

Bibliography

Ackerman, Bruce, *Reconstructing American Law* (Cambridge: Harvard University Press, 1984).

Ackerman, Bruce, *We the People. Foundations* (Cambridge: Harvard University Press, 1991).

Ackerman, Bruce, *We the People. Transformations* (Cambridge: Harvard University Press, 2000).

Ackerman, Bruce, *We the People. The Civil Rights Revolution* (Cambridge: Harvard University Press, 2014).

Ackerman, Bruce, 'The New Separation of Powers.' *Harvard Law Review*, 113(3) (2000), 633–729.

Agresto, John, *The Supreme Court and Constitutional Democracy* (Ithaca: Cornell University Press, 1984).

Alexy, Robert, *A Theory of Constitutional Rights* (Oxford: Oxford University Press, 2002).

Altman, Scott, 'Beyond Candor', *Michigan Law Review*, 89 (1990), 296–351.

Anschütz, Gerhard, *Die Verfassung des Deutschen Reiches vom 11. August 1919. Ein Kommentar für Wissenschaft und Praxis*, 14th edn (Berlin, 1933).

Atiyah, Patrick S. and Robert S. Summers, *Form and Substance in Anglo-American Law: A Comparative Study of Legal Reasoning, Legal Theory, and Legal Institutions* (Oxford: Clarendon Press, 1991).

Baldus, Manfred, 'Wer war und wofür steht Martin Drath?', *Recht und Politik*, 43 (2007), 86.

Barkow, Rachel E., 'More Supreme than Court? The Fall of the Political Question Doctrine and the Rise of Judicial Supremacy', *Columbia Law Review*, 102(2) (2002), 237–336.

Bassok, Or, 'The Supreme Court's New Source of Legitimacy', *University of Pennsylvania Journal of Constitutional Law*, 16 (2013), 153.

Baxi, Upendra, 'Taking Suffering Seriously: Social Action Litigation in the Supreme Court of India', *Third World Legal Studies* (1985), 107–32.

Berman, Harold J., *Law and Revolution: The Formation of the Western Legal Tradition* (Cambridge: Harvard University Press, 1983).

Bickel, Alexander M., *The Least Dangerous Branch: The Supreme Court at the Bar of Politics* (New Haven: Yale University Press, 1962).

Black, Charles L., *Structure and Relationship in Constitutional Law* (Woodbridge: Ox Bow Press, 1985).

Böckenförde, Ernst-Wolfgang, 'Entstehung und Wandel des Rechtsstaatsbegriffs', in H. Ehmke and H. Scharoun (eds), *Festschrift für Adolf Arndt zum 65. Geburtstag* (Frankfurt am Main: Europäische Verlagsanstalt, 1969), 53–76.

Böckenförde, Ernst-Wolfgang, 'Die Methoden der Verfassungsinterpretation-Bestandsaufnahme und Kritik', *Neue Juristische Wochenschrift*, 46 (1976), 2089–99.

Böckenförde, Ernst-Wolfgang, 'Grundrechtstheorie und Grundrechtsinterpretation', in Ernst-Wolfgang Böckenförde (ed.), *Staat, Verfassung, Demokratie: Studien zur Verfassungstheorie und zum Verfassungsrecht* (Frankfurt am Main: Suhrkamp, 1991), 115–45.

Bode, Ingo, Adalbert Evers, and Ansgar Klein, *Bürgergesellschaft als Projekt: Eine Bestandsaufnahme zu Entwicklung und Förderung zivilgesellschaftlicher Potenziale in Deutschland* (Heidelberg: Springer, 2009).

Bogdandy, Armin von, 'The Past and Promise of Doctrinal Constructivism: A Strategy for Responding to the Challenges Facing Constitutional Scholarship in Europe', *International Journal of Constitutional Law*, 7(3) (2009), 364.

Bogdandy, Armin von, 'Europäische und nationale Identität', *Vereinigung der deutschen Staatsrechtslehrer*, 62 (2002), 156.

Bomhoff, Jacco, *Balancing Constitutional Rights. The Origins and Meanings of Postwar Legal Discourse* (Cambridge: Cambridge University Press, 2013).

Brinks, Daniel M and Varun Gauri, 'Human Rights as Demands for Communicative Action', *World Bank Policy Research Working Paper*, 5951 (2012), <http://ssrn.com/abstract=1988039>.

Brinks, Daniel M and Varun Gauri, 'Transforming Legal Theory in the Light of Practice: the Judicial Application of Social and Economic Rights to Private Orderings', in *Courting Social Justice: Judicial Enforcement of Social and Economic Rights in the Developing World*, ed. Daniel M. Brinks and Varun Gauri (Cambridge: Cambridge University Press, 2010).

Brodocz, André, *Die Macht der Judikative* (Heidelberg: Springer, 2009).

Brodocz, André and Steven Schäller, 'Hinter der Blende der Richterbank—Über den Tag der offenen Tür am Bundesverfassungsgericht', in Hans Vorländer (ed.), *Die Deutungsmacht der Verfassungsgerichtsbarkeit* (Wiesbaden: Verlag für Sozialwissenschaften, 2006), 235–58.

Bumke, Christian, *Der Grundrechtsvorbehalt. Untersuchungen über die Begrenzung und Ausgestaltung der Grundrechte* (Baden-Baden: C. H. Beck, 1998).

Bülow, Birgit von, *Die Staatsrechtslehre Der Nachkriegszeit (1945–1952)* (Berlin: Berlin Verlag Arno Spitz GmbH, 1996).

Bushell, Allison and Peter Hogg. 'The Charter Dialogue between Courts and Legislatures', *Osgoode Hall Law Journal*, 35 (1997), 75–105.

Cameron, Edwin, 'Legal Chauvinism, Executive-Mindedness and Justice-LC Steyn's Impact on South African Law', *South African Law Journal*, 99 (1982), 38–75.

Carolan, Eoin, *The New Separation of Powers. A Theory for the Modern State* (Oxford: Oxford University Press, 2009).

Chayes, Abram, 'The Role of the Judge in Public Law Litigation', *Harvard Law Review*, 89 (1976), 1281–316.

Chayes, Abram, 'The Supreme Court 1981 Term—Foreword: Public Law Litigation and the Burger Court', *Harvard Law Review*, 96 (1982), 4–60.

Cockrell, Alfred, 'Rainbow Jurisprudence', *South African Journal on Human Rights*, 12 (1996), 1–38.

Cohen-Eliya, Moshe and Iddo Porat, 'American Balancing and German Proportionality: The Historical Origins', *International Journal of Constitutional Law*, 8 (2010), 263–86.

Cohen-Eliya, Moshe and Iddo Porat, *Proportionality and Constitutional Culture* (Cambridge: Cambridge University Press, 2013).

Collings, Justin, *Democracy's Guardians: Constitutional Justice in Postwar Germany, 1951–1989* (Oxford: Oxford University Press, forthcoming 2015).

Corder, Hugh, *Judges at Work: The Role and Attitude of the South African Appellate Judiciary, 1910–1950* (Cape Town: Juta, 1984).

Dahl, Robert A., 'Decision-Making in a Democracy: The Supreme Court as National Policy-Maker', *Journal of Public Law*, 6 (1957), 279.

Damaška, Mirjan R., *The Faces of Justice and State Authority: A Comparative Approach to the Legal Process* (New Haven: Yale University Press, 1986).

Damaška, Mirjan R., 'Reflections on American Constitutionalism', *American Journal of Comparative Law*, Supp. 38 (1990), 421–44.

Davis, Dennis, 'Private Law after 1994: Progressive Development or Schizoid Confusion', *South African Journal on Human Rights*, 24 (2008), 318–29.

Davis, Dennis and Michelle le Roux, *Precedent and Possibility: The (Ab)use of Law in South Africa* (Cape Town: Double Storey, 2009).

Davis, Dennis and Karl Klare, Transformative Constitutionalism and the Common Law and Customary Law', *South African Journal on Human Rights*, 26(3) (2010), 403–509.

Deutscher Bundestag und Bundesarchiv under guidance from Hans-Joachim Stelzl and Hartmut Weber (eds), *Der Parlamentarische Rat 1948–1949. Akten Und Protokolle. Band 9: Plenum* (München: Oldenbourg, 1996).

Deutscher Bundestag und Bundesarchiv under guidance from Hans-Joachim Stelzl and Hartmut Weber (eds), *Der Parlamentarische Rat 1948–1949. Akten Und Protokolle. Band 13: Ausschuß für Organisation des Bundes / Ausschuß für Verfassungsgerichtshof und Rechtspflege* (München: Oldenbourg, 2002).

Deutscher Bundestag und Bundesarchiv under guidance from Horst Risse and Hartmut Weber (eds), *Der Parlamentarische Rat 1948–1949. Akten und Protokolle. Band 14: Hauptausschuß, Teilband 1* (München: Oldenbourg, 2009).

Dicey, Albert V., *Lectures Introductory to the Study of the Law of the Constitution* (London: Macmillan, 1885).

Di Fabio, Udo, 'Grundrechte als Werteordnung', *Juristenzeitung* (2004), 1–8.

Dixon, Rosalind, 'The Supreme Court of Canada, Charter Dialogue, and Deference', *Osgoode Hall Law Journal*, 47 (2009), 235–86.

Dobbs, Dan D., 'Contempt of Court: A Survey', *Cornell Law Review*, 56 (1971), 183–235.

Drath, Martin, 'Die Grenzen der Verfassungsgerichtsbarkeit', *Vereinigung der deutschen Staatsrechtslehrer*, 9 (1950), 17–111.

Dreier, Horst, *Rechtslehre, Staatssoziologie Und Demokratietheorie bei Hans Kelsen* (Baden-Baden: Nomos, 1990).

Dreier, Horst and Hartmut Bauer (eds), *Grundgesetz. Kommentar*, 3rd edn (Tübingen: Mohr Siebeck, 2012).

Drosdeck, Thomas, *Die herrschende Meinung—Autorität als Rechtsquelle* (Berlin: Duncker & Humblot, 1989).

Du Plessis, Lourens, 'The Evolution of Constitutionalism and the Emergence of a Constitutional Jurisprudence in South Africa: An Evaluation of the South African Constitutional Court's Approach to Interpretation', *Saskatchewan Law Review*, 62 (1999), 299–328.

Dürig, Günther, 'Der Grundrechtssatz der Menschenwürde. Entwurf eines praktikablen Wertsystems der Grundrechte aus Art. 1 Abs. I in Verbindung mit Art. 19 Abs. II des Grundgesetzes', *Archiv für öffentliches Recht*, 81 (1956), 117.

Dworkin, Ronald M., *Law's Empire* (Cambridge: Harvard University Press, 1986).

Dyzenhaus, David, *Hard Cases in Wicked Legal Systems: Pathologies of Legality* (Oxford: Oxford University Press, 2010).

Ebsen, Ingwer, *Das Bundesverfassungsgericht als Element gesellschaftlicher Selbstregulierung* (Berlin: Duncker & Humblot, 1983).

Ehmke, Horst, 'Prinzipien der Verfassungsinterpretation', *Vereinigung der Deutschen Staatsrechtslehrer*, 20 (1963), 53–102.

Ellmann, Stephen, *In a Time of Trouble: Law and Liberty in South Africa's State of Emergency* (New York: Oxford University Press, 1992).

Ely, John H., *Democracy and Distrust: A Theory of Judicial Review* (Cambridge: Harvard University Press, 1980).

Engstrom, Kristin M., 'Establishment Clause Jurisprudence: The Souring of Lemon and the Search for a New Test', *Pacific Law Journal*, 27 (1995), 121–60.

Epp, Charles R., *The Rights Revolution: Lawyers, Activists, and Supreme Courts in Comparative Perspective* (Chicago: University of Chicago Press, 1998).

Eskridge, Jr., William N. and John Ferejohn. *A Republic of Statues: The New American Constitution* (New Haven: Yale University Press, 2013).

Fallon, Jr., Richard H., 'The Core of an Uneasy Case for Judicial Review', *Harvard Law Review*, 121 (2008), 1693–736.

Fikentscher, Wolfgang, *Methoden des Rechts in vergleichender Darstellung. Band II: Anglo-amerikanischer Rechtskreis* (Tübingen: Mohr Siebeck, 1975); *Methoden des Rechts Band III: Mitteleuropäischer Rechtskreis* (Tübingen: Mohr Siebeck, 1976).

Fleming, James E., 'Judicial Review Without Judicial Supremacy: Taking the Constitution Seriously Outside the Courts', *Fordham Law Review*, 73 (2005), 1377–400.

Forsthoff, Ernst, *Verfassungsprobleme Des Sozialstaates* (Münster: Aschendorff, 1954).

Forsthoff, Ernst, 'Die Umbildung des Verfassungsgesetzes', in Klaus Frey (ed.), *Rechtsstaat im Wandel* (München: C. H. Beck, 1976), pp. 130–52.

Forsthoff, Ernst, 'Zur Problematik der Verfassungsauslegung, in Klaus Frey (ed.), *Rechtsstaat im Wandel* (München: C. H. Beck, 1976), pp. 153–74.

Forsthoff, Ernst, *Recht und Sprache* (Halle: Niemeyer, 1940).

Forsthoff, Ernst, 'Das Bundesverfassungsgericht und das Berufsbeamtentum', *Deutsche Verwaltungsblätter*, (1954), 69.

Fowkes, James, *Building the Constitution: The Practice of Constitutional Interpretation in South Africa Since 1994* (Cambridge: Cambridge University Press, forthcoming 2016).

Fowkes, James, 'Socio-economic Rights and the Newness Hypothesis', Max Planck Lecture, delivered 29 January 2014.

Fowkes, James, 'Civil Procedure in Public Interest Litigation: Tradition, Collaboration and the Managerial Judge', *Cambridge Journal of International & Comparative Law*, 1 (2012), 235.

Fraenkel, Ernst, *The Dual State* (Oxford: Oxford University Press, 1941).

Fowkes, James and Michaela Hailbronner, 'Courts as the Nation's Conscience: Empirically Testing the Intuitions Behind Ethicalization', in *Ethik und Recht—Die Ethisierung des Rechts/Ethics and Law—The Ethicalization of Law*, ed. Silja Vöneky, Britta Beylage-Haarmann, Anja Höfelmeier, and Anna-Katharina Hübler (Heidelberg: Springer, 2013).

Frankenberg, Günter, 'Vorsicht Demokratie! Kritik der juridischen Versicherung einer Gesellschaft gegen die Risiken der Selbstregierung', in Redaktion Kritische Justiz (ed.), *Demokratie und Grundgesetz* (Baden-Baden: Nomos, 2000), pp. 177–82.

Friedman, Barry, *The Will of the People. How Public Opinion Has Influenced the Supreme Court and Shaped the Meaning of the Constitution* (London: Macmillan, 2010).

Friedman, Barry, 'The Birth of an Academic Obsession: The History of the Countermajoritarian Difficulty, Part Five', *Yale Law Journal*, 112 (2002), 153.

Gawron, Thomas and Ralph Rogowski, 'Introduction. Constitutional Litigation as Dispute Processing: Comparing the U.S. Supreme Court and the German Federal Constitutional Court', in Ralph Rogowski and Thomas Gawron (eds), *Constitutional Courts in Comparison* (New York: Berghahn Books, 2002).

Gebhardt, Jürgen, 'Verfassungspatriotismus als Identitätskonzept der Nation', *Aus Politik und Zeitgeschichte*, 43 (1993), 29–37.

Gilliomee, Herrmann, *The Afrikaners: Biography of a People* (London: C. Hurst & Co., 2003).

Ginsburg, Tom and Tokujin Matsudaira, 'The Judicialization of Japanese Politics?', in Tom Ginsburg and Harry N. Schreiber (eds), *The Japanese Legal System: An Era of Transition* (Berkeley: University of California Press, 2012).

Goerlich, Helmut, *Wertordnung und Grundgesetz. Kritik einer Argumentationsfigur des Bundesverfassungsgerichts* (Baden-Baden: Nomos, 1973).

Goldmann, Matthias, 'Adjudicating Economics? Central Bank Independence and the Appropriate Standard of Judicial Review', *German Law Journal*, 15 (2014), 265.

Görtemaker, Manfred, *Geschichte der Bundesrepublik Deutschland. Von der Gründung bis zur Gegenwart* (München: Beck, 1999).

Grabenwarter, Christoph, 'Verfassungsinterpretation, Verfassungswandel, Verfassungsfortbildung', in Hedwig Kopetz , Josef Marko, and Klaus Poier (eds), *Soziokultureller Wandel im Verfassungsstaat: Phänomene politischer Transformation. Festschrift für Wolfgang Mantl zum 65. Geburtstag* (Wien: Böhlau, 2004).

Grechenig, Kristoffel R. and Martin Gelter, 'The Transatlantic Divergence in Legal Thought: American Law and Economics vs. German Doctrinalism', paper presented at the American Law and Economics Association Annual Meetings, 2008.

Greve, Michael S., 'The Non-Reformation of Administrative Law: Standing to Sue and Public Interest Litigation in West German Environmental Law', *Cornell International Law Journal*, 22 (1989), 197–243.

Grigoleit, Klaus J., *Bundesverfassungsgericht und deutsche Frage. Eine dogmatische und historische Untersuchung zum judikativen Anteil an der Staatsleitung* (Tübingen: Mohr Siebeck, 2004).

Grigoleit, Klaus J., 'Bundesverfassungsgericht und sozialliberale Koalition unter Willy Brandt: Der Streit um den Grundvertrag', in Martin Möllers and Rober C. Ooyen (eds), *Das Bundesverfassungsgericht im politischen System* (Wiesbaden: Verlag für Sozialwissenschaften, 2006), 163–74.

Grimm, Dieter, 'Reformalisierung des Rechtsstaats als Demokratiepostulat?', *Juristische Schulung*, 20 (1980), 704–9.

Grimm, Dieter, 'Integration by Constitution', *International Journal of Constitutional Law*, 3 (2005), 193–208.

Grimm, Dieter, 'Proportionality in Canadian and German Constitutional Jurisprudence', *University of Toronto Law Journal*, 57 (2007), 383–97.

Günther, Frieder, *Denken vom Staat her: Die bundesdeutsche Staatsrechtslehre zwischen Dezision und Integration 1949–1970* (München: Oldenbourg, 2004).

Gusy, Christoph, *Die Weimarer Reichsverfassung* (Tübingen: Mohr Siebeck, 1997).

Häberle, Peter, 'Die offene Gesellschaft der Verfassungsinterpreten', *Juristenzeitung* (1975), 297–305.

Habermas, Jürgen, 'Verfassungspatriotismus', in Jürgen Habermas (ed.), *Die nachholende Revolution* (Frankfurt: Suhrkamp, 1990).

Habermas, Jürgen, *Between Facts and Norms: Contributions to a Discourse Theory of Law and Democracy*, trans. W. Rehg (Cambridge: MIT Press, 1996).

Habermas, Jürgen, 'Apologetische Tendenzen', in Jürgen Habermas (ed.), *Eine Art Schadensabwicklung* (Frankfurt: Suhrkamp, 1987).

Hailbronner, Michaela, 'Rethinking the Rise of the German Constitutional Court: From Anti-Nazism to Value Formalism', *International Journal of Constitutional Law*, 12(3) (2014), 626–49.

Hailbronner, Michaela, 'We the Experts. Die geschlossene Gesellschaft der Verfassungsinterpreten', *Der Staat*, 53(3) (2014), 425–43.

Hailbronner, Michaela and Stefan Martini, 'Germany', in Andras Jakab, Arthur Dyevre, and Giulio Itzcovich (eds), *Comparative Constitutional Reasoning* (Cambridge: Cambridge University Press, forthcoming 2015).

Halberstam, Daniel and Christoph Möllers, 'The German Constitutional Court says Ja zu Deutschland', *German Law Journal*, 10 (2009), 1241–57.

Haley, John O., 'The Japanese Judiciary: Maintaining Integrity, Autonomy and the Public Trust', in Daniel J. Foote (ed.), *Law in Japan: A Turning Point* (Seattle: University of Washington Press, 2007), 99–135.

Haley, John O., 'Constitutional Adjudication in Japan: Context, Structures, and Values', *Washington University Law Review*, 88 (2011), 1467–91.

Haltern, Ulrich R., *Verfassungsgerichtsbarkeit, Demokratie und Mißtrauen: Das Bundesverfassungsgericht in einer Verfassungstheorie zwischen Populismus und Progressivismus* (Berlin: Duncker & Humblot, 1998).

Haltern, Ulrich R., *Was bedeutet Souveränität* (Tübingen: Mohr Siebeck, 2007).

Haltern, Ulrich R., *Europarecht und das Politische* (Tübingen: Mohr Siebeck, 2005).

Häußler, Richard, *Der Konflikt zwischen Bundesverfassungsgericht und politischer Führung* (Berlin: Duncker & Humblot, 1994).

Hegel, Georg W. F., *Grundlinien Der Philosophie des Rechts*, ed. Georg Lasson (Leipzig: F. Meiner, 1911).

Henkel, Michael and Oliver Lembcke, 'Staat als Lebensaufgabe: Martin Drath', *Kritische Justiz*, 36(4) (2003), 445–61.

Henne, Thomas, 'Erich Lüth vs. Veit Harlan—Sechs Göttinger Beiträge zum Lüth-Urteil des Bundesverfassungsgerichts von 1958', in Eva Schumann (ed.), *Kontinuitäten und Zäsuren. Rechtswissenschaft und Justiz im "Dritten Reich" und in der Nachkriegszeit* (Göttingen: Wallstein, 2008), pp. 213–32.

Hennis, Wilhelm, 'Verfassung und Verfassungswirklichkeit—ein deutsches Problem', in *Regieren im modernen Staat* (Tübingen: Mohr Siebeck, 1999), pp. 183–213.

Herbert, Ulrich, 'Integration Der Jungen Republik Durch Verfassungsrecht?', in Michael Stolleis (ed.), *Das Bonner Grundgesetz: Altes Recht und neue Verfassung in den ersten Jahrzehnten der Bundesrepublik Deutschland (1949–1969)* (Berlin: BWV, 2006), pp. 85–102.

Herbert, Ulrich, *Geschichte Deutschlands im 20. Jahrhundert* (München: Beck, 2014).

Herdegen, Matthias, Roman Herzog, Hans H. Klein, and Rupert Scholz (eds), *Maunz/Dürig: Grundgesetz Kommentar* (München: C. H. Beck, 2013).

Herget, James E. and Stephen Wallace, 'German Free Law Movement As the Source of American Legal Realism', *Virginia Law Review*, 73 (1987), 399–456.

Hillgruber, Christian, 'Die Leistungsfähigkeit der Wissenschaft vom Öffentlichen Recht', *Vereinigung der deutschen Staatsrechtslehrer*, 67 (2008), 8–56.

Hirsch, Martin, Diemut Majer, and Jürgen Meinck (eds), *Recht, Verwaltung und Justiz im Nationalsozialismus: ausgewählte Schriften, Gesetze und Gerichtsentscheidungen von 1933 bis 1945* (Baden-Baden: Nomos, 1997).

Holmes, Jr., Oliver W., *The Common Law* (Boston: Little, Brown and Company, 1881).

Höltl, Johanna, *Die Lückenfüllung der klassisch-europäischen Kodifikationen: zur Analogie im ALR, Code Civil und ABGB* (Wien: Lit-Verlag, 2005).

Hönnige, Christoph, Sascha Kneip, and Astrid Lorenz (eds), *Verfassungswandel im Mehrebenensystem* (Wiesbaden: Springer, 2011).

Hufen, Friedhelm, *Staatsrecht II. Grundrechte* (München: Beck, 2007).

Hwang, Shu-Perng, *Verfassungsgerichtlicher Jurisdiktionsstaat? Eine Rechtsvergleichende Analyse zur Kompetenzabgrenzung von Verfassungsgericht und Gesetzgeber in den USA und der Bundesrepublik Deutschland* (Berlin: Duncker & Humblot, 2005).

Iles, Kevin, 'Limiting Socio-Economic Rights: Beyond the Internal Limitations Clauses', *South African Journal on Human Rights*, 20 (2004), 448–65.

Iles, Kevin, 'A Fresh Look at Limitations: Unpacking Section 36', *South African Journal on Human Rights*, 23 (2007), 68–92.

Itoh, Hiroshi, 'Judicial Review and Judicial Activism in Japan', *Law and Contemporary Problems*, 53(1) (1990), 169–79.

Jacobson, Arthur J. and Bernhard Schlink, *Weimar: A Jurisprudence of Crisis* (Berkeley: University of California Press, 2000).

Jaggi, Stephan, 'The Forgotten Revolution? Rediscovering the 1989 Revolution in the GDR and its Impact on Unified Germany's Constitutional Law', PhD thesis, Yale University, 2012.

Jestaedt, Matthias, Oliver Lepsius, Christoph Möllers, and Christoph Schönberger, *Das entgrenzte Gericht: Eine kritische Bilanz nach sechzig Jahren Bundesverfassungsgericht* (Berlin: Suhrkamp, 2011).

Kahan, Dan M., 'The Supreme Court 2010 Term—Foreword: Neutral Principles, Motivated Cognition, and Some Problems for Constitutional Law', *Harvard Law Review*, 125 (2011), 1.

Kahn, Paul W., *The Cultural Study of Law: Reconstructing Legal Scholarship* (Chicago: University of Chicago Press, 2000).

Kahn, Paul W., *Political Theology: Four New Chapters on the Concept of Sovereignty* (New York: Columbia University Press, 2011).

Kaiser, Anna-Bettina, *Die Kommunikation der Verwaltung: Diskurse zu den Kommunikationsbeziehungen zwischen staatlicher Verwaltung und Privaten in der Verwaltungsrechtswissenschaft der Bundesrepublik Deutschland* (Baden-Baden: Nomos, 2007).

Kantorowicz, Herrmann, *Der Kampf um die Rechtswissenschaft* (Berlin: Berliner Wissenschaftsverlag, reprinted 2003).

Kelsen, Hans, *Wer soll der Hüter der Verfassung sein?: Abhandlungen zur Theorie der Verfassungsgerichtsbarkeit in der pluralistischen, parlamentarischen Demokratie* (Tübingen: Mohr Siebeck, 2008).

Kern, Ernst, 'Probleme der Rechtsprechung des Bundesverfassungsgerichts', *Deutsche Verwaltungsblätter* (1954), 211.

Kirchhof, Gregor, Stefan Magen, and Karsten Schneider (eds), *Was weiß Dogmatik? Was leistet und wie steuert die Dogmatik des Öffentlichen Rechts?* (Tübingen: Mohr Siebeck, 2012).

Kirchhof, Paul, 'Der demokratische Rechtsstaat—Die Staatsform der Zugehörigen', in Josef Isensee and Paul Kirchhof (eds), *Handbuch Des Staatsrechts IX* (Heidelberg: C. F. Müller, 1997).

Kischel, Uwe, 'Darf der Gesetzgeber das Bundesverfassungsgericht igonorieren? Zum erneuten Erlaß für nichtig erklärter Gesetze', *Archiv des öffentlichen Rechts*, 131 (2006), 219–54.

Klare, Karl E., 'Legal Culture and Transformative Constitutionalism', *South African Journal on Human Rights*, 14 (1998), 146–88.

Klein, Eckard, 'Grundrechtliche Schutzpflicht des Staates', *Neue Juristische Wochenzeitschrift* (1989), 1633.

Klein, Oliver, *Verfassungsprozessrecht: ein Lehr-und Handbuch* (Heidelberg: C. F. Müller, 2012).

Kneip, Sascha, *Verfassungsgerichte als demokratische Akteure: Der Beitrag des Bundesverfassungsgerichts zur Qualität der bundesdeutschen Demokratie* (Baden-Baden: Nomos, 2009).

Kommers, Donald P. and Russell A. Miller, *The Constitutional Jurisprudence of the Federal Republic of Germany*, 3rd edn (Durham: Duke University Press, 2012).

Korioth, Klaus and Stefan Schlaich, *Das Bundesverfassungsgericht: Stellung, Verfahren, Entscheidungen*, 9th edn (München: C. H. Beck, 2012).

Köttgen, Arnold, *Deutsche Verwaltung*, 3rd edn (Berlin: F. Vahlen, 1944).

Köttgen, Arnold, 'Das Beamtenurteil des Bundesverfassungsgerichts', *Archiv des öffentlichen Rechts*, 79 (1954), 351.

Kramer, Larry, *The People Themselves: Popular Constitutionalism and Judicial Review* (New York: Oxford University Press, 2004).

Kranenpohl, Uwe, *Hinter dem Schleier des Beratungsgeheimnisses: Der Willensbildungs- und Entscheidungsprozess des Bundesverfassungsgerichts* (Wiesbaden: Verlag für Sozialwissenschaften, 2010).

Kronenberg, Volker, *Patriotismus in Deutschland: Perspektiven für eine weltoffene Nation* (Wiesbaden: Verlag für Sozialwissenschaften, 2006).

Lamprecht, Rolf, *Ich Gehe bis nach Karlsruhe: Eine Geschichte des Bundesverfassungsgerichts* (München: Deutsche Verlagsanstalt, 2011).

Langbein, John H., Renée Lettow Lerner, and Bruce P. Smith, *History of the Common Law: The Development of Anglo-American Legal Institutions* (New York: Aspen Publishers, 2009).

Lange, Friederike V., *Grundrechtsbindung des Gesetzgebers: Eine Rechtsvergleichende Studie zu Deutschland, Frankreich und den USA* (Tübingen: Mohr Siebeck, 2010).

Lasser, Mitchel de S.-O.-l'E., *Judicial Deliberations: A Comparative Analysis of Transparency and Legitimacy* (Oxford: Oxford University Press, 2004).

Latour, Bruno, *The Making of Law: An Ethnography of the Conseil D'état*, trans. Marina Brilman and Alain Pottage (Cambridge: Polity Press, 2010).

Laufer, Heinz, *Verfassungsgerichtsbarkeit und politischer Prozess: Studien zum Bundesverfassungsgericht der Bundesrepublik Deutschland* (Tübingen: Mohr Siebeck, 1968).

Law, David S., 'The Anatomy of a Conservative Court: Judicial Review in Japan', *Texas Law Review*, 87 (2009), 1545–89.

Lembcke, Oliver W., *Über das Ansehen Des Bundesverfassungsgerichts: Ans ichten und Meinungen in der Öffentlichkeit 1951–2001* (Berlin: Berliner Wissenschafts-Verlag, 2006).

Lembcke, Oliver W., *Hüter der Verfassung. Eine institutionentheoretische Studie zur Autorität des Bundesverfassungsgerichts* (Tübingen: Mohr Siebeck, 2007).

Lepsius, Oliver, *Die gegensatzaufhebende Begriffsbildung* (München: C. H. Beck, 1994).

Lepsius, Oliver, 'Die Religionsfreiheit als Minderheitenrecht in Deutschland, Frankreich und den USA', *Leviathan*, 34 (2006), 321–49.

Lepsius, Oliver, 'Rezension von: Frieder Günther: Denken Vom Staat Her. Die Bundesdeutsche Staatsrechtslehre Zwischen Dezision Und Integration 1949-1970', *Sehepunkte*, 4 (2004), <http://www.sehepunkte.de/2004/05/5714.html>.

Levinson, Sanford, *Constitutional Faith* (Princeton: Princeton University Press, 2011).

Liebenberg, Sandra, *Socio-Economic Rights: Adjudication Under a Transformative Constitution* (Cape Town: Juta, 2010).

Loewenstein, Karl, 'Militant Democracy and Fundamental Rights', in András Sájo (ed.), *Militant Democracy* (Utrecht: Eleven International Publishing, 2004), 231–62.

Lorz, Alexander, *Interorganrespekt im Verfassungsrecht: Funktionenzuordnung, Rücksichtnahme und Kooperationsverpflichtungen: eine rechtsvergleichende Analyse anhand der Verfassungssysteme der Bundesrepublik Deutschland, der Europäischen Union un der Vereinigten Staaten* (Tübingen: Mohr Siebeck, 2001).

Luhmann, Niklas, *Law As a Social System, trans. Klaus A. Ziegert, ed. Fatima Kastner, Richard Nobles, David Schiff, and Rosamund Ziegert* (Oxford: Oxford University Press, 2004).

Madison, James, Alexander Hamilton, and John Jay, *The Federalist Papers*, ed. Isaac Kramnick (England: Penguin, 1987).

Manow, Philip, 'Entwicklungslinien Ost- und Westdeutscher Gesundheitspolitik Zwischen Doppelter Staatsgründung, Deutscher Einigung und Europäischer Integration', *Zeitschrift für Sozialreform*, 43 (1997), 101–31.

Manssen, Gerrit. *Staatsrecht II Grundrechte* (München: Beck, 2002).

Mantei, Simone, *Nein und Ja zur Abtreibung: Die evangelische Kirche in der Reformdebatte um [Paragraph] 218 StGB (1970–1976)* (Göttingen: Vandenhoeck & Ruprecht, 2004).

Markesinis, Basil, *Engaging with Foreign Law*. In cooperation with Jörg Fedtke (Portland: Hart Publishing, 2009).

Mashaw, Jerry L., *Creating the Administrative Constitution: The Lost One Hundred Years of American Administrative Law* (New Haven: Yale University Press, 2012).

Matsui, Shigenori, *The Constitution of Japan: A Contextual Analysis* (Portland: Hart Publishing, 2011).

Maus, Ingeborg, 'Liberties and Popular Sovereignty: On Jürgen Habermas's Reconstruction of the System of Rights', *Cardozo Law Review*, 17 (1995), 825–1082.

Maxeiner, James R., 'Legal Certainty: A European Alternative to American Legal Indeterminacy?', *Tulane Journal of International and Comparative Law*, 15 (2007), 541–607.

Mishra, Robin, *Zulässigkeit und Grenzen der Urteilsschelte* (Berlin: Duncker & Humblot, 1997).

Möller, Martin and Robert C. Ooyen (eds), *Das Bundesverfassungsgericht im politischen System* (Wiesbaden: Verlag für Sozialwissenschaften, 2006).

Möllers, Christoph, *Gewaltengliederung* (Tübingen: Mohr Siebeck, 2005).

Möllers, Christoph, *Der vermisste Leviathan: Staatstheorie in der Bundesrepublik* (Frankfurt am Main: Suhrkamp, 2008).

Möllers, Christoph, *Staat als Argument* (Tübingen: Mohr Siebeck, 2011).

Möllers, Christoph, *Die drei Gewalten* (Weilerswist: Velbrück, 2008).

Möllers, Christoph, (for a shortened English account of *Die drei Gewalten*) *The Three Branches. A Comparative Model of Separation of Powers* (Oxford: Oxford University Press, 2013).

Möllers, Christoph and Hannah Birkenkötter, 'Towards a New Conceptualism in Comparative Constitutional Law or: Reviving the German Tradition of the Lehrbuch, *International Journal of Constitutional Law*, 12(3) (2014), 603–25.

Müller, Doreen, *Flucht und Asyl in europäischen Migrationsregimen: Metamorphosen einer umkämpften Kategorie am Beispiel der EU, Deutschlands und Polens* (Universitätsverlag Göttingen, 2010).

Müller, Jan-Werner, *Constitutional Patriotism* (Princeton: Princeton University Press, 2007).

Münch, Ursula, 'Vorgeschichte, Probleme und Auswirkungen der Asylrechtsänderung 1993', in Carsten Tessmer (ed.), *Deutschland und das Weltflüchtlingsproblem*, (Opladen: Leske & Budrich, 1994).

Mureinik, Etienne, 'A Bridge to Where? Introducing the Interim Bill of Rights', *South African Journal on Human Rights*, 10 (1994), 31.

Neumann, Franz, 'Der Funktionswandel des Gesetzes im Recht der bürgerlichen Gesellschaft', in *Demokratischer und autoritärer Staat* (Frankfurt am Main: Europäische Verlagsanstalt, 1967).

O'Brien, David M. and Yasuo Ohkoshi, *To Dream of Dreams: Religious Freedom and Constituitonal Politics in Postwar Japan* (Hawaii: University of Hawaii Press, 1996).

Papier, Hans-Jürgen, Das Mitbestimmungsurteil des Bundesverfassungsgerichts–Eine kritische Würdigung aus verfassungsrechtlicher Sicht', *Zeitschrift für Unternehmens-und Gesellschaftsrecht*, 8(4) (1979), 444–70.

Patzelt, Werner, 'Warum verachten die Deutschen ihr Parlament und lieben ihr Verfassungsgericht?—Ergebnisse einer vergleichenden demoskopischen Studie', *Zeitschrift für Parlamentsfragen*, 36 (2005), 517–38.

Paulson, Stanley L., 'The Theory of Public Law in Germany 1914–1945', *Oxford Journal of Legal Studies*, 25(3) (2005), 525–45.

Payandeh, Mehrdad, Das Gebot der Folgerichtigkeit: Rationalitatsgewinn oder Irrweg der Grundrechtsdogmatik?', *Archiv des öffentlichen Rechts*, 136 (2011), 578–615.

Petersen, Niels, 'Proportionality and the Incommensurability Challenge—Some Lessons from the South African Constitutional Court', *New York University Public Law and Legal Theory Working Papers* (2013), 1–23.

Pickerill, Mitchell J., *Constitutional Deliberation in Congress. The Impact of Judicial Review in a Separated System* (Durham: Duke, 2004).

Posner, Richard, *How Judges Think* (Cambridge: Harvard University Press, 2008).

Post, Robert C., 'Racist Speech, Democracy, and the First Amendment', *William and Mary Law Review*, 32 (1990), 267–327.

Post, Robert C. and Reva B. Siegel, 'Roe Rage: Democratic Constitutionalism and Backlash', *Harvard Civil Rights–Civil Liberties Law Review*, 42 (2007), 373–433.

Radbruch, Gustav, 'Statutory Lawlessness and Supra-Statutory Law (1946)', *Oxford Journal of Legal Studies*, 26(1) (2006), 1–11.

Ramnath, Kalyani, 'The Runaway Judgement: Law as Literature, Courtcraft and Constitutional Visions', *Journal of Indian Law and Society*, 3 (2012), 1–28.

Rau, Christian, *Selbst entwickelte Grenzen in der Rechtsprechung des United States Supreme Court und des Bundesverfassungsgerichts* (Berlin: Duncker & Humblot, 1996).

Rausch, Heinz, 'Politisches Bewußtsein Und Politische Einstellungen Im Wandel', in Werner Weidenfeld (ed.), *Die Identität der Deutschen* (Berlin: Bundeszentrale für politische Bildung, 1983), 119–53.

Ray, Brian, 'Evictions, Aspirations and Avoidance', *Constitutional Court Review*, 5 (2013), 172.

Reinthal, Angelika and Reinhard Mußgnug (eds), *Briefwechsel Ernst Forsthoff—Carl Schmitt 1926–1974* (Berlin: Akademie Verlag, 2007).

Reitz, John C., 'Political Economy as a Major Architectural Principle of Public Law', *Tulane Law Review*, 75 (2001), 1121–58.

Renner, Moritz, 'Kontingenz, Redundanz, Transzendenz? Zum Gerechtigkeitsbegriff Niklas Luhmanns', *Ancilla Juris* (2008), 62–72.

Rennert, Dominik, 'Die verdrängte Werttheorie und ihre Historisierung. Zu "Lüth" und den Eigenheiten bundesrepublikanischer Grundrechtstheorie', *Der Staat*, 53(1) (2014), 31–59.

Rennert, Klaus, *Die geisteswissenschaftliche Richtung in der Staatsrechtslehre der Weimarer Republik: Untersuchungen zu Erich Kaufmann, Günther Holstein und Rudolf Smend*, vol. 518 (Berlin: Duncker & Humblot, 1987).

Rensmann, Thilo, *Wertordnung und Verfassung: Das Grundgesetz im Kontext grenzüberschreitender Konstitutionalisierung* (Tübingen: Mohr Siebeck, 2007).

Rinken, Alfred, 'Demokratie und Hierarchie. Zum Demokratieverständnis des Zweiten Senats des Bundesverfassungsgerichts', in Redaktion Kritische Justiz (ed.), *Demokratie und Grundgesetz* (Baden-Baden: Nomos, 2000), pp. 125–47.

Rojahn, Gunther, 'Elfes—Mehr als ein Urteil, Aufladung und Entladung eines Politikums', Doctoral thesis, FU Berlin, 2009.

Rose-Ackerman, Susan, Stefanie Egidy, and James Fowkes, *'Due Process of Lawmaking': United States, South Africa, Germany and the European Union* (New York: Cambridge University Press, 2014).

Roux, Theunis, 'Principle and Pragmatism on the Constitutional Court of South Africa', *International Journal of Constitutional Law*, 7(1) (2009), 106–38.

Roux, Theunis, The Politics of Principle, The First South African Constitutional Court, 1995–2005 (Cambridge: Cambridge University Press, 2013).

Rubenfeld, Jed, 'Unilateralism and Constitutionalism', *New York University Law Review*, 79 (2004), 1971–2028.

Rusteberg, Benjamin, *Der Grundrechtliche Gewährleistungsgehalt* (Tübingen: Mohr Siebeck, 2009).

Rüthers, Bernd, *Die unbegrenzte Auslegung* (Tübingen: Mohr Siebeck, 2005).

Rüthers, Bernd, *Die heimliche Revolution. Vom Rechtsstaat zum Richterstaat* (Tübingen: Mohr Siebeck, 2014).

Scalia, Antonin, 'The Doctrine of Standing as an Essential Element of the Separation of Powers', *Suffolk University Law Review*, 17 (1983), 881–900.

Schaal, Gary S., *Integration durch Verfassung und Verfassungsrechtsprechung?: Über den Zusammenhang von Demokratie, Verfassung und Integration* (Berlin: BWV, 2000).

Schauer, Frederick F., 'English Natural Justice and American Due Process: An Analytical Comparison', *William and Mary Law Review*, 18 (1976), 47–72.

Scheppele, Kim L., 'Constitutional Interpretation after Regimes of Horror', *University of Pennsylvania Law School Public Law Working Paper* 05, <file:///Users/mhailbronner/Downloads/SSRN-id236219.pdf>.

Scheppele, Kim L., 'Jack Balkin Is an American', *Yale Journal of Law and the Humanities*, 25 (2013), 23–42.

Schlink, Bernhard, *Abwägung im Verfassungsrecht* (Berlin: Duncker & Humblot, 1976).

Schlink, Bernhard, 'Die Entthronung der Staatsrechtswissenschaft durch die Verfassungsgerichtsbarkeit', *Der Staat*, 28 (1989), 161.

Schlink, Bernhard and Bodo Pieroth, *Grundrechte. Staatsrecht II* (Heidelberg: C. F. Müller, 2012).

Schmitt, Carl, *Verfassungslehre* (München: Duncker & Humblot, 1928).

Schmitt, Carl, *Die Hüter der Verfassung* (Tübingen: Mohr Siebeck, 1931).

Schmitt, Carl, *Die Tyrannei der Werte*, 3rd edn., ed. Christoph Schönberger (Berlin: Duncker & Humblot, 2011).

Scholz, Richard, *Analyse der Entstehungsbedingungen der reichsgerichtlichen Aufwertungsrechtsprechung* (Oxford: Lang, 2001).

Schönberger, Christoph, *Das Parlament im Anstaltsstaat: Zur Theorie Parlamentarischer Repräsentation in der Staatsrechtslehre des Kaiserreichs (1871–1918)* (Frankfurt am Main: Vittorio Klostermann, 1997).

Schönberger, Christoph, 'Verwaltungsrecht als Konkretisiertes Verfassungsrecht', in Michael Stolleis (ed.), *Das Bonner Grundgesetz: Altes Recht Und Neue Verfassung in Den Ersten Jahrzehnten Der Bundesrepublik Deutschland (1949–1969)* (Berlin: Berliner Wissenschafts-Verlag, 2006), pp. 53–83.

Schweber, Howard and Jennifer Williams, 'US Report', in *Comparative Constitutional Reasoning*, ed. A. Jakab, A. Dyevre, and G. Itzcovich (Cambridge University Press, forthcoming).

Siegel, Reva B., 'Constitutional Culture, Social Movement Conflict and Constitutional Change: The Case of the De Facto Era. 2005–06 Brennan Center Symposium Lecture', California Law Review, 94 (2006), 1323–419.

Siegel, Reva B., 'Dignity and Sexuality: Claims on Dignity in Transnational Debates over Abortion and Same-Sex Marriage', *International Journal of Constitutional Law*, 10(2) (2012), 355–79.

Skowronek, Stephen, *Building a New American State: The Expansion of National Administrative Capacities, 1877–1920* (Cambridge: Cambridge University Press, 1982).

Smend, Rudolf, *Verfassung und Verfassungsrecht* (München: Duncker & Humblot, 1928).

Soifer, Aviam, 'The Paradox of Paternalism and Laissez-Faire Constitutionalism: United States Supreme Court, 1888–1921', *Law and History Review*, 5 (1987), 249–79.

Spevack, Edmund, *Allied Control and German Freedom: American Political and Ideological Influences on the Framing of the West German Basic Law (Grundgesetz)* (Münster: Lit, 2001).

Spranger, Tade M., 'Soldaten sind Mörder', in *Verfassungsrechtsprechung: Hundert Entscheidungen des Bundesverfassungsgerichts in Retrospektive*, ed. Jörg Menzel and Thomas Ackermann (Tübingen: Mohr Siebeck, 2000), 592–8.

Sternberger, Dolf, 'Rede zur Hundertjahrfeier der Sozialdemokratischen Partei Deutschlands', in *Schriften Band 4: Staatsfreundschaft* (Frankfurt am Main: Insel, 1990), pp. 17–31.

Sternberger, Dolf, 'Verfassungpatriotismus: Rede bei der 25-Jahr Feier der "Akademie für politische Bildung"', in *Verfassungspatriotismus, Schriften Band 10* (Frankfurt am Main: Insel, 1990).

Stolleis, Michael, *Geschichte des öffentlichen Rechts in Deutschland: Erster Band 1600–1800* (München: C. H. Beck, 1988); *Zweiter Band 1800–1914* (München: C. H. Beck, 1992); *Dritter Band Weimarer Republik und Nationalsozialismus* (München: C. H. Beck, 2002); *Vierter Band 1945–1990* (München: C. H. Beck, 2012).

Stolleis, Michael, (for an English account) *The Law Under the Swastika: Studies on Legal History in Nazi Germany*, trans. Thomas Dunlap (Chicago: University of Chicago Press, 1998).

Stolleis, Michael (ed.), *Das Bonner Grundgesetz: Altes Recht und neue Verfassung in den ersten Jahrzehnten der Bundesrepublik Deutschland (1949–1969)* (Berlin: Berliner Wissenschaftsverlag, 2006).

Stone-Sweet, Alec, *Governing with Judges: Constitutional Politics in Europe* (Oxford: Oxford University Press, 2000).
Stone-Sweet, Alec, 'All Things in Proportion? American Rights Doctrine and the Problem of Balancing', *Emory Law Journal*, 60 (2011), 101–79.
Stone-Sweet, Alec and Jud Mathews, 'Proportionality Balancing and Global Constitutionalism', *Columbia Journal of Transnational Law*, 47 (2008), 73–165.
Sunstein, Cass R., 'What's Standing after Lujan? Of Citizen Suits, "Injuries," and Article III', *Michigan Law Review*, 91 (1992), 163–236.
Sunstein, Cass R., *One Case at a Time: Judicial Minimalism on the Supreme Court* (Cambridge: Harvard University Press, 2001).
Sunstein, Cass R., *Designing Democracy: What Constitutions Do* (New York: Oxford University Press, 2001).
Tamanaha, Brian Z., *Beyond the Formalist–Realist Divide: the Role of Politics in Judging* (Princeton: Princeton University Press, 2009).
Teitel, Ruti G., *Transitional Justice* (Oxford: Oxford University Press, 2000).
Thurn, John Philipp, *Welcher Sozialstaat? Ideologie und Wissenschaftsverständnis in den Debatten der bundesdeutschen Staatsrechtslehre 1949–1990* (Tübingen: Mohr Siebeck, 2013).
Toobin, Jeffrey, *The Nine: Inside the Secret World of the Supreme Court* (New York: Doubleday, 2007).
Tushnet, Mark, 'Policy Distortion and Democratic Debilitation: Comparative Illumination of the Countermajoritarian Difficulty', *Michigan Law Review*, 94 (1995), 245–301.
Tushnet, Mark, 'The Possibilities of Comparative Law', *Yale Law Journal*, 108 (1999), 1225–309.
Tushnet, Mark, *Taking the Constitution Away from the Courts* (Princeton: Princeton University Press, 1999).
Twining, William, *Karl Llewellyn and the Realist Movement*, 2nd edn (Cambridge: Cambridge University Press, 2012).
Vanberg, Georg, *The Politics of Constitutional Review in Germany* (Cambridge: Cambridge University Press, 2005).
Vermeule, Adrian, *Judging under Uncertainty: An Institutional Theory of Legal Interpretation* (Cambridge: Harvard University Press, 2006).
Von der Pfordten, Dietmar, 'Zum Begriff des Staates bei Kant und Hegel', in *Internationales Jahrbuch des Deutschen Idealismus: Der Begriff des Staates* (Berlin: W. de Gruyter, 2004), 103–20.
Von Stein, Freiherr, *Lebenserinnerungen und Denkschriften* (Altenmünster: Jazzybee-Verlag, 2011).
Vorländer, Hans (ed.), *Die Deutungsmacht der Verfassungsgerichtsbarkeit* (Wiesbaden: Verlag für Sozialwissenschaften, 2006).
Voßkuhle, Andreas, 'Der Grundsatz der Verfassungsorgantreue und die Kritik am BVerfG', *Neue Juristische Wochenschrift*, (1997), 2216–19.
Wahl, Rainer, *Herausforderungen und Antworten: Das öffentliche Recht der letzten fünf Jahrzehnte* (Berlin: de Gruyter, 2006).

Waldron, Jeremy, *Law and Disagreement* (Oxford: Oxford University Press, 2001).

Weber, Max, *Grundriss Der Sozialökonomik. III. Abteilung: Wirtschaft und Gesellschaft* (Tübingen: Mohr Siebeck, 1922).

Wengst, Udo, *Staatsaufbau und Regierungspraxis 1948–1953: Zur Geschichte Der Verfassungsorgane der Bundesrepublik Deutschland* (Düsseldorf: Droste-Verlag, 1984).

Wesel, Uwe, *Der Gang nach Karlsruhe: Das Bundesverfassungsgericht in der Geschichte der Bundesrepublik* (München: Karl Blessing Verlag, 2004).

Whitman, James Q., 'Separating Church and State: The Atlantic Divide', *Historical Reflections*, 34 (2008), 86–104.

Whittington, Keith E. *Political Foundations of Judicial Supremacy : The Presidency, the Supreme Court, and Constitutional Leadership in U.S. History* (Princeton: Princeton University Press, 2007).

Whittington, Keith E., 'James Madison Has Left the Building', *University of Chicago Law Review*, 72(3) (2005), 1137–58.

Wilson, Stuart and Jackie Dugard, 'Taking Poverty Seriously: The South African Constitutional Court and Socio-economic Rights', *Stellenbosch Law Review*, 22(3) (2011), 664.

Winkler, Heinrich August, *Der lange Weg nach Westen. Deutsche Geschichte vom 'Dritten Reich' bis zur Wiedervereinigung* (München: C. H. Beck, 2000).

Wood, Gordon S., *Empire of Liberty: A History of the Early Republic, 1789–1815* (New York: Oxford University Press, 2009).

Wood, Gordon S., *The Radicalism of the American Revolution* (New York: A. A. Knopf, 1992).

Wunder, Bernd, *Geschichte der Bürokratie in Deutschland* (Frankfurt am Main: Suhrkamp, 1986).

Index

The manufacturer's authorised representative in the EU for product safety is Oxford University Press España S.A. of El Parque Empresarial San Fernando de Henares, Avenida de Castilla, 2 - 28830 Madrid (www.oup.es/en or product.safety@oup.com). OUP España S.A. also acts as importer into Spain of products made by the manufacturer.
Printed and bound by CPI Group (UK) Ltd, Croydon, CR0 4YY
14/09/2026
02216308-0005